BIS ZUM DACH DER WELT

LAND ROVER EXPERIENCE TOUR

TO THE TOP OF THE WORLD

teNeues

INHALTSVERZEICHNIS
TABLE OF CONTENTS

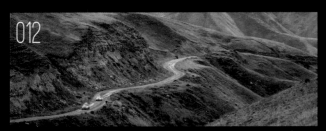

SEIDENSTRASSE / SILK ROAD
2013

JORDANIEN / JORDAN
2000

ISLAND / ICELAND
2001

NAMIBIA / NAMIBIA
2002

VORWORT
FOREWORD

ie Land Rover Experience Tour ist einmalig in der Automobilwelt und eine Erfolgsgeschichte für die Marke Land Rover in Deutschland. Von Anfang an war es das Ziel, die Marke in ihrer eigentlichen Umgebung für eine breitere Öffentlichkeit erlebbar zu machen und gleichzeitig die Bandbreite an Fähigkeiten der Fahrzeuge unter Beweis zu stellen.

Die Offroad-Welt hat sich seit dem Start der Land Rover Experience Tour im Jahr 2000 dramatisch geändert. Seitdem die Camel Trophy den Abenteurer mit kaputten Schuhen und einem Land Rover an seiner Seite erfunden hatte und in unzähligen Werbespots präsentierte, wurden viele neue Nischen besetzt, neue Player haben den SUV- und Geländewagenmarkt stark erweitert. Aber schon immer hat die automobile Konkurrenz respektvoll auf die Experience-Aktivitäten von Land Rover geschaut. Auch der einhellige Tenor der Journalisten war: „So eine Tour kann nur Land Rover durchführen, nur diese Marke steht authentisch für dieses Abenteuer."

Durch die Finanz- und Wirtschaftskrise ab 2007 wurden viele „Abenteuer-Projekte" in der Industrie eingestellt. Auch Land Rover Deutschland musste die Land Rover Experience Tour (LET) vehement gegenüber der Zentrale in Großbritannien verteidigen, aber mit dem Jaguar-Land-Rover-Besitzerwechsel von Ford zu Tata Motors war die LET wieder im Fokus und ist heute eine der wichtigsten Säulen der globalen Marketingstrategie von Land Rover.

Das schlüssige und kontinuierlich verfolgte Konzept ist das Erfolgsrezept für die Tour: Zunächst die Qualifikation mit teils mehr als 30 000 Bewerbungen, den intensiven Offroad-Testfahrten der Bewerber bei den nationalen Qualifikations-camps und der Zielgruppenansprache, die auch weitestgehend der Käufer-zielgruppe entspricht. Wer hier dabei ist (insgesamt mehr als 2 400 Teilnehmer), hat zwar das Tourziel vor Augen, ist aber alleine schon durch den Tag mit Land Rover und all den Modellen vom Defender bis zum Range Rover nachhaltig begeistert. Diejenigen, die sich durchgesetzt haben und als besonderes Extra dann bei der Endqualifikation in unserem Center in Wülfrath dabei sein dürfen (in diesen Genuss kommen 60 Personen bei jeder Tour), sind schon fast auf dem Offroad-Olymp. Ein einmaliges Erlebnis, das man nie mehr vergisst. Drei Tage im Gelände, sich mit anderen messen, immer nach dem Motto: „Dabei sein ist alles." Wer dann zu den sechs Finalisten gehört – bei der Seidenstraßentour sind es wegen der Länge zwölf – hat viele Neider, denn diese Tour kann man für Geld nicht kaufen. Die Tour ist das Faszinosum, das einen ganz besonderen Reiz ausübt.

Wenn wir behaupten, die Tour sei nicht zu kaufen, ist das nicht ganz richtig, denn auch die Jubiläumstour ist im Angebot, quasi als Rückreise in sechs einzeln buchbaren Etappen von Mumbai nach Berlin „auf den Spuren der Tour". Dabei nutzen wir das durch unsere Profis erworbene Know-how in den Tourländern in Form eines exklusiven und individuellen Reiseprogramms. Erfolgreiche Beispiele für Experience-Reisen sind die Tourziele Island und Namibia, die seit Jahren im Programm sind und weiterhin sehr stark nachgefragt werden.

Wir sind überzeugt, dass unser Konzept so stark und einzigartig ist, dass es zahlreiche weitere Touren geben wird und wir gemeinsam mit Dag Rogge auch weiterhin neue Experience-Destinationen finden werden. Denn es gibt immer wieder ein neues faszinierendes Ziel, an dem Träume wahr werden können.

Schwalbach/Taunus, den 10.10.2013
Christian Uhrig
Leiter Marketing Land Rover Deutschland

In the automotive industry, the Land Rover Experience Tour is both unique and a runaway success for the Land Rover brand in Germany. From the start, it was intended to open up the brand to a greater portion of the general public by enabling them to experience Land Rover in its natural environment – and to demonstrate the sheer breadth of capability inherent in the vehicles themselves.

The world of off-road and 4x4 has changed dramatically since the first Experience Tour in 2000. After Camel Trophy virtually invented the globetrotter with his worn-out shoes and trusty Land Rover at his side in countless advertising slots, many new niches have sprung up. The SUV (Sport Utility Vehicle) and off-road vehicle market has seen a lot of newcomers providing much more choice. The Experience programme, however, has always enjoyed the respect of the competition, with journalists agreeing unanimously that "only Land Rover can do this kind of tour as it is the only brand which truly stands for adventure."

From 2007 onwards, however, the global, economic and financial crisis resulted in the cancellation of many car-industry-driven adventure projects. Land Rover Germany had to fight the good fight with the head office in Great Britain in order to keep the Land Rover Experience Tour (LET) alive. When Ford sold Jaguar Land Rover to Tata Motors, though, things looked up for the LET, and today it has become one of the most important cornerstones of Land Rover's global marketing strategy.

A coherent and rigorously applied concept is the secret behind the tour's success. Over 30,000 candidates apply to take part in national selection camps that involve intensive off-road driving and a target-group communication methodology that fits the Land Rover customer profile almost like a glove. Those who make it to this stage (well over 2,400 participants) are obviously focussed on taking part in the tour, but by virtue of having participated in the selection phase, they have also had the privilege to drive the full range of Land Rover products, from Defender to Range Rover. Those who make it to the final selection camp held at our centre in Wülfrath (usually around 60 participants per tour), which is itself a highlight of the tour selection process, have nearly made it to the off-road equivalent of the 100 metres in the Olympic Games.

The experience is unique and unforgettable. Three days of total off-road, measuring up against your competitors and driven by the maxim: "It isn't winning that counts; it's taking part that matters." The final six – or, in the case of the current tour along the Silk Road, twelve because of the sheer length of the event – will be the target of more than their fair share of envy, as the tour is something money can't buy. It is a fascinating journey with its own individual charm and appeal.

Of course when we say the tour is something that money can't buy, that's not strictly accurate. This year's anniversary tour can also be booked by paying customers keen to follow the route – broken down into six individual sections from Mumbai to Berlin. Our professional teams use the knowledge gained in the countries we explore to provide the backbone to a very exclusive made-to-measure adventure holiday. Iceland and Namibia are very good examples of our Experience adventure tour destinations which have been in the programme for years and continue to be booked up year after year.

We are convinced that our concept has stood the test of time and will provide the basis for Dag Rogge to create many more Experience Tours in the future. For one thing is clear, there will always be a dream destination just waiting for people to wake up to.

Schwalbach/Taunus, Germany, 10 October 2013
Christian Uhrig
Head of Marketing Land Rover Germany

...da war es noch cool, zu rauchen. Lässig die Fluppe im Mundwinkel, dazu noch ein bisschen Abenteuer und Cowboy-Märchen, fertig war das Camel-Image vom weit reisenden, unerschütterlichen Weltenbummler. Den höchstens ein Loch im Schuh bremste, wenn er im wildesten Westen, Osten, Süden oder Norden unterwegs war.

Deswegen brauchte er Helfer.

Die stellte die gelbe Zigarettenmarke aus dem Hause Reynolds Tobacco Company zunächst in Form von uramerikanischen Jeeps. Die erste Camel Trophy im Jahr 1980 – der Versuch, harte und hart rauchende Männer durch noch härteres Gelände zu treiben, um sich das allerhärteste Image zu verleihen – führte mit vier Mietwagen entlang der Transamazônica, teils direkt durch den Urwald. Einzige Aufgabenstellung: Fahre bei A los und versuche, B zu erreichen. Es gab keine lokalen Scouts und Guides, die mit Wissen, Sprache und landestypischen Lösungen aushelfen konnten. Es gab keine Vortouren zum Eruieren von Pisten, Hotels, Verkehr und Gefahren. Und es gab keine geplante Sicherheit – als würde harten Männern schon nichts passieren. Man brach durch den Dschungel, wo es ging. Zum Beispiel auf Forststraßen. Wo es nicht ging, musste man umkehren und man merkte: B ist manchmal ganz schön weit weg. 1981 stand plötzlich in der Kinowerbung kein Jeep mehr neben dem immer noch sehr abenteuerlustig wirkenden Herren mit Loch in der Schuhsohle, sondern ein bis dato in Deutschland wenig beachteter Land Rover. Dass neben der Zigarette auch ein Land Rover plötzlich in aller Munde war, ermutigte den englischen Offroad-Spezialisten, 1982 fester Sponsor der Camel Trophy zu werden und die Autos für die Touren zu stellen. Um nicht nur mit schwerem Gasfuß irgendwo durch eine Gegend zu toben, waren nun auch spezielle Aufgaben in die Touren eingebaut worden: besonders schwierige Offroad-Parcours meistern, auf Zeit fahren, nach Roadbook navigieren.

Der Aufwand für die Camel Trophy wuchs stetig: Hubschrauber wurden zum Transport der Lead Scouts eingesetzt, und wenn die Aufgaben zum Beispiel auf der Insel Borneo stattfanden und Regen den Weg unpassierbar machte, wurden schon mal alle teilnehmenden 90er-Defender in ihre Einzelteile zerlegt, ums Hindernis herum geflogen und nach der Landung von den Teilnehmern wieder zusammengebaut. Geld spielte keine Rolle. Es war einfach da.

1990 reichte es den Veranstaltern nicht mehr, mit kleinen Spielchen im Gepäck durch die Gegend zu touren – sie stellten neue, diesmal sehr sportliche Aufgaben, zum Beispiel Kanufahrten, Orientierungsläufe oder Mountainbiken in den abenteuerlichsten Ecken der Welt. Diese Trophy gilt als letzte „Zigaretten-Trophy". Hier wurden noch Sieger und Vizemeister gekürt – ein gewisser Hans Hermann Ruthe erhielt als Teilnehmer den Master Driver Award und belegte in der Gesamtwertung Platz zwei.

Die Umfänge der folgenden Touren nahmen gigantische Ausmaße an: 1996 in Argentinien und Chile bestand der Tross aus 56 Land Rover. Allein 36 davon bildeten einen Konvoi, inklusive zwei Ambulanzen, drei Technikwagen, 2 Teamfahrzeugen, drei Fotowagen und noch mal drei Autos für Videofilmer. Ende des Jahrtausends war es allerdings nicht mehr cool, in Schlammschlachten durch die Welt zu pflügen. Die Trophy entwickelte sich mehr und mehr zum Adventure, die Autos wurden zu reinen Transportmitteln. Sport stand jetzt im Vordergrund: Biken, Snowboarden, Laufen – extrem zuschauerunfreundlich, weil kein Journalist den Top-Athleten – welche die Teilnehmer inzwischen sein mussten – folgen konnte. Außerdem wetterte ein Teil der Öffentlichkeit gegen diese Form von Tourismus, würde man doch nur die Umwelt plattwalzen. Was die wenigsten wussten oder wissen wollten: Die Land Rover haben nie neue Wege geschaffen, sondern immer nur vorhandene genutzt und stets einen Benefit im Land gelassen. Zum Beispiel vier Millionen Dollar für den Nationalpark Baikalsee oder eine komplette Forschungsstation in Malaysia.

1998 wurde Reynolds nach Japan verkauft. Da war Land Rover als Sponsor bereits seit einem Jahr ausgestiegen, weil das Raucherumfeld nicht zum Land-Rover-Image passte und der neue Eigner, BMW, anderes mit der Marke vorhatte. Im Jahr 2000 wurde eine letzte Camel Trophy organisiert, die alle anderen in den Schatten stellen sollte: Samoa. Autos gab es gar nicht mehr, nun wurde in Booten um Punkte und Platzierungen gekämpft. 46 Teamschiffe düsten durchs Wasser, begleitet von einem Tankschiff, Kriegsschiffen als Sicherung, Beobachterschiffen und natürlich auch zwei Hubschraubern.

Dann war Schluss.

Aber Land Rover ohne Abenteuer? Niemals.

1999 bestand das Portfolio der Marke aus Range Rover, Discovery, Freelander und Defender. Eigentlich perfekt für die Eroberung der Welt – aber dazu mussten wir reisen. Metaphorisch ausgedrückt: Wir hatten eine tolle Torte, doch es fehlte die Kirsche obendrauf.

So entwickelten wir 1999 ein neues Konzept. Basis war die Idee, dass sich nur Menschen für eine Tour bewerben können, die früher bei der Camel Trophy nur vorm Fernseher saßen und bedauerten, dass sie weder das richtige Alter noch die richtige Statur für so eine harte Rallye besaßen. Die Tortur schafften damals wirklich nur gestählte GSG-9-Beamte, Jet-Piloten oder Extremsportler. Außerdem erschien uns die ganz harte Tour nicht mehr zeitgemäß. Der Trend ging zum Nichtrauchen, zum ökologisch verantwortbaren Offroaden, zu Menschen und Kultur statt mit der Brechstange durch den Dschungel. Wir stellten uns ein kontrolliertes und kontrollierbares Abenteuer vor, die Entdeckung von Land und Leuten abseits touristischer Pfade mit hohem Erlebniswert.

Der Weg dorthin: Bekanntmachung einer solchen Tour über die damals rund 160 Land-Rover-Händler sowie Presse und Radio. Danach die Einrichtung von verschiedenen Qualifikationscamps, bei denen die Aufgaben niemanden abschrecken oder überfordern sollten. Nach denen aber auch diejenigen, die nicht ausgewählt wurden, zufrieden nach Hause fahren konnten – und das Erlebnis, in einem Land Rover gefahren zu sein, nicht vergaßen. Letztendlich sollten stets sechs geeignete Menschen mit uns auf die jeweilige Tour gehen.

1999 präsentierten wir das Konzept dem damaligen Eigner BMW. Von dort kam ein klares „Nein". Niemand dort konnte sich solche Touren als imagefördernde Marketinginstrument vorstellen.

Doch kurz darauf, im April 2000, verkaufte BMW die Marke Land Rover an Ford. Die Amerikaner forderten noch in der Übergangsphase verkaufsunterstützende Marketingaktivitäten für die Offroad-Marke, für die zu dem Zeitpunkt noch eine BMW-Abteilung zuständig war. So bekam Land Rover im April/Mai 2000 einen Anruf aus Bayern: Konzept nun doch genehmigt. Die erste Tour führte – noch unter dem Namen „Land Rover Entdecker-Tour" – nach Jordanien.

Die englische Land-Rover-Sektion versuchte übrigens ebenfalls, ein eigenes Event auf die Beine zu stellen. 2003 und 2006 gab es die G4 Challenge (G4 = Global Four), eine Tour in vier Zeitzonen auf vier Kontinenten. Das Projekt erwies sich aber als zu aufwendig, für Journalisten war es so gut wie nicht mehr verfolgbar. Und: Die Medienvertreter durften nie – wie schon bei allen früheren Camel Trophys – selbst ans Steuer. Was für die eher Komfort gewohnten Lifestyle-Schreiber nicht so dramatisch war, für die erlebnisorientierten Auto-Journalisten jedoch umso schlimmer. So oder so: Auf diese Weise war es für sie nur schwer vermittelbar, was so eine G4-Tour ausmachte.

2001 kam Christian Uhrig ins Land Rover Marketing, mit ihm zusammen entwickelten wir das aktuelle Tour-Konzept aus Qualifikation, Tour und Reiseprogramm weiter. Im gleichen Jahr wurde die Land Rover Experience gegründet – als „Fahrschule" für Neukunden. Nach Festsetzung von Qualitätsstandards sollten alle Land Rover Experience Center die exakt gleichen Aus- und Fortbildungskriterien an die Kunden weitergeben, Händler schulen, die hohe Verantwortung beim Offroad-Fahren vermitteln und ein optimales Trainingsareal zur Verfügung stellen.

Die Ur-Ausbildungsstätten heißen Eastnor Castle und Solihull – die „homes of the legend". Hier waren Hans und ich schon in den 80er Jahren zu Schulungen. Mittlerweile werden hier die neuen Instruktoren der Experience Center ausgebildet. Heute existieren weltweit 27 Experience Center. Die „Land Rover Experience Tour" aber gibt es nur in Deutschland. Darauf bin ich ein bisschen stolz.

Unseren Rückblick auf zehn Land Rover Experience Touren und eine unvergessliche Winter-Veranstaltung für Journalisten beginnen wir mit der aufwendigsten und längsten Tour: die Jubiläumstour durch elf Länder über Teile der legendären Seidenstraße von Deutschland nach Indien. Danach blicken wir auf die Anfänge zurück und reisen chronologisch in die Neuzeit.

Sie werden sehen: Wir haben zwar die Abenteuertouren mit den besten Offroadern der Welt nicht neu erfunden – aber dramatisch professionalisiert, präzisiert und kultiviert.

Wülfrath, den 16.10.2013
Dag Rogge
Geschäftsführer der Land Rover Experience Germany

...when smoking was still cool. Nonchalant, the cigarette dangling from the corner of one's mouth, a bit of adventure and cowboy chic thrown in, and there you had it – Camel's image of the intrepid globetrotter. The only thing that stopped him on his way west, east, south or north was a hole in his shoe.

It was time to get help.

Reynolds Tobacco Company, which owned the Camel brand, initially found help in the form of American Jeeps. The first Camel Trophy in 1980 was an attempt to get tough, smoking guys through even tougher terrain to bolster the tough-guy image in the ad campaign. Four rented vehicles battled their way along the Trans-Amazonian Highway, partly cutting their way through rain forest. The task was simple: start in A and try to get to B. There were no scouts or guides on hand to contribute local knowledge, language or any other skills indigenous to the region. There was no pre-scouting to determine the best possible routes, accommodation, traffic situation or possible dangers. And there was no risk management – where the going gets tough, the tough get going. Where necessary, the route was hacked through the jungle using forestry roads, for example, and where that wasn't possible, one simply turned round, noting that B was quite a long way away.

From 1981, however cinema advertising no longer featured a Jeep alongside the globetrotting adventurer with the hole in his shoe. On display instead was a Land Rover, which thus far in Germany had not exactly been a sales or even PR success story. As people began talking not only about cigarettes but about Land Rover as well, it prompted the English maker of specialist off-road vehicles to become official sponsor of the Camel Trophy in 1982 and furnish the vehicles used in the competition. To avoid simply flattening the countryside, special tasks were now integrated into the event, including mastering particularly challenging off-road driving sections, time trials and road book navigation.

The logistics of the Camel Trophy grew exponentially year on year. Helicopters were used to transport the lead scouts; when, for example, during the event on the island of Borneo, incessant rain made the route impassable, the participating Defender 90s were taken apart, flown around the obstacle and rebuilt by the competitors. Money was no object.

By 1990, as far as the event organizers were concerned, simply driving through the countryside, with all manner of mini tasks for the participants, would no longer suffice. This time the focus was on real sporting tasks – with canoeing, orienteering and mountain bike events scheduled in the most exotic "back of beyond" locations on the planet. The 1990 event was known as the last "Cigarette Trophy". Winner and runner-up titles were awarded, with a certain Hans Hermann Ruthe winning the Master Driver Award and second place overall.

The following tours grew increasingly complex, assuming gargantuan dimensions. The 1996 event in Argentina and Chile had a fleet of 56 Land Rovers, of which 16 alone made up the main convoy with two ambulances, three technical support vehicles, 22 team cars, three photography cars and another three cars for video crews.

By the end of the century, global mud-plugging was no longer cool. The Trophy was increasingly adventure-focused, the vehicles reduced to the status of mere transport. The emphasis was on sport: biking, snowboarding, running – all of which was difficult for audience participation, as no journalist could keep up with the top athletes (who now made up the majority of the competitors). For the scribes, covering the event proved a struggle. Additionally, some sections of the general public were increasingly prone to rant and rail at this kind of tourism, which appeared to have no respect whatsoever for the environment. At the time, people were either unaware, or wished to remain ignorant, of the fact that the Land Rovers never hacked their way through virgin jungle. Instead, they drove routes that already existed and always made sure that when they left a country, some form of benefit remained, such as a four million dollar donation for the Lake Baikal national park or a complete research station in Malaysia.

In 1998 Reynolds was sold to a company in Japan. The year prior, Land Rover had ended its sponsorship deal, as smoking no longer suited Land Rover's image and new owner BMW had other plans for the brand. In 2000, the final Camel Trophy event, designed to put all the previous Trophies in the shade, took part on Samoa. This time there were no vehicles involved. The competition was fought out in high-speed dirigibles. 46 team boats shot across the Pacific Ocean, supported by their own tanker and protected by warships, with the usual entourage of observers and of course two helicopters.

And then it was over.

In 1999 the brand consisted of four vehicle types: Range Rover, Discovery, Freelander and Defender. All designed to conquer the world – but to do so, you had to go travelling. Metaphorically speaking, the cake looked delicious but still needed the icing on top.

In 1999 we developed a new idea. The idea was that there were people out there who had seen Camel Trophy on TV but had been unable to take part because they were either too old or lacked the appropriate physique for such a demanding tour. Indeed, by the final running of the Camel Trophy, only jet fighter pilots, marines and extreme athletes were up to the task. Besides, we felt that the extreme tour was no longer in keeping with the Zeitgeist. Not smoking was the new trend, and off-roading had gone ecologically responsible, with greater focus on understanding communities and culture rather than just ploughing one's way through the jungle. We planned a controlled and manageable adventure trip, one that would be a rich and varied experience, exploring countries and their ways of life off the beaten touristic trails.

How to get there: we had to spread the word about the new tour to the approximately 160 Land Rover dealers in Germany, and we had to generate the necessary PR through the media. After that, we had to set up a series of selection camps in which no one would be scared off by tasks deemed impossible but that would also leave those not selected with a positive impression of the experience of having driven a Land Rover as they made their way home. In 1999 we presented the concept to the owner of Land Rover at the time – BMW. The answer was a very clear "No". Such tours were not seen in Munich as an appropriate image-building marketing tool.

Shortly afterwards, however, in April 2000, BMW sold the Land Rover brand to Ford. During the handover period, the Americans requested marketing events to directly support the off-road brand's sales operations in Germany. As this effort was still being run by a BMW department, Land Rover received a phone call in April/May 2000 from the Bavarians informing them that the concept had been approved after all. The first Tour, which ran under the name "Land Rover Entdecker (Discoverer) Tour", was to Jordan.

Land Rover's head office in Great Britain was also planning its own event. 2003 and 2006 saw the global marketing department putting on the G4 Challenge (G4 stood for "Global Four"): an event held in four time zones on four continents. The logistics of the project were, as it turned out, too complex for the journalists to follow the entire competition. And to add insult to injury, the media weren't allowed to drive themselves (as had been the case on all the Camel Trophy events). For cosseted-lifestyle journalists, this wasn't too great a sacrifice, but for the automobile press focusing on the experience aspect of the event, it was a PR nightmare. Either way, it was difficult for them to convey to audiences what the buzz of the G4 Tour really was.

Christian Uhrig joined the marketing department at Land Rover Germany in 2001 and together we developed the current tour concept, consisting of selection, tour and travel programme. That same year, the Land Rover Experience was founded as a form of Driving Academy for new customers. Following centrally assigned quality standards, Land Rover Experience Centres the world over were to offer a common standard of driver and off-road training courses for customers and dealers, teaching people the need to act responsibly when driving off-road while also providing ideal locations in which to conduct training.

The original Land Rover training centres are located at Eastnor Castle (on the border between England and Wales) and at the home of Land Rover in Solihull, Birmingham, where they operate under the title "Home of the Legend". Hans and I completed our respective training courses there in the '80s. Today, all Experience Centre instructors complete their training at Eastnor Castle. There are 27 Experience Centres in operation across the world. However, the "Land Rover Experience Tour" is a purely German operation, which leaves me with a sense of pride.

Our review of ten Land Rover Experience Tours and an unforgettable winter drive for journalists begins with the most complicated and longest tour we have undertaken thus far: the anniversary tour crosses through eleven countries and takes in elements of the legendary Silk Road from Germany to India. In the following chapter, we go back to our first event and then proceed from one tour to the next in chronological order to the present day. Obviously we haven't re-invented the adventure tour with the best off-road vehicles on the planet – what we have achieved, however, is this: an adventure tour with new impetus and significant improvements in the levels of professionalism and attention to detail.

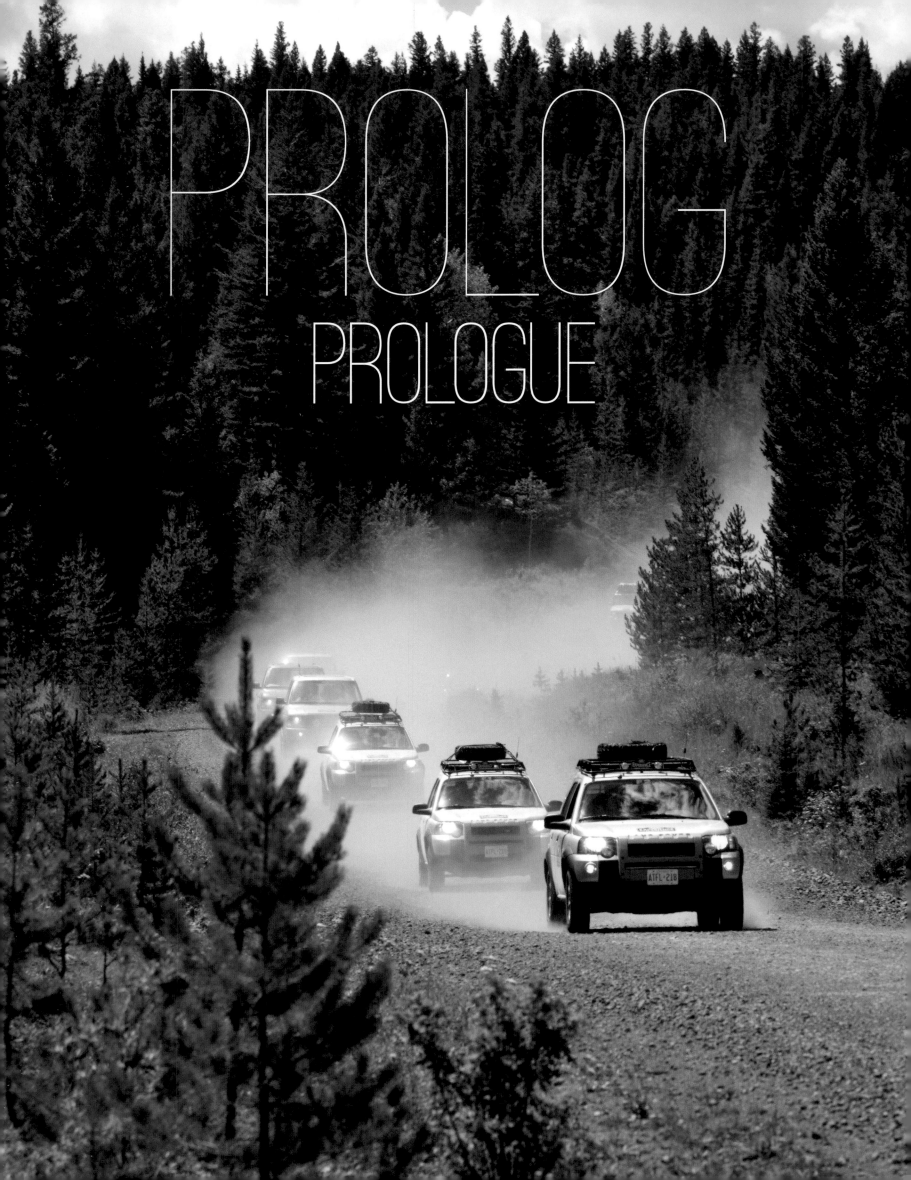

PROLOG

PROLOGUE

„Hans, Hans – Dag, Dag!
„Dag, Hans!"
„Hans, geht's da weiter?"
„Dag, sieht so aus."
„Danke Hans, Dag."
„Dag, Dag – Hans, Hans?"
„Dag hört."
„Oder auch nicht."
„Danke Hans. Hans, Dag, Dag?"
„Hier Hans. Dag?"
„Hans, also was?"
„Dag, Hans, weiter."
„Hans, Dag, klar."
„Dag, Dag, Hans, Hans?"
„Hans, Dag."
„Wie immer."
„Genau, Hans. Bis später. Dag Ende."
„Bis später. Hans Ende."

"Hans, Hans – Dag, Dag!
"Dag, Hans!"
"Hans, any movement up there?"
"Dag, looks like it."
"Thanks Hans, Dag."
"Dag, Dag – Hans, Hans?"
"Dag's listening."
"Or maybe not."
"Thanks Hans. Hans, Dag, Dag?"
"Hans here. Dag?"
"Hans, so what's happening?"
"Dag, Hans, off we go."
"Hans, Dag, understood."
"Dag, Dag, Hans, Hans?"
"Hans, Dag."
"As usual."
"Exactly, Hans. See you later. Dag out."
"See you later. Hans out."

Ich gebe zu, ob diese Unterhaltung über Funk tatsächlich so verlaufen ist und wann das war, vermag ich nicht mit hundertprozentiger Sicherheit zu sagen. Aber wer zum ersten Mal eine unserer Touren begleitet, hat zumindest den Eindruck, Hans und ich würden uns nur so unterhalten. Und da ist eine Menge Wahres dran.

Wir beide sind seelenverwandte, der Hans Hermann Ruthe und ich, und wäre es anders, gäbe es vielleicht die Land Rover Experience Touren nicht. Dieser begnadete Werkzeugbauer organisierte seit 1991 die Camel Trophy mit, wurde 1992 Adjutant des Eventdirektors und ist heute bei den Land Rover Experience Touren nicht mehr wegzudenken – meine rechte und manchmal auch linke Hand, mein gutes und manchmal auch mein schlechtes Gewissen.

Aber selbst wenn wir viel Spaß an unseren Touren haben – es steckt unendlich viel Arbeit darin, die wir alleine gar nicht leisten könnten. Deshalb möchte ich mich hier ganz besonders bei dem Team von Jaguar Land Rover Deutschland bedanken, das die Touren finanziert; bei meinem gesamten Land Rover Experience Team; bei den Ärzten, die seit Jahren die Touren begleiten; bei den Fotografen und Journalisten, die dafür sorgen, dass die Welt von unseren unvergleichlichen Touren erfährt; bei den lokalen Guides, ohne die wir niemals die unvergesslichen Tracks und Pisten gefunden hätten; und bei den unzähligen anderen Helfern, die zum Erfolg der Land Rover Experience Touren beigetragen haben. Einige von ihnen lernen Sie in diesem Buch durch persönliche Interviews kennen.

Übrigens: Oft werde ich gefragt, ob wir uns schon mal so richtig verfahren haben. Erst seit der Jubiläumstour – der Seidenstraße – muss ich zugeben: Ja. Und peinlicherweise ausgerechnet in Deutschland. Am Startpunkt Wülfrath hatten wir Krakau in Polen ins von uns sonst nie benutzte Navigationssystem eingegeben und als es uns in Dortmund „abbiegen" befahl, haben wir den Hinweis ignoriert. Wie sollte ein Navi es denn auch besser wissen können als gewiefte Weltreisende? Kurz: Es wusste es besser. Wir sind über Berlin nach Polen gereist statt über den kürzesten Weg.

Aber das ist wirklich nur eine Petitesse gegenüber den Anekdoten, Geschichten und Dramen, die ich als Leiter der Land Rover Experience in mehr als zehn Jahren Experience Tour erleben durfte. Lassen Sie sich in Wort und Bild einfach ein auf die zehn „geilsten Touren der Welt" in insgesamt 23 Länder sowie den Versuch einer „Winter-Experience" für Journalisten, die ich hier zusammengetragen habe – natürlich aus persönlichem Blickwinkel erzählt, aber immer hart an der Wahrheit. Ich habe nichts hinzugedichtet und keine Problematik, Unter- und Überschätzung ausgelassen.

Sie werden sehen: Trotz aller Erfahrung bin auch ich nicht unfehlbar.

I will admit that I can't recall with any certainty when or whether this conversation actually took place at all. However, anyone joining Hans and myself for the first time on a tour rapidly comes to the conclusion that this is how we talk to each other all the time. And there is a lot of truth in that.

Hans Hermann Ruthe and I are soulmates, and were this not the case, then we probably wouldn't have the Land Rover Experience Tour at all. From 1991 onwards, this gifted toolmaker was involved in the organization of the Camel Trophy, becoming adjutant to the event director in 1992. Today I can't imagine the Land Rover Experience Tour without him – he is my right hand and sometimes even my left. He is my conscience in the good times and the bad.

However much fun we have on the tours – there is a phenomenal amount of work involved in the organization of the event, which we couldn't achieve on our own. For this reason I would like to extend my thanks to the team at Jaguar Land Rover Germany, which finances the tours; to my own team at Land Rover Experience; to the doctors who have accompanied the tours for years; to the photographers and journalists who have seen to it that the world experiences our incomparable tours; to the local guides without whom we would never have discovered the unforgettable routes and tracks; and to countless others who have contributed to the success of the Land Rover Experience Tours. You will get to know some of them in interviews conducted for this book.

By the way, I have often been asked whether we have taken a wrong turn on a tour. Since the anniversary event on the Silk Road, I have to admit: yes. Embarrassingly enough, it happened in Germany. At our point of departure in Wülfrath we tapped Krakow in Poland into the navigation system (which we otherwise never really use), and as we approached Dortmund we ignored the instruction to turn off the motorway – as if a computer were better informed than two globetrotting professionals. Fact is, the computer was better informed, and we ended up driving to Poland via Berlin instead of taking the shorter route.

This, however, is a mere trifle when weighed up against the plethora of anecdotes, tales and dramas that I have been privileged to witness first-hand as head of the Land Rover Experience in over ten years of the tour. Enjoy the words and pictures I have put together from ten of the most awesome tours on the planet, crossing through a total of 23 countries and including a Media Winter Experience Tour we once attempted. Always from my personal perspective but as close to what really happened as possible. Nothing has been made up, and no problem, under- or overestimation of a situation has been omitted from the story.

As you will see, despite all my experience, I'm human, too.

SEIDEN — STRASSE

SILK ROAD
2013
GERMANY, POLAND, UKRAINE, RUSSIA,
KAZAKHSTAN, UZBEKISTAN,
KYRGYZSTAN, CHINA, TIBET, NEPAL, INDIA
7 EVOQUE, 4 DISCOVERY
STRECKE / DISTANCE: 16 000 KM / 10,000 MILES

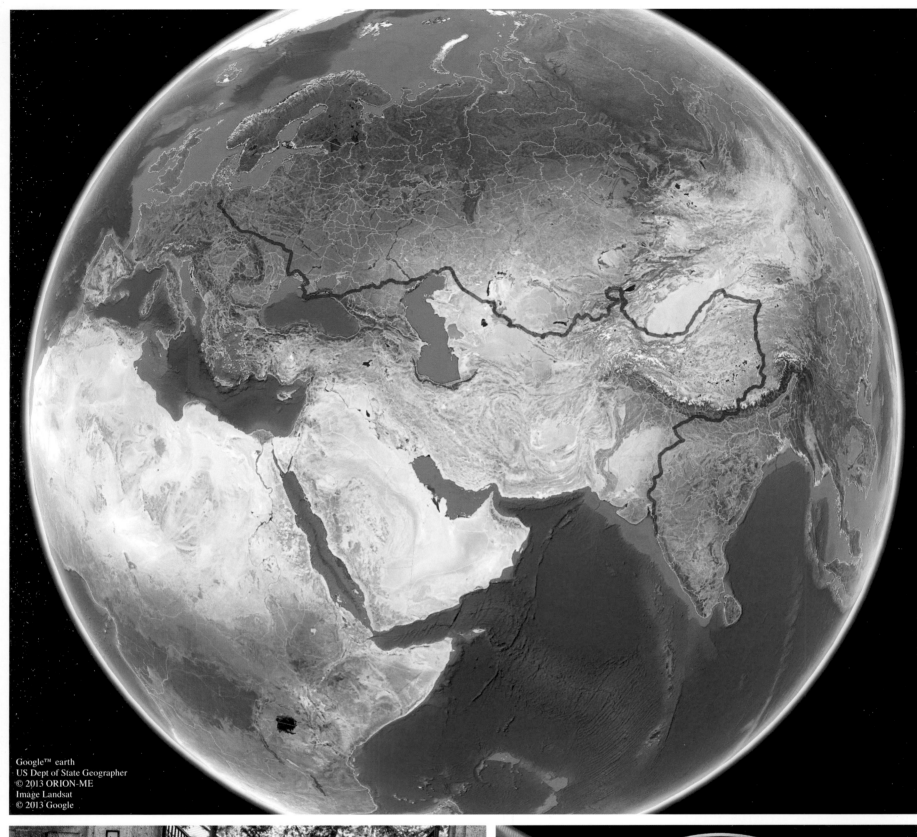

DER TRIUMPH
THE VICTORY

Unglaublich – es ist geschafft. In 50 Tagen elf Länder durchfahren, inklusive der durchaus nicht selbstverständlichen Passagen durch China und Tibet. Alle elf Autos sind in Berlin gestartet und – fast – ohne Kratzer in Mumbai angekommen. Zwölf Teilnehmer kommen gesund zurück, rund 50 Journalisten ebenso und mein Team auch. Bis auf den Doc. Ausgerechnet er muss einen Tag früher abreisen mit Verdacht auf Denguefieber. So verpasst er mit der großen Abschlussparty den letzten Höhepunkt dieser Tour – der Königin aller Experience Touren: Es ist die längste, anstrengendste, aufwendigste, aber vielleicht auch schönste. Und vor allem: die zehnte. Die Jubiläumstour.

Die Einfahrt nach Mumbai werde ich nie vergessen. So wie man (wenn überhaupt) so eine Tour nur einmal im Leben macht – und immer davon zehren kann. Ich bin noch zu aufgewühlt, um mich zu erinnern, wo genau wir langgefahren sind, zum Ziel der 16 000-Kilometer-Tour. Es war irgendwo am Strand von Mumbai, Richtung Taj Mahal Palace Hotel, das zum Tata-Konzern gehört. Ich weiß noch: Die Straße ist gesperrt, es wird getanzt, viele Leute schwenken Fahnen, eine indische Rhythmusgruppe trommelt, was das Zeug hält. Und ich höre darunter trotzdem noch mein Herz klopfen.

Und jetzt sitze ich hier alleine in meinem Zimmer, einen Gin Tonic in der Hand, und denke an alle Touren, die ich jemals geleitet habe, und an die vielen Hürden, die genommen werden mussten, bis die Jubiläumstour stand.

It's unbelievable – we made it. Eleven countries in 50 days including driving through China and Tibet, which is anything but a walk in the park. All eleven vehicles started in Berlin and arrived almost without a scratch in Mumbai. Twelve participants returned to Germany as healthy as when they left, and the same went for around 50 journalists and my team. Except for the doctor, that is. How ironic that he should be the one to have to leave early with suspected dengue fever and miss the final highlight: the end-of-tour party celebrating this, the queen of all Experience Tours. It was the longest, most tiring, most complex, but perhaps the most stunning of all the tours. And it was the tenth. The Anniversary Tour.

I will never forget driving into Mumbai. A tour like this is a once-in-a-lifetime (and most don't even manage that) opportunity, and it provides a tale for a lifetime. As I write this, I am still too exhausted to remember exactly where we drove to get to our destination at the end of the 10,000 miles. It was somewhere on Mumbai's beach towards the Taj Mahal Palace Hotel, which belongs to Tata. I can remember that the road was blocked off for us, there was dancing, lots of people were waving flags, and an Indian rhythmic band were banging their drums for all they were worth – but I could still hear my own heart beating.

And now I am sitting in my room on my own, with a gin & tonic in my hand, thinking about all the tours I have led and all the obstacles that had to be overcome to make the Anniversary Tour happen.

Die Entscheidung, wo die zehnte Tour der Land Rover Experience enden soll, ist nicht schwer zu fällen: Indien. Denn dort firmiert mit Tata die Muttergesellschaft von Jaguar Land Rover, die es möglich machte, dass es seit der Übernahme im Jahr 2008 sowohl mit Land Rover als auch mit Jaguar stetig bergauf geht. Klar, dass Mumbai – Stammsitz von Tata – das Ziel sein muss.

Aber die Tour ausschließlich in Indien zu fahren, bietet sich nicht an. Aus mehreren Gründen: Dort leben die Menschen mehr auf der Straße als in Häusern, es ist also immer und überall voll. Dazwischen stehen und laufen noch die heiligen Kühe, die man tunlichst nicht anrempeln sollte, will man heil aus der jeweiligen Ortschaft wieder herauskommen. Außerdem sind die meisten Menschen in Indien zwar überaus hilfsbereit und liebenswert, aber sie lieben auch Körperkontakt, kennen keine Scheu und kommen Mensch und Maschine oftmals so nahe, wie man das in unseren Kulturkreisen nicht kennt und schätzt. Und wer schon mal ein paar so neugierige wie gut gelaunte Inder am Auto hängen hatte, weiß, dass das zwar sehr spaßig sein kann, ein Vorankommen aber doch deutlich behindert. Aus ähnlichem Grund können wir Campsites ebenfalls nicht guten Gewissens aufbauen.

Die Lösung des Problems liegt deshalb nahe, auch wenn so eine Strecke einen von uns bislang noch nicht ausprobierten und bewältigten Organisationsaufwand bedeutet: Wir fahren von Deutschland nach Indien und wandeln damit auf den Spuren der Seidenstraße. Das hat noch niemand gemacht.

Seidenstraße – schon der Name hat einen besonderen Klang. Die Seidenstraße gehört zu den ältesten Handelsrouten der Welt: ein Netz von Karawanenwegen, auf denen über Land Waren wie Gewürze, Glas, Porzellan und natürlich Seide gehandelt wurden, aber auch Religions-, Zivilisations- und Techniktransfer zwischen Morgenland und Abendland stattfand. Heute bedeutet eine Reise auf ihren Spuren vor allem massenhaft Eindrücke fremder Kulturen.

Aber wir wären schlechte Planer, würden wir nicht ein paar Bedenken anmelden, um sie genauso zügig wieder zu verwerfen: Sind elf Länder am Stück – Deutschland, Polen, Ukraine, Russland, Kasachstan, Usbekistan, Kirgisistan, China, Tibet, Nepal, Indien – logistisch machbar? Wird so etwas nicht zu teuer – denn höhere finanzielle Mittel als für die vergangene Tour nach Bolivien lässt das Budget nicht zu? Mal eben über den Daumen gepeilte 16 000 Kilometer in 50 Tagen – finden wir überhaupt jemanden, der das mitmacht?

Unsere Antworten sind ermutigend. Wir setzen nur elf statt 14 Autos ein, somit brauchen wir auch weniger Personal. Und wir machen im Gegensatz zu einigen anderen aufwendigen Touren nur eine Vortour. Da hilft es, dass wir nicht lange nach einem Guide suchen müssen: Kostja ist der richtige. Mein Freund und Kollege Hans Hermann Ruthe – wer sonst – kennt ihn bereits von einer Reise nach China, die er (selbstverständlich mit dem Auto) bereits gemacht hat. Kostja ist Spezialist und Veranstalter für Weltreisen mit Wohnmobilen. Was wollen wir mehr?

Zum Beispiel ganz offiziell am Brandenburger Tor in Berlin starten. Allerdings gibt es dafür von den Behörden vor Ort nicht die Spur einer Genehmigung. Begründung: zu großer Aufwand, Einladung für Nachahmer, Störung des Verkehrsflusses. So erteilt uns die Stadt eine klare Absage, uns dort mit Bannern, Autos und viel Tamtam zu postieren. Aber: Sich zwischen Siegessäule und Brandenburger Tor auf dem Parkstreifen zu treffen und sich von dort im Konvoi gemäß der StVO gen Polen zu bewegen, dagegen könne man überhaupt nichts einwenden.

Somit ist der Startpunkt klar, ebenso das Ziel – der Rest dazwischen pures Abenteuer.

Deciding the destination of the Land Rover Experience Anniversary Tour hadn't been difficult: India. This is the home of Jaguar Land Rover's parent company, Tata, which, after taking over the British companies in 2008, is the reason why both Land Rover and Jaguar have been able to build on their success ever since. It was patently obvious that Mumbai – where Tata is based – would have to be the culmination of the tour.

However, taking the tour to India alone was out of the question. There were numerous reasons for this: because the majority of its population spends most of their time on the streets rather than in buildings, roads everywhere are constantly teeming with people. In between are the famous sacred cows, which are to be avoided at all costs, assuming of course you want to leave that particular town in one piece. Additionally, most people are incredibly helpful and genuine in their affection, which leads us to the next point – they are very tactile people, not at all shy, and that goes for getting very close to both man and machine, the kind of proximity rightly unheard of in our culture. If you have ever had a few Indians hanging onto your car, then you will probably confirm that while it was quite entertaining, it does slow you down somewhat. Similar reasons led us to conclude that building campsites would be ill-advised.

The solution to the problem was simple, even if the route required a level of planning and organisation far beyond the planning required for previous tours. We were going to drive from Germany to India following the route of the original Silk Road. This hadn't been done before.

The Silk Road – even the name has a special ring to it. The Silk Road is one of the world's oldest trade routes: a network of caravan trails along which goods such as spices, glass, porcelain and of course silk were transported – but also a network in which religion, civilisation and technology made the leap from Orient to Occident. To travel the Silk Road today is an opportunity to experience cultural diversity en masse.

Good planning requires considering all the possible obstacles and potential problems, even if some can be dealt with quickly. Were the eleven countries – Germany, Poland, Ukraine, Russia, Kazakhstan, Uzbekistan, Kyrgyzstan, China, Tibet, Nepal and India – logistically feasible in a single trip? Could we afford such an undertaking – we wouldn't be able to stretch our budget beyond that allocated for the Bolivia tour the previous year? We reckoned on approximately 10,000 miles in 50 days – was there anyone prepared to join us?

The answers were encouraging. Instead of 14 vehicles, we would take eleven. That would save staff. And in comparison to previous complex tours, this time only one pre-scout recce drive would be necessary. Fortunately we found a guide almost immediately. Kostja was perfect. Not surprisingly, my friend and co-worker Hans Hermann knew him from a trip he had recently undertaken to China (naturally by car). Kostja organises global RV tours. Things were really looking up.

Except that we wanted to start from the Brandenburg Gate in Berlin, and the city authorities were not particularly interested in helping us with the necessary permits. Their argumentation: too complex, the danger of copycat events, interference with traffic flow. Our plans to put up banners, position the cars and generally give the tour a great send-off received short shrift from the town hall. However, they had nothing against our parking between the Victory Column on Straße des 17. Juni and the Brandenburg Gate before heading for Poland in convoy while strictly observing German traffic regulations.

So we knew where to start and where to finish. In between was adventure pure and simple.

DAG ROGGE

geb. 6.7.1962
gelernter Fernmeldetechniker,
Geschäftsführer der Land Rover Experience Germany,
Land Rover Lead Instructor, Jäger, Hubschrauberpilot,
Pferdezüchter

born 6 July 1962
trained telecommunications specialist,
Head of Land Rover Experience Germany,
Land Rover Lead Instructor, hunter, helicopter pilot,
horse breeder

Bei deinem Job kommt man sofort auf die Idee, du bist ein geborener Outdoorer und Offroader. Stimmt das?

Dag: Überhaupt nicht. Nach der Realschule habe ich Fernmeldetechniker gelernt, dann das Fachabitur nachgemacht, ein internes BWL-Studium absolviert und beim Fernmeldeamt 1 in Düsseldorf gearbeitet. Allerdings war mir das dann bald zu wenig.

Wovon hast du geträumt?

Dag: Zumindest von mehr, als ein Beamter zu sein. Ich eröffnete daraufhin parallel zum Postjob 1983 meine eigene Promotionsfirma. Ein Bekannter arbeitete zu der Zeit schon mit seiner Agentur für Land Rover, und er suchte manchmal jemanden zum Aushelfen. Als die Post 1988 ihr Personal verringerte und Abfindungen anbot, habe ich den sicheren Job aufgegeben und mich völlig selbstständig gemacht. 1990 konnte ich dann das Land-Rover-Geschäft übernehmen – da war mein Büro noch ein Raum im Haus meiner Eltern. 1994, mit der Einfüh▮▮▮des Defender in Deutschland, habe ich dann meinen ersten Steinbruch gepach▮▮▮eute sitzt hier die Zentrale meiner Firma APS und damit die der Land Rover Experience Germany.

Also bist du Chef über ...?

Dag: ... 17 Festangestellte und rund 130 Freelancer, davon etwa 100 Fahrtrainer. Von 27 Land Rover Experience Centern weltweit ist unseres inzwischen das größte.

Welche Land Rover fährst du selber?

Dag: Viel zu selten meinen ganz frühen Land Rover Serie I aus dem Jahr 1949. Der Wagen ist voll restauriert und immer wieder bei Klassik-Rallyes zu sehen. Ein früher Serie-II-Landy wird gerade von Grund auf restauriert, und eines meiner Alltagsfahrzeuge ist ein moderner Discovery. Und dann hatte ich noch einen Defender, den ich als Winterdienstfahrzeug mit Räumschild umgebaut habe, um zu zeigen, dass es nicht immer gleich ein Unimog sein muss. Den hat allerdings ein Pflanzbetrieb gekauft – natürlich für den Winterdienst.

Wie viele Tage im Jahr bist du für die Land Rover Experience Tour unterwegs? Und wie verkraftest du den ständigen Wechsel von Zeit- und Klimazonen körperlich?

Dag: In Spitzenzeiten bis zu 200 Tage. Zeitumstellung gibt es nicht. Es ist immer Experience Zeit.

Hand aufs Herz: Wie kommt man zum Vornamen „Dag"?

Dag: Ganz einfach: Mein Vater verehrte Dag Hammarskjöld, den schwedischen Staatssekretär, UN-Generalsekretär und Friedensnobelpreisträger, der ein Jahr vor meiner Geburt starb.

Looking at your job, anyone would think that you were the born off-roading outdoors type. Any truth in that?

Dag: None at all. After secondary school, I was apprenticed as a telecommunications specialist, and then I went back to school to graduate, after which I completed a business studies course before starting work at the telephone exchange in Düsseldorf. Mind you, it wasn't long before I was bored.

What did you dream of doing?

Dag: I certainly wasn't dreaming of being a civil servant. I started my own event company in 1983 while I was still working for the post office. The agency of an acquaintance of mine was working for Land Rover, and every once in a while he needed assistance. In 1988, when the post office started eliminating positions they offered me voluntary redundancy so I gave up what was a secure job and went into business for myself. In 1990 I took over the Land Rover contract with my own agency – at that time I was still working from an office in my parents' house. When Defender was launched in Germany in 1994, I leased my first quarry which is where the headquarters of my firm APS and of course Land Rover Experience Germany is based.

So you're in charge of...?

Dag: 17 full-time staff and around 130 freelancers, of which around 100 are trained instructors. Of the 27 Land Rover Experience Centres across the globe, ours is the biggest.

Do you drive a Land Rover yourself?

Dag: I have a very early 1949 Series I that I get to drive every once in a while. It is fully restored and often takes part in classic car rallies. I'm in the process of restoring a Series II Landy, and one of my daily vehicles is a Discovery. I also had a Defender that I had converted into a snowplough just to show that vehicles other than Unimogs are capable of the task. It has been bought by a vegetable garden – they need it to keep the road open in winter.

How many days per year do you spend travelling on the Land Rover Experience Tour? And how do you cope with the constant changes in climate and time zones?

Dag: When it gets intense, I can be away for up to 200 days a year. Time zones don't mean anything to me. It is always "Experience Time".

Let's be honest. Where does the name "Dag" come from?

Dag: Simple: My father worshipped Dag Hammarskjöld, the Swedish State Secretary, Secretary-General of the UN and Winner of the Nobel Prize for peace who died a year before I was born.

Faszinierendes Usbekistan – trotzdem sind wir froh, unsere Tour in den zuverlässigen Evoque zu absolvieren und nicht in den abenteuerlichen Flugzeugen.

Fascinating Uzbekistan – nevertheless, we were happy to be driving the tour in our reliable Evoques and not flying in these somewhat antiquated aircraft.

DIE MAFIA
THE MAFIA

Rund 30000 Menschen wollen uns auf dieser einmaligen Abenteuertour begleiten – wir könnten ein Auswahlcamp in der Größe von Buxtehude veranstalten. Sorry, das sind zu viele, aber eine tolle Bestätigung für unsere Auswahl der Tour und für den Hunger nach Freiheit und Abenteuer, für Reiselust und Wissensdurst. Immerhin ein Dutzend Land-Rover-Freunde haben die Chance, einen Teil der alten Handelsstraßen und die Kulturen drumherum kennenzulernen. Aber weil die Tour so lang ist und niemand 50 Tage Zeit hat, splitten wir erstmals eine Tour in drei Sektionen, wobei in jeder Sektion zwei Teams mitfahren. Die Anforderungen sind hoch: Es kommen Tagesetappen von 1 200 Kilometern vor, und wer schon mal 500 Kilometer schnurgerade Piste durch die kasachische Wüste gefahren ist, weiß, was Eintönigkeit bedeutet und wie gefährlich sie sein kann.

Aber nicht nur das legt uns die Vortour offen – vor allem das Spritproblem holt uns ein (mal wieder, siehe Bolivien-Tour 2011), besonders auffällig in Usbekistan und an den innerchinesischen Grenzen. Schade eigentlich, dass selbst unsere Autos noch nicht nur mit Luft und Liebe fahren.

Während Kasachstan (nach Fläche der neuntgrößte Staat der Erde) zwar extrem wenige Tankstellen besitzt, können immerhin alle, die existieren, auch Kraftstoff anbieten. Im Nachbarland Usbekistan scheint es genau umgekehrt zu sein. Das Tankstellennetz in dem Land, von dem noch gut fünf Prozent zum äußersten Osteuropa gerechnet werden, ist wohl dichter als das in der Bundesrepublik, aber die wenigsten haben tatsächlich Kraftstoff in den Tanks. Von den zehn Prozent der Tankstellen, die in der glücklichen Lage sind, überhaupt Kraftstoff anbieten zu können, haben etwa 90 Prozent nur Gas auf Lager. Der magere Rest wartet auf den nächsten Tankwagen. Der kommt eben, wenn er kommt, und das auch nicht früher, sondern meistens später. Immerhin funktioniert der usbekische Flurfunk ausgezeichnet, denn immer wieder treffen wir auf kilometerlange Schlangen von wartenden Pkw, deren Fahrer uns erzählen, gleich käme ein Lastwagen und fülle die Tanks der Tankstelle wieder auf. Tatsächlich sehen wir einmal, wie eine Lieferung kommt, die allerdings nicht mal für einen Bruchteil der wartenden Benzinschlucker reicht.

Womit ich unser Problem auch nur halb umrissen habe. Alle Wagen dieser Experience Tour benötigen Diesel – und das ist in Usbekistan ein noch selteneres Gut als Benzin. Selbst wenn das ölige Gemisch tatsächlich irgendwo vorhanden ist, handelt es sich oft nur um den sogenannten „schwarzen" Diesel – ein Treibstoffderivat aus Erdölrückständen mit einem Schuss Diesel, gedacht für die allesfressenden Kamaz-Laster, die durch das Land stänkern. Im Herbst potenziert sich das Problem. Dann wird der gesamte Dieselvorrat Usbekistans an die Fahrzeuge ausgegeben, die bei der landesweiten großen Baumwollernte helfen. Wir müssen also dringend Diesel-Depots einrichten, denn wir können es uns bei der langen Haupttour nicht leisten, irgendwo lange untätig herumzustehen oder Kraftstoff zu suchen.

Was also tun eines Nachts auf der Vortour? Wir wenden uns vertrauensvoll an die so heimische wie freundliche Sprit-Mafia. Das dauert seine Zeit, aber mit den richtigen Guides, die wiederum die richtigen Fragen bei den richtigen Personen stellen, landen wir irgendwann an den richtigen Zapfsäulen. Die stehen zwar in einem stockdunklen Hinterhof, sind mit Teppichen abgedeckt und sehen aus, als sei durch ihre Schläuche seit Sowjetzeiten nichts Flüssiges mehr durchgekrochen, aber plötzlich sprudelt hier reinster Dieselsaft hervor. Der Preis ist gepfeffert, aber da Sprit das Salz in der Suppe von Automobilreisen ist, nehmen wir das hin.

Noch mehr Würze wird dem Deal verliehen (wie übrigens auch jedem anderen usbekischen Deal) durch das Begleichen der Rechnung mit der Landeswährung Sum. Der größte Schein zeigt 1 000 Sum. Das sind zum Reisezeitpunkt (offiziell) etwa 40 Eurocent (schwarz getauscht bei der ebenso heimischen wie freundlichen Bargeld-Mafia etwa 30 Eurocent). Die Folge: Die Usbeken laufen beim Einkaufen mit schwarzen Tüten voller Geld herum und zahlen selbst ihr Mittagessen in den vielen Garküchen aus 100 000er-Einheiten (ein vollständiges Bündel ist gleich 40 Euro), die kein Mensch nachzählt – bis auf die noch nicht sehr zahlreichen Touristen. Die damit aber überhaupt nicht klarkommen.

Mit Benzinproblemen ganz anderer Art werden wir an der Provinzgrenze von China zu Tibet konfrontiert. Aufgrund der langen Strecken, die wir fahren müssen, ist jedes Auto mit zwei bis drei 20-Liter-Kanistern Diesel auf dem Dach bestückt. Insgesamt führen wir auf der Vortour etwa 200 Liter Extrasprit mit. Er ist als Notfallration gedacht, weil die Kraftstoffqualität zum Beispiel in Lhasa und Nepal nach unseren Informationen grottenschlecht ist. So haben wir zur Sicherheit auch Helikopterfilter samt Wasserabscheider und Partikelfänger im Gepäck.

Schon bei der Ankunft an der Grenze fällt uns ein riesiger Berg von Blech- und Plastikkanistern auf, die neben der Zollstation aufgetürmt sind. Ich ahne es schon: Hier will uns jemand an die Vorräte. Und tatsächlich kommen wir nicht an den Zöllnern vorbei, ohne uns der Kanister entledigt zu haben. Der Grund ist nicht Mangel an eigenem Kraftstoff oder Schikane von Weltreisenden, sondern die absolute Kraftstoffkontrolle der Chinesen in Tibet wegen der immer wieder vorkommenden Selbstverbrennungen von Mönchen.

Also keine Chance, den kostbaren Saft mitzunehmen. Allerdings möchte ich den guten Diesel nun auch nicht unbedingt den wirtschaftsboomenden Chinesen schenken. Also verteilen wir ihn an die tibetanischen Truckerfahrer, die in langer Schlange an der Grenze warteten. So happy sind die Jungs beim Warten wahrscheinlich lange nicht mehr gewesen.

Around 30,000 people applied to join us on this once-in-a-lifetime adventure tour. We'd have to build a selection camp the size of a small airport to fit them all in. Sorry, folks, we can't take you all, even if it does confirm that the interest in the tour and the hunger people have for adventure travel and new and different cultures is still enormous. Nevertheless, a dozen Land Rover fans have the opportunity to explore the trade routes of old and experience the different cultures along the way for themselves. For the first time, though, because the tour is so long and nobody has 50 days to spare, we have split the tour into three sections with two teams driving each section. It is demanding. There are days when 750 miles have to be driven in one go, and anyone who has driven 300 miles in a straight line through the Kazakh desert knows the meaning of monotony and just how dangerous that can be.

The pre-scout also revealed that fuel would be an issue again (as we experienced on the 2011 Bolivia Tour), particularly in Uzbekistan and on the borders between provinces in China. It is a pity that our vehicles still don't run on love and air alone.

While Kazakhstan (which according to its percentage of the earth's surface is the ninth largest country on the planet) has very few fuel stations, at least all of them have fuel to sell. Across the border in Uzbekistan, the situation is exactly the opposite. The fuel-station network in a country of which five percent is considered the easternmost periphery of Europe is, on paper, more extensive than its German counterpart – but only a very few have fuel of any kind in their tanks. Of the ten percent with fuel available for sale, 90 percent can offer only gas. Everybody else must wait for the fuel lorry that turns up on an "as and when" basis, with the emphasis more on "as" than on "when". Fortunately, the Uzbek "grapevine" is excellent, as we repeatedly encountered mile-long queues of cars whose drivers told us that a fuel lorry would be along shortly to replenish the fuel station. Once, we actually witnessed a delivery, but it turned out not to have been ample enough for even a fraction of the waiting gas-guzzlers.

And this brings me to the next part of the fuel problem. All our Experience Tour vehicles run on diesel, and that is even harder to find than petrol. And should you actually find something that looks like fuel oil, more often than not it is the so-called "black" diesel – a fuel derivative made from the residue of crude oil with a dash of diesel, originally manufactured for the Kamaz lorries known for their ability to run on anything and which can be found everywhere. The issue really comes to a head in the fall. Uzbekistan's complete supply of diesel is held over for the vehicles used to bring in the national cotton harvest. We would need to set up diesel storage depots, as we can't afford to hang around or hunt for fuel during the main event.

How does one spend an evening on the pre-scout recce? Naturally a friendly chat with the equally friendly local fuel mafia. It takes time, but with the right guides asking the right people the right questions, we finally made it to the right fuel pumps. They were in some gloomy backyard, covered with carpets, and looked as if nothing had flowed through their hoses since the days of the Soviet Union, but all of a sudden Rudolf's finest started pouring out of the pistol. The prices are outrageous, of course, but given that a tour without diesel is like a car without wheels, we have to live with it.

The deal (like every other Uzbek deal, incidentally) gets more outrageous when paying the bill in the local Sum currency. The largest-denomination banknote is for 1,000 Sum. At the official exchange rate when we are travelling, this is worth 40 Euro cents (on the black market with the local, friendly cash mafia, around 30 Euro cents). The result: the Uzbeks go shopping with large black bags full of bank notes, and even lunch in one of the many hot food stalls is paid for using 1,000 Sum notes bundled into a roll to make 100,000 Sum (a complete roll is worth around £34 or $54). Nobody ever bothers to check, other than the small number of tourists who don't understand the system at all.

A different kind of fuel problem awaits us on the provincial border between China and Tibet. As a consequence of the distances we are travelling each vehicle has an additional two or three 20-litre jerry cans of diesel on the roof. On the pre-scout recce, that equated to a total of approximately 200 litres of extra fuel. According to our sources, the quality of the diesel in Lhasa and Nepal is so poor that we decided it was prudent to carry an emergency supply on board the vehicles. For the same reason we also had water separators, helicopter filters and dust filters on board.

On arriving at the border, we couldn't help noticing a huge mountain of steel and plastic jerry cans at the side of the customs post. It dawned on me that someone out there wanted our reserve diesel. And so it came to pass – the customs officers wouldn't let us by without relieving us of our jerry cans. The reason is not the lack of diesel or the desire to victimize the globetrotting community; no, it is simply the Chinese insistence on having their hands on every drop of fuel in Tibet because of the monks' reliance on self-immolation as a form of protest.

So taking our precious diesel with us was completely out of the question. At the same time, I was disinclined to hand it over as a gift to an economic powerhouse such as China. Instead, we shared it among the Tibetan lorry drivers waiting in the long queue at the border. Judging by the smiles on their faces, the gift was probably a rare highlight during the long wait.

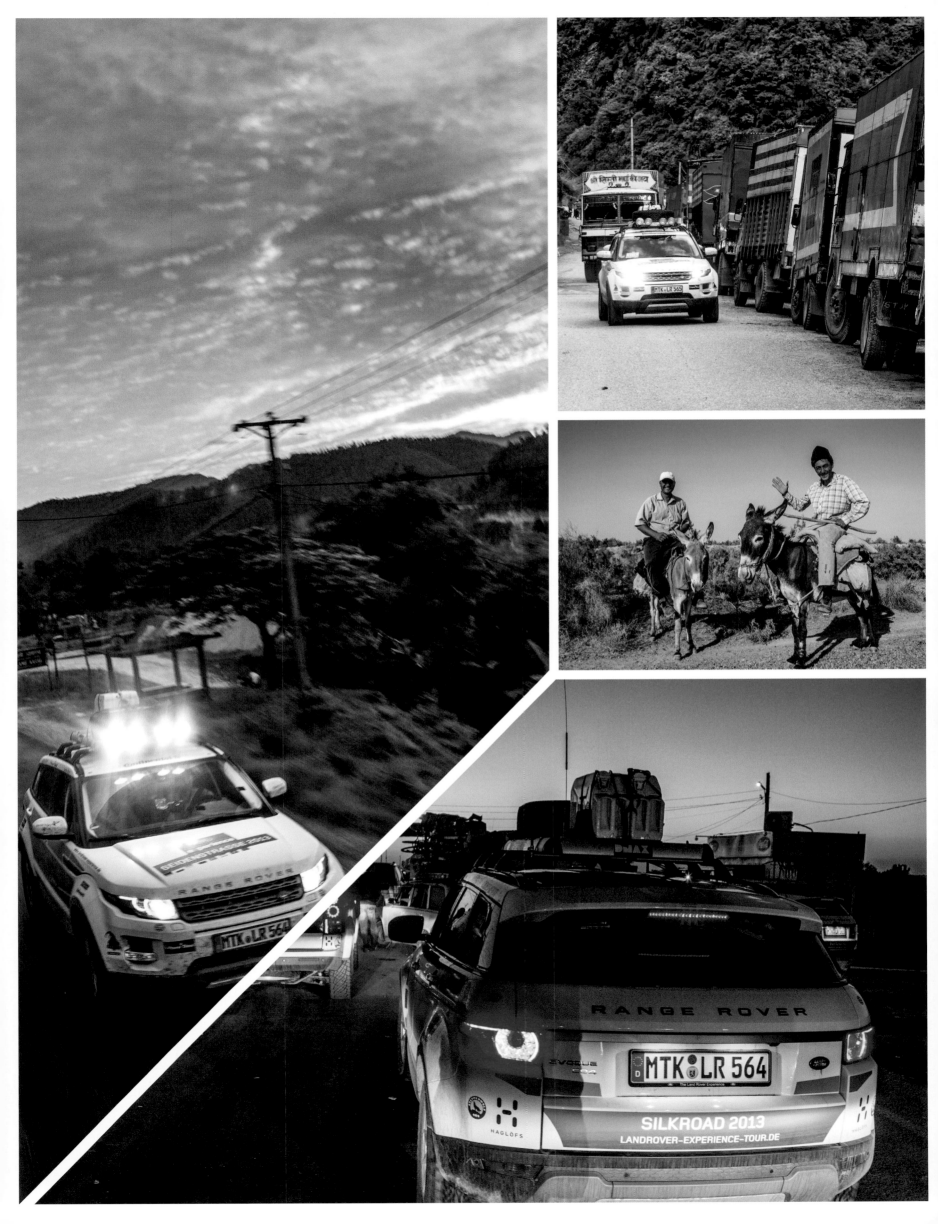

DER SCHNEE
THE SNOW

Es ist April, es ist Vortour und es ist ganz und gar ungewöhnlich: In Kasachstan schneit es. Als ich aus unserem einfachen Hotel zum Parkplatz gehe, bekomme ich einen mächtigen Schreck: Wir müssen am Morgen die Autos freischaufeln – 30 Zentimeter Schnee überraschen uns total. Das bedeutet schon mal Zeitverzug, und Zeit ist das einzige, was wir nicht haben. Hinzu kommt: Weder unsere Kleidung noch die Bereifung der Wagen sind irgendwie einem Wintereinbruch angepasst. An der nächsten Tankstelle frage ich vorsichtig, ob das Wetter Richtung Süden ähnlich ist. Die ernüchternde Antwort: „Die nächsten 1000 Kilometer bleibt es so." Dazu muss man wissen: Kasachstan ist gut 2,7 Millionen Quadratkilometer groß.

Na klasse. Uns ist erstmals auf dieser Tour nicht mehr nach Späßchen zumute. Es bleibt nichts anderes, als rein in die Autos und los. Das Schneetreiben wird dichter, die Sicht beträgt zeitweise nicht mehr als 100 Meter. Und das auf kasachischen Straßen, kein Zuckerschlecken. Langsame, unbeleuchtete Autos und Trucks machen die Fahrt genauso gefährlich wie nicht mehr sichtbare Pistenbegrenzungen, Schlaglöcher oder plötzliche Kurven nach kilometerlanger Fahrt geradeaus. Hier muss jeder für jeden mitdenken. Der Leader im Führungsfahrzeug sagt über Funk an, wenn der Rest des Konvois überholen kann – eine Fahrhilfe, die sich unter anderem schon auf den engen Bergstraßen Boliviens bewährt hat. Gerade noch rechtzeitig sehe ich nach langer und ereignisloser Kilometerfresserei als Fahrer des ersten Wagens, dass die Straße blockiert ist. Eine Ansammlung von Lkw behindert unsere Weiterfahrt. Und jetzt sehen wir auch das Dilemma: Der erste Kamaz hat sich eingedreht und ist mit dem Zugfahrzeug in einer Schneewehe hängen geblieben, der Hänger hat sich quer gestellt. Das Schlimmste: die Ratlosigkeit der Trucker. Es wird viel geredet und wenig getan.

Ein Großteil der russischen und kasachischen Laster ist nicht nur alt, achsenlahm und rostgeschwächt, sondern auch noch sehr schlecht mit Hilfsmitteln aller Art ausgerüstet. Aber unser Bergeequipment ist auf dem neuesten Stand. Und da wir es eilig haben, siehe oben, koordiniere ich sofort die Bergung. Oder zumindest das Vorhaben, irgendwie eine Gasse zum Passieren zu öffnen. Wir laden die Trucker ein, zu Schaufeln zu greifen, schieben selber Schnee weg und zerren dann mit Bergegurten, die an unsere Land Rover gebunden sind, an dem Lastwagen. Es braucht viele Ansätze, Versuche und noch mehr Schweiß, bis wir eine Schneise neben der Fahrbahn geschlagen haben, um passieren zu können. Das Angebot der Lastwagenfahrer, die Schneise noch zu vergrößern, damit auch sie mit ihren Uralt-Trucks vorbeikommen, müssen wir ausschlagen. Die Aktion hat bereits jetzt schon drei wertvolle Stunden gekostet. Stunden, die unsere Nachtruhe minimieren. Wie immer bei solchen Aktionen.

It's April, we're on our pre-scout recce, and how about this for bizarre: Kazakhstan was experiencing a snowstorm. As I walked from our basic hotel to the car park, I realized that the following morning we would have to dig our cars out of the snow. An impressive 12 inches of snow had caught us completely unawares. This put us behind schedule – and our schedule had no time buffer built in. We lacked appropriate winter clothing, and our vehicles had no winter tires. At the next filling station I tentatively asked whether the weather in the south was any different. The sober response: "It's like this for the next 600 miles." Just to put that in perspective, however, Kazakhstan is a good 1 million square miles in size. Wonderful. For the first time on this trip, no one was laughing. We had no choice but to get into the cars and hit the road. The driving snow started getting thicker, reducing visibility at times to no more than 300 feet, and on Kazakh roads this was no walk in the park. Slow-moving cars and lorries without lights are a constant hazard and no less dangerous than the hard shoulder marker poles that have disappeared in the blizzard, the potholes and the sudden curves after mile-long straights. Teamwork is critical. The lead vehicle communicates to the rest of the convoy when it is safe to overtake – a method that had proved its worth on the narrow mountain passes in Bolivia.

I was in the lead car on a particularly long section that had thus far been without incident when at the last minute I noticed that the road ahead was blocked. A line of lorries prevented us from continuing on our journey. Upon closer investigation, we saw what the problem was: the first Kamaz in the convoy had lost traction in the snow, and the tractor unit was stuck in a snowdrift while the trailer had jack-knifed. The worst part was that the lorry drivers hadn't a clue what to do. The standard approach to the problem appears to be to discuss at length without actually undertaking anything to solve the problem.

Most Russian and Kazakh lorries are not only old, with years of overloading and rust having taken their toll, but they also lack recovery gear (and for that matter any other kind of on-board emergency equipment.) That said, our recovery equipment was brand new and state-of-the-art. Also we had a deadline to meet (see above), so I set about coordinating the recovery – or, at the very least, freeing up a lane so that vehicles could get past. We managed to persuade the lorry drivers to grab whatever shovels they could find and started shovelling snow ourselves before attaching the recovery straps we carried on the Land Rovers to the lorry and pulling it out of the drift. A number of strategies, attempts and a great deal of sweat were required before we finally managed to clear a way next to the road enabling us to get by. We had to refuse the lorry drivers' proposal to increase the size of the passage so that they could get their old-timers back on the road again, too. The hold-up had already cost us three valuable hours. Three hours fewer in the sack. As usual, the same old story.

DIE PAPIERE
THE DOCUMENTS

Niemandsländer sind für mich extrem anstrengend. Das, was in Europa kaum existiert, ist zwischen den Staaten des ehemaligen Ostblocks üblich: Landstreifen von bis zu 20 Kilometern Länge, um die sich niemand kümmert, die scheinbar keinem gehören – eine Art Pufferzone zwischen Ländern, die sich nie kannten und sich deswegen auch heute noch kaum kennen. Nach Passieren einer Grenze kann man nicht zurück; auf der anderen Seite weiß man nicht, ob die Zöllner des nächsten Landes einen hineinlassen. Bei Vortouren bin ich entspannter, da habe ich Profis bei mir und wir sind nur zwei bis drei Wagen. Auf einer Haupttour wie hier auf der Seidenstraße mit elf Autos ist das etwas anderes. Erst recht, wenn etwas völlig Unerwartetes passiert. Wie auf der Fähre zwischen der Ukraine und Russland.

Will man die Grenze am Schwarzen Meer überwinden, muss man in den Zollhof der Ukraine, zeigt dort seine Fahrzeugpapiere und Pässe, fährt von dort auf eine stets volle Fähre, tuckert eine halbe Stunde übers Wasser und landet im russischen Zollhof, wo sich die Papier-Prozedur wiederholt. Damit wir mit allen elf Autos auf ein und dieselbe Fähre passen, habe ich ein paar Scheine lockergemacht. Der Zollbeamte dort hat mich sofort wiedererkannt, mir freundlich auf die Schulter geklopft und gut gelaunt gesagt: „Du weißt doch, wie das geht …" Erst mal auf dem Wasser, entspanne ich mich auf dem Fahrersitz meines Discovery, die Beine locker auf die geöffnete Tür gelegt. Da kommt unser Kameramann Medi angeschlendert und fragt im Vorbeigehen, wie denn die Unterlagen für die Autos eigentlich aussehen. „Wieso interessiert dich das?", frage ich ihn misstrauisch. „Ich will nur gucken", sagt er. Das kommt mir spanisch vor und ich setze ihn auf den Topf. Was er erzählt, belustigt mich: „Da schwamm eben so eine DIN-A5-Klarsichthülle im Wasser vorbei, und ich dachte, ich hätte ein Land-Rover-Logo drauf gesehen." Ich schicke ihn weg mit den Worten, er solle sich bitte bessere Witze ausdenken.

Aber eigentlich weiß ich ja aus Erfahrung, dass es nichts gibt, was es nicht gibt, und so bitte ich dann doch kurz darauf jede Autobesatzung, nachzusehen, ob ihre Papiere noch vorhanden sind. Alle ziehen sie lässig aus irgendwelchen Taschen – nur Teilnehmer Andre klopft seine Klamotten immer hektischer ab. Und muss gestehen: Sie sind weg. Wie sich herausstellt: Locker an der oberen Reling stehend wollte er sie in seine Haglöfs-Weste stecken, um sie nicht im Auto zu lassen. Hat er auch gemacht – aber das Netz auf der Innenseite der Jacke dient ausschließlich dem Tragekomfort, ist also oben und unten offen und damit keine Tasche. So fanden die Dokumente den Weg ins Schwarze Meer.

Das ist nun wirklich nicht witzig: Mitten im Niemandsland plötzlich ohne Unterlagen zu stehen, zumal an einem Sonnabend, ist vielmehr prekär. In jedem Kuvert befinden sich die originalen Versicherungsunterlagen des betreffenden Autos, die originalen Fahrzeugscheine und mit der Apostille eine beglaubigte Abschrift, dass ich die Verantwortung für jedes Auto des Konvois trage. Auch die diversen Vorschläge, um sich aus dieser misslichen Lage zu befreien, halte ich eher für kontraproduktiv: „Rettungsboot zu Wasser lassen", „Käpt'n zum Umkehren und zur Suche überreden" und so weiter.

Zum Glück habe ich vor der Tour vom Büro alle Unterlagen in Farbe kopieren lassen und mitgenommen. So nutze ich also die restlichen zehn Minuten auf der Fähre, um die Kopien auf Fahrzeugpapiergröße zurechtzuschneiden und ein bisschen zu beten, die Russen mögen das nicht bemerken.

Ich gebe zu, an der russischen Grenze habe ich leicht geschwitzt und vielleicht noch etwas auf die Grenzer (in diesem Fall zwei attraktive russische Grenzerinnen) eingeredet, als ich es sonst tue, um sie von den falschen Unterlagen, zu viel Medizin oder anderen nicht in jedem Land erlaubten Dingen abzulenken. Und tatsächlich: Sie bemerken den Trick nicht. Kaum in Russland eingereist, bitte ich mein Büro zuhause in Wülfrath um die Ausstellung neuer Originaldokumente, und kurz vor der Ausreise aus Russland bringen die neu angekommenen Journalisten die Papiere mit.

Permits, Urkunden, Passierscheine, Autopapiere, Pässe mit Visa – das sind neben Autos, Wasser und Brot die wohl wichtigsten Dinge auf so einer Tour. Wenn da etwas nicht stimmt, werde ich sofort nervös. Und selbst, wenn diesmal das Problem trickreich gelöst wurde: Das wird wohl so bleiben, solange ich die Welt erkunde.

I find no-man's-land extremely tedious. Almost completely unknown in Europe, it is the norm between the states of the former Eastern Bloc. Strips of land that can extend to up to 12 miles, for which no one is responsible, apparently belonging to nobody. A buffer zone between countries that have never had relations with one another and that aren't very concerned to change the status quo today. You pass one border, meaning there is no turning back; and on the other side there is no guarantee that the customs officials will let you in at all. On a pre-scout I am more relaxed, as I am surrounded by professionals and we have two, maybe three vehicles. During a main event such as this one, we had eleven vehicles, and that is very different, especially when something unexpected happens. Such as on the ferry between the Ukraine and Russia.

If you intend to cross the border at the Black Sea then you have to enter the Ukraine customs area, show your vehicle documentation and your passport. Then you drive onto a ferry, which is always full, and steam for half an hour across the water before landing in the Russian customs area, where the whole papers thing repeats itself. Getting all eleven vehicles onto one and the same ferry had cost me. The customs official had recognised my face, patted me on the shoulder and, while smiling, said, "You know how it works…" On the water, I was relaxing for a few minutes, feet up on the open door of my Discovery, when along came our cameraman Medi and asked in an off-the-cuff kind of way what our vehicle documentation actually looked like. I was a little suspicious and asked him why he needed to know. "I just wanted to have a look," he replied. This sounded like a fairy tale to me, so I decided to grill him. What he said made me laugh. "I saw an A5 plastic folder in the water and I thought I saw a Land Rover logo on it." I packed him off, telling him to think up a better joke.

However, as I know from bitter experience, anything is possible. So I asked every team to check their papers. Cool as cucumbers, everyone pulled them out of some bag in their respective vehicle. Everyone, that is, except the participant Andre, who looked increasingly nervous as he checked his clothes. Then he had to admit that the papers were missing. This is how it had happened: standing up on deck, he had put the documentation in his Haglöfs vest to ensure that they wouldn't be left in the vehicle. The jacket's inside mesh, however, is a comfort feature and was open at both ends – i.e. it wasn't a pocket. This is how the documentation landed in the Black Sea.

This wasn't funny. In the middle of no-man's-land without papers, on a Saturday, is a worrying predicament for a number of reasons. Each vehicle had an envelope with the following papers: the original insurance documentation for each vehicle; the original vehicle registration document; and a certified legal copy of a document confirming that I was responsible for every vehicle in the convoy. The various methods suggested to extricate us from our plight – such as "use a rescue boat to hunt for the envelope" or "persuade the captain to turn around and look for the documents" – clearly weren't helpful.

Fortunately, I had made colour copies of all our documentation beforehand, so I used the remaining ten minutes on the ferry to cut the copies to the right size and prayed a little that the Russians wouldn't notice.

Admittedly on the Russian border I was sweating a little and spent more time than I usually would chatting with the border guards (in this case, two attractive Russian women) to divert their attention from the falsified documents, excess medication or anything else that wasn't allowed in every country on the planet. Fortunately, it worked – they didn't notice the difference. Once in Russia proper, I contacted my office to organise new copies of all the documents, which the next group of journalists to join the tour brought with them.

Permits, certificates, passes, vehicle documentation, passports with visa – along with the cars, bread and water, these are the most important things on an expedition like this. If something is not one hundred percent, I get nervous. Even if the problem had been solved with a bit of trickery this time, I will always be like this as long as I spent my time exploring the world.

DAS BAKSCHISCH

THE BAKSHEESH

Es war mir schon bei der Planung glasklar, dass wir mit diversen merkwürdigen Zöllnern, diversen merkwürdigen Regeln, diversen merkwürdigen Formularen und diversen merkwürdigen Landessitten an den verschiedenen Grenzen konfrontiert werden würden. Deswegen habe ich in weiser Voraussicht – erstmals auf einer Tour – ein „Bakschisch-Budget" eingerichtet. Nur, dass ich die Bestechungsgeld-Reserve bereits an der Grenze Polen-Ukraine anbrechen muss, damit habe ich nicht gerechnet.

Spätestens, wenn noch in Polen die Holzhütten und die Panjepferde auftauchen, die Straßen fühlbar schlechter und die Rauchsäulen aus den Schornsteinen dunkler werden, landet man in einer anderen, älteren Welt. Hier lebt der graue Osten noch, der immer farbloser wird, je weiter man sich vom Westen entfernt.

Wir haben keine Waren mit, die wir anmelden müssten – das sieht sogar der Zöllner an der polnisch-ukrainischen Grenze bei unserer Einreise ein. Aber leider stehen wir auf der falschen Wartespur, wie er uns zu verstehen gibt. Nun, denken wir, wechseln wir sie eben – rein technisch kein Problem. Dagegen hat der gute Mann allerdings etwas. Mit Nachdruck untersagt er uns den nötigen Spurwechsel. Und brummt uns ein ordentliches Strafgeld auf. So macht man sich Freunde.

Die Einreise aus der Ukraine nach Russland verläuft dagegen erstaunlich entspannt. Unser Pfefferspray wird zwar konfisziert, aber wir verteilen dafür Modellautos und T-Shirts, die wir extra für diesen Zweck in beträchtlicher Anzahl eingepackt haben.

In dem Riesenreich sind es nämlich Polizisten und nicht Zöllner, die uns ans Portemonnaie wollen. Mitten in Russland wird Hans angehalten, weil er angeblich eine weiße Linie überfahren habe. Die Strafe: Konfiszierung des Passes für einen Monat, wahlweise Zahlung von 200 Dollar, dann bekäme er seinen Pass sofort wieder. 200 Dollar? Nee, das finden wir zu viel. Hans legt einen 100-Dollar-Schein in den Pass und wartet auf die Reaktion. Die kommt prompt: Weiter geht's Richtung Osten.

Die nächste Kontrolle: „Du Germansky?"

Ich nicke.

„Du Schnaps?"

Ich schüttele den Knopf. Doch das überzeugt den freundlichen Polizisten nicht.

„Du Germansky, du Schnaps!"

Und dann fordert er uns alle auf, ihm in seine Polizeistation am Straßenrand zu folgen. Dort müssen wir blasen.

Das Messgerät sieht höchst modern und funktionstüchtig aus. Und es scheint die Wahrheit zu sprechen: Ich kein Schnaps, meine Kollegen kein Schnaps. Aber Hans, der als letzter bläst, hat angeblich 0,48 Promille im Blut. Was definitiv gelogen ist.

Jetzt werden wir laut. Schiebung! Schmu! Allesamt protestieren wir mächtig. Hans besteht auf seine unnachahmliche, weltgewandte Weise auf einen Bluttest. Bluttest! Bluuuuuutteeeeest!!! Der Lärm, den wir veranstalten, lockt nun endlich den Vorgesetzten des geldgierigen Beamten heraus. Was denn los sei? Wir beschweren uns über die Manipulation am Messgerät. Manipulation! Maaaaaanipulatioooooooon! Und der Chef sieht ein: Hier hat er ein paar zu harte Nüsse vor sich. Und lässt uns gehen.

When we started planning, we knew full well that we would have dealings with all manner of weird and wonderful customs officials with their equally weird and wonderful rules, forms and national traits on the numerous borders we had to cross. Prudently, and for the first time ever for a tour, I established a "bribes budget". That said, I hadn't anticipated breaking into this reserve quite as early as the Polish-Ukrainian border.

Wooden huts, the traditional pack horses, roads barely worthy of the name and chimneys emitting clouds of thick, sooty smoke are the clearest indication that one has landed in a very different, older world, where the colour grey grows more prominent the further east one drives.

We had no goods on board requiring declaration – this fact was registered by the customs official on the Polish-Ukrainian border. Unfortunately, we were parked in the wrong queue, as he was at pains to point out. We thought all we needed to do was change lanes, which was, technically speaking, easily accomplished. Our friendly customs official saw it differently, though, forbidding us from moving from the spot at all and immediately issuing a large fine. A lesson in how to make friends.

Entering into Russia from the Ukraine was a comparatively relaxed affair. Our pepper sprays were confiscated, but the model cars and T-shirts with which we were particularly well equipped proved to be very popular.

The thing is, in the former Soviet Union it is the police and not the customs authorities that are interested in emptying our wallets. Somewhere in the middle of Russia, Hans was pulled over for allegedly crossing a solid white line. The penalty: confiscation of his passport for a month or a no-questions-asked payment of 200 dollars and his passport would be returned immediately. 200 dollars? We thought that was over the top. Hans slipped a 100-dollar bill in his passport and waited for the reaction. It was immediate – we were free to head east.

At the next checkpoint: "You Germansky?"

I nodded.

"You schnapps?"

I shook my head. But our smiling policeman wasn't convinced.

"You Germansky. You schnapps!"

At which point we were asked to accompany him to the police station at the side of the road and subjected to a breath test. The breathalyzer looked modern enough, appeared to be in working order and seemed to be telling the truth. I, no schnapps, my colleagues also no schnapps. Hans, however, who was last up to be tested, allegedly had a blood-alcohol level of 0.48. This was clearly the stuff of fiction.

We started shouting. This is a set-up! We were being taken for a ride. We upped the tone of our protest. Hans insisted in his own inimitable and cosmopolitan way on having a blood test. By now the noise we were making had even drawn the greedy police officer's superior out of his office. We complained bitterly about the manipulation of the breathalyzer and lo and behold the boss decided to back down and let the obstreperous foreigners on their way.

Ich bin erleichtert, als wir Russland hinter uns lassen. Wer des Kyrillischen nicht mächtig ist, kann hier nichts lesen; wer bislang immer mal wieder auf den Rechtsstaat schimpfte, weiß plötzlich, was er an ihm hat, weil Russland damit so gar nichts gemein hat – hier zerfallen die Sitten genauso schnell wie die Häuser. Kann uns noch irgendeine Grenze überraschen? Nicht wirklich, nur die Art der Abzocke. Wie an der Grenze Russland-Kasachstan.

Dabei haben wir diesmal alles richtig gemacht. Korrekte Grenze, korrekte Spur, korrekte Papiere. Der Grenzbeamte will natürlich die Unterlagen sehen – ihn macht es stutzig, dass die Wagen einer Company gehören, aber Privatfahrer am Steuer sitzen. Er will die Urkunden sehen, die besagen, dass das alles seine Richtigkeit hat. Wir geben sie ihm, zunächst die deutsche Version. Er nickt, dann will er sie auf Englisch sehen. Haben wir auch dabei – seine Laune verschlechtert sich. Er nickt wiederum, dann will er sie auf Russisch sehen. Haben wir auch – wir sind wirklich bestens vorbereitet. Jetzt ist seine Laune ganz im Keller. Er gibt uns zu verstehen, dass die Papiere okay sind und wir nicht ausreisen können.

Noch schwieriger, als mit korrupten Beamten zu diskutieren, die irgendeinen Grund für die Verweigerung der Weiterfahrt vortäuschen, ist es, mit Beamten zu diskutieren, die nicht mal einen Grund vortäuschen, sondern die Weiterfahrt ohne Begründung verbieten. Ich berate mich mit Hans und dem Team und wir beschließen, als letztes Mittel die klassische Überzeugungsformel anzuwenden: ein 100-Dollar-Schein im Reisepass. Damit gehe ich zu dem Beamten zurück und bitte ihn, sich den Ausweis noch einmal genau anzusehen. Vielleicht findet er ja doch noch den richtigen Stempel, das richtige Formular, den richtigen Durchfahrts-S-c-h-e-i-n. Tatsächlich wird er fündig – und lässt uns ohne weitere Fragen ausreisen.

In dieser Form ist uns das tatsächlich nur an den Grenzen der Ukraine, Russlands und Kasachstans passiert, andere Grenzen bergen andere Überraschungen. Zum Beispiel das interessante Schauspiel an einem kleinen kasachisch-usbekischen Grenzübergang, den wir auf der Vortour gewählt haben in der Annahme, hier wäre nicht so viel los. Die Straße gleicht einem monströsen, matschigen Kraterfeld. Hier stehen große Berge-Lkw, um die vielen dort havarierten Lastwagen über die Grenze zu ziehen. In den Zollhof darf aber nur eine gewisse Anzahl an Fahrzeugen, sodass davor eine riesige Schlange an Trucks auf Einlass wartet. Warum das alles Willy-Betz-Laster sind, weiß ich bis heute nicht.

Während uns die Kasachen problemlos ausreisen lassen, kommen wir in Usbekistan an einen höchst peniblen Grenzer, der seine Ausbildung anscheinend bei der Stasi genossen hat. Im Zöllnerhaus werde ich in einen neonbeleuchteten Raum geführt, den ich guten Gewissens als Verhörzimmer bezeichnen kann. Der Mann, in Zivil, will alles von mir wissen, und zwar jedes Detail der Reise. Weil so ein Vorhaben wie die Land Rover Experience Jubiläumstour durch elf Länder mit Vortour, Teilnehmern und Journalisten schwer zu vermitteln ist, behaupte ich, wir seien eine Freundesgruppe auf Sightseeing-Reise. Wir haben uns die Autos geliehen und fahren gut gelaunt durch diverse Länder, um schöne Fotos zu machen – so etwas wie eine Kaffeefahrt für Laien-Knipser. So hätten wir das auch vor kurzem in Bolivien gemacht und ein Büchlein für den Freundeskreis darüber verfasst. Mit netten Bildern vom Urlaub.

Mr. Hundertprozent will das Buch sehen – rein zufällig habe ich natürlich eines im Auto. Ein Soldat begleitet mich nach draußen, da steht zufällig Hans gerade. Dem teile ich in knappsten deutschen Worten und seltsam anmutenden Gesten mit, was ich dem Grenzer gerade erzählt habe, damit Hans die gleiche Geschichte erzählt, falls er auch noch verhört wird. Hans kapiert sofort – wie immer.

Der Zöllner vertieft sich in das Buch mit den fantastischen Aufnahmen von Craig Pusey, unserem Profi-Fotografen. Der Usbeke will jedes Bild erklärt haben – tatsächlich jedes einzelne. Und hat noch ein paar Zusatzfragen: Warum wir keine Mädels dabeihaben?

I was glad to put Russia behind us. If you can't read the Cyrillic alphabet, then you are up a gum tree in Russia and no mistake. Anyone who has ever complained about the rule of law at home should take a trip there, because the rule of law in Russia is meaningless. In Russia customs and conventions fall apart more quickly than the housing. Were there any more border surprises waiting for us? Not really, just the nature of the rip-off. Such as what we experienced on the Russia-Kazakhstan border.

I must emphasize that this time we had done everything correctly. The right border, the right lane, the right papers. The border guard naturally wanted to see the documentation. He was suspicious that the vehicles belonged to a company, but that they were being driven by private individuals. He wanted to see the certificates confirming that everything was right and proper. We initially handed over the German documentation. He nodded and then said he wanted to see the English documentation. We handed that over, too. His mood worsened visibly. He nodded and said he wanted the documentation in Russian. No problem, he could have that, too – we had done our homework. Our border guard was furious. Yes, our papers were fine. No, we couldn't leave the country.

Dealing with a corrupt official who conjures up any old reason not to let you across their border is bad enough. But it's worse when said official doesn't even bother to say why they're not prepared to let you pass. After a quick head-to-head with Hans and the team, we decide to use the classic currency of influence: the 100-dollar-bill-in-the-passport trick. I walked back to the same official, asked him to check the passport once again in the hope that this time he might find the right stamp and the right form. As it turned out, he found what he was looking for and we were free to continue on our journey without further ado.

This particular form of harassment actually only happened on the borders of the Ukraine, Russia and Kazakhstan. Elsewhere there were different surprises lying in wait. On the pre-scout recce, for example, we were part of the following sitcom after deciding on a particular border crossing between Kazakhstan and Uzbekistan, as we thought it would be relatively quiet. The road looked like something out of a First World War battlefield – one huge, muddy crater after the next. Equally huge recovery lorries were parked and ready to pull the many broken-down lorries over the border. The number of vehicles allowed to enter the customs area, however, is limited. Hence the long queues of lorries. To this day I couldn't tell you why they were all Willy-Betz lorries (a well known German haulage company.)

While leaving Kazakhstan was trouble-free, upon entering Uzbekistan we encountered a particularly fastidious border guard who had clearly learnt his craft in the East German Secret State Police. In the customs building I was led into a neon-lit office that I can describe with some confidence as an interrogation room. The man, dressed in civilian clothing wanted to know everything about the tour. Trying to explain a project such as the Land Rover Experience Anniversary Tour, which takes in eleven countries, a pre-scout recce, participants and media is not easy, so I chose a different tack and claimed we were a group of amateur photographers on a sightseeing trip. We had hired the vehicles and were enjoying a very pleasant photo tour through these countries. We had recently undertaken a similar tour to Bolivia and put together a book full of nice holiday pics for our friends.

Mr. Perfect wanted to see the book – by chance I had a copy in the car. A soldier accompanied me to the car where Hans was standing waiting. I passed on my story to Hans in reduced form and using gestures that would have appeared rather strange to anyone observing the situation so that he would have the same story to tell the border guard in case he were asked. Hans immediately understood what I was trying to achieve – as always.

Wann ich geboren bin? Wo Wuppertal liegt, ob eher bei Düsseldorf oder bei Köln? „Köln hat gutes Bier", sagt er plötzlich in bestem Ostdeutsch – und ich bin froh, keine dummen Sprüche während des Verhörs gemacht zu haben. Der Mann war – welch Überraschung! – einst in Ostberlin stationiert und hatte dort Deutsch gelernt. Nach vier Stunden können wir die Grenze überqueren.

Noch mehr Grenzerfahrungen? Kein Problem. Besonders die Prozeduren bei der Ein- und Ausreise nach und aus China werde ich nie vergessen. Schon während der Vortour habe ich lernen müssen, dass wir hier in einer anderen Welt sind. Bei der Haupttour verschärft sich die Situation noch. Weil in China zu Feiertagen die Grenzen geschlossen werden und wir das nicht berücksichtigt haben, streichen wir einen freien Tag in der kirgisischen Hauptstadt Bischkek und brechen vom Jurtencamp morgens um 4 Uhr auf. Die Ausreise aus Kirgisistan mit drei Kontrollstellen klappt völlig problemlos. Weitere drei erwarten uns auf chinesischer Seite bei der Einreise über den Torugart-Pass. Die erste besteht aus einem schlichten Eisentor mit müden Soldaten und wachen Schäferhunden, 10 Kilometer später müssen wir ein paar Stunden warten, um unsere Papiere checken zu lassen. Die dritte ist 70 Kilometer weiter – hier werden ausgiebig das Reisegepäck und die Autos gefilzt sowie die persönlichen Papiere ein drittes Mal gefordert. Mit der Fahrt durch eine Desinfektionsdusche betreten wir nach elfeinhalb Stunden Grenzübertritt (leicht schnappatmend, denn wir befinden uns bereits auf 3 700 Metern Höhe) endlich chinesischen Boden. In unserem Hotel in Kashgar erhalten wir dann unsere chinesischen Führerscheine, ohne die wir hier nicht fahren dürfen – später ein wunderbares Souvenir.

Die Ausreise gestaltet sich kein bisschen einfacher. Grenzübergang Zhangmu nach Kodari, Nepal: Morgens um 9 Uhr schleicht unser Konvoi durch die an einen Hang gebaute Grenzstadt, in der schon viele Lastwagen auf die Erlaubnis zur Ausreise warten. Parkende Autos blockieren den Verkehr der viel zu engen Straße, die eigentlich nur einspurig ist, aber Fahrzeuge in beide Richtungen bewältigen muss. Nach fünf Stunden Warten schauen die Offiziellen kurz auf die Fahrgestellnummern. Dann dürfen wir über eine völlig kaputte Piste zum nächsten Posten rollen, der sich unsere Pässe vornimmt. Der Fahrer muss im Auto sitzen bleiben, der Beifahrer geht zu Fuß durch ein Haus, um nach einer Serpentine wieder ins Auto zu steigen. Bei der letzten Stelle regiert nur noch das Chaos: Dicht an dicht warten Lastwagen auf die Ausreise, unser Konvoi mittendrin. Es wuselt nur so von Einwohnern dieses eigenwilligen Ortes sowie Tagelöhnerinnen, die bis zu 40 Kilo schwere Ballen mit Textilien nach Nepal tragen. Dazu noch wenig vertrauensvolle Gestalten, die immer mal wieder die eine oder andere Autotür testen – ob sie sich nicht öffnen lassen und fette Beute dahinter wartet.

Die Grenzer arbeiten erst mal nicht. Angeblich ist der Strom ausgefallen (bei der Ausreise zwei Stunden später sehen wir allerdings keinen einzigen Computer, sämtliche Arbeiten werden händisch getätigt. Das Gepäck wird übrigens akribisch nach unerwünschten Tibet-Reiseführern gecheckt). Dann geht es weiter Richtung Nepal, ab hier wirklich einspurig. Einige Autos werden durchsucht, andere nicht – ein System ist nicht erkennbar. Endlich dürfen alle – die Fahrer im Auto, die Beifahrer zu Fuß – über die „Freundschaftsbrücke". Der Weg führt durch bewaffnete Soldaten sowie bereitstehende Feuerlöscher mit Niederhaltegabeln zur Bekämpfung von aufsehenerregenden Selbstverbrennungen nach Nepal. Dort atmen wir auf. Nicht nur, weil jetzt die Hochlandetappe hinter uns liegt, sondern eher, weil wir wieder in der Freiheit sind. Zivilpolizisten legen uns zur Begrüßung einen leichten Schal um den Hals, stempeln ohne Fragen die Pässe, und schon dürfen wir in dieses bitterarme, aber wunderschöne, warmherzige und gastfreundliche Land. Für die rund 130 Kilometer von Nyalam (China) bis nach Kathmandu brauchen wir übrigens insgesamt satte 15 Stunden.

The border guard was getting more into the book with Craig Pusey's amazing photography. The Uzbek wanted to know the background behind every individual picture and had a few additional questions up his sleeve. Why are no women on the tour? When was I born? Where is Wuppertal, is it nearer to Düsseldorf or Cologne? "Cologne has good beer," he suddenly said with a very strong East German accent, and I was very happy not to have said anything stupid during the interrogation. The man had indeed been stationed in East Berlin (what a surprise!), where he had learned to speak German. Four hours later we were able to cross the border.

Any more border experiences? No problem. I will never forget the experience of entering and exiting China. On the pre-scout we had learned that we were in a different world. On the main event things got more complicated. In China the borders are closed on public holidays. As we had forgotten to factor this in, we decided to drop our day off in the Kyrgyzstani capital of Bishkek, breaking our yurt camp at 4 in the morning.

Departing Kyrgyzstan with its three checkpoints went by without incident. Three more were waiting for us on the Chinese side over the Torugart Pass. The checkpoint consisted of a simple iron gate guarded by tired soldiers and not-so-tired German Shepherd dogs. 6 miles further on, we had to wait for a few hours as our papers were being checked. The third checkpoint was another 40 miles down the road. This time our luggage and the vehicles were thoroughly checked, and we had to hand our passports over for a third time. Crossing into China had taken a total of 11.5 hours, and, slightly out of breath (we were after all at an altitude of 12,000 feet), we were then subjected to a disinfectant shower. In our hotel in Kashgar, we received our Chinese driving licences without which we wouldn't be able to drive here at all. Later this will be a wonderful souvenir.

Departing China was no easier. The border crossing point at Zhangmu to Kodari in Nepal. At 9 o'clock in the morning, our convoy crawled through the border town built into the side of a hill where many trucks were already waiting to depart the country. Parked cars make it even more difficult to drive along the street, which in reality is a one-track road but must service traffic in both directions. After waiting for five hours, the officials briefly checked the vehicle identification numbers. This was followed by a drive along a dreadful track to the next checkpoint, which took our passports. While the driver was expected to remain in the vehicle, the co-driver had to enter a building and, after a serpentine route, was permitted to climb back into the car. The last checkpoint was just pure chaos. Truck after truck parked up, awaiting permission to leave, and our convoy stuck right in the middle. Locals abound in this very strange place, as do day labourers carrying huge balls of textiles weighing up to 90 lbs. to Nepal. Not to mention the suspicious-looking figures who, every once in a while, test a car door in the hope that there might be something worth stealing inside.

The border guards weren't working. Apparently there had been a power cut. (Two hours later, as we departed the country we didn't see a single computer. All the paperwork was done by hand. The luggage was meticulously checked for the highly unpopular – with the Chinese at least – guidebooks to Tibet.) After that, we were able to head in the direction of Nepal along what really is a single-track road. Some vehicles were checked, others ignored – there didn't appear to be any system to it. Finally, we were allowed to cross the "Bridge of Friendship", the drivers in the vehicles, while the co-drivers had to walk. Our route took us past armed soldiers as well as fire extinguishers and pitchforks, which were lined up just in case any one decided on self-immolation on the way to Nepal. We could breathe again. Not because the mountainous stage was now behind us, but also because we were in a free country again. Police welcomed us with light scarves around our necks, stamped our passports without asking any questions, and with that we were free to enter this dreadfully poor, but beautiful, warm-hearted and hospitable country. The 80 miles from Nyalam in China to Kathmandu had taken us a healthy 15 hours.

DER GUIDE
THE GUIDE

Normalerweise suchen wir auf den Vortouren neben Hotels und Strecken grundsätzlich auch aus, wer unser Guide ein soll, um den Konvoi mit seiner Hilfe (Landessprache, spezielle Sitten und Gebräuche, nicht gleich ersichtliche Verbote, Zoll-Abwicklung etc.) unbeschwerter durch das betreffende Land führen zu können. Allerdings gibt es bei den bislang zehn Land Rover Experience Touren eine Ausnahme: China. Dort stellt die Regierung die jeweiligen „Helfer". Einer ist Tenzin – ein sehr offener Insider, der weiß, wie das Land tickt, und der uns durch das politisch nicht einfache Tibet führt. Für den großen Teil Chinas aber ist Adil zuständig – und der ist wohl die schrägste Type, die ich auf den zehn Experience Touren inklusive der elf Länder umfassenden Seidenstraßen-Tour erlebt habe.

Wir lernen Adil an der zweiten Grenzkontrolle von Kirgisistan nach China kennen. Er kommt drei Stunden zu spät, ist klein, leicht untersetzt, hat einen wiegenden Gang und versteckt in seiner oft zur Vase geformten Hand grundsätzlich eine brennende Zigarette. Sein Englisch ist passabel, seine Arbeitsweise unergründlich. Er ist eigentlich nie dort, wo man ihn braucht, aber immer da, wo man ihn nicht vermutet. Der Mann aus Kashgar verträgt angeblich das chinesische Essen nicht, was ihn unterwegs oft in die Büsche treibt, wo wir ihn allerdings genüsslich rauchen sehen. Wenn er nicht laut schnarchend im ersten Auto auf dem Rücksitz hängt und tief schläft (nicht ein einziger anderer Guide hat sich während seiner Arbeitszeit erlaubt, die Augen auch nur länger als zum Zwinkern zu schließen), lernt er Deutsch oder spricht es einfach lautmalerisch nach, singt türkische Unterhaltungslieder oder telefoniert so laut, dass die deutsche Wagenmannschaft weder Musik hören noch die Gespräche über Funk verstehen kann. Allerdings gelingt es ihm einmal, schon mittags im Restaurant am Zielort kaltes Bier zu ordern, obwohl die Chinesen normalerweise kalte Getränke meiden. Dass dann bei der Hälfte der Bierflaschen der Inhalt zum Eisblock gefroren ist und beim Öffnen der Flaschen Gerstensaft am Stück durchs Restaurant schießt, können wir ihm nicht ankreiden. Und eines muss man ihm lassen: Er hat Einfluss. Auf wen auch immer.

Das merken wir besonders auf der Strecke zwischen Hotan und Qiemo. Die Fahrt über das nicht enden wollende Hochland (ständig auf rund 2 000 Metern Höhe) ermüdet, auch wenn wir bald bemerken, dass sich ganz offizielle Inoffizielle um uns sorgen – sie überholen immer mal wieder, meist in weißen Toyota Land-Cruiser-Sondereditionen. Sie filmen und fotografieren den gesamten Konvoi und die Autoinsassen. Das fällt ihnen leicht, denn die chinesischen Tempovorschriften sind rigide: Auf den meist gut ausgebauten Straßen sind höchstens 80 km/h erlaubt. Und manchmal auch nur 60.

So ein 60-km/h-Schild übersehen die ersten fünf Wagen ein einziges Mal. Wie auch die dazugehörige, in einem Baum versteckte Speed-Kamera. Das bedeutet: Bei der nächsten (von unzähligen) Polizeikontrollen mitten auf dem platten Land dürfen wir nicht weiterfahren. Adil muss alle extra angefertigten chinesischen Kennzeichen der fünf Frontautos abliefern, ebenso die extra angefertigten chinesischen Führerscheine der fünf deutschen Fahrer. Dann heißt es: warten. Schließlich kommt ein Polizist und verlangt 8 000 Yuan, rund 1 000 Dollar.

Das ist auch für uns verdammt viel Geld. Wie immer in solchen Fällen behaupte ich erst mal, dass das gar nicht sein könne – wir wollen die Blitzfotos sehen, in den chinesischen Bußgeldkatalog schauen und überhaupt. Doch die Beamten können den Verkehrsverstoß tatsächlich mit Bildern samt Messdaten auf dem Laptop nachweisen. Okay: Wenn man Bockmist baut, sollte man auch dazu stehen – das ist zuhause nicht anders. Also bin ich schon bereit, die fünf Fahrer auszulösen. Da sagt Adil: „Ich frag mal nach Discount."

Auch wenn ich ihn nie freiwillig ausgewählt hätte: Der Typ ist unschlagbar. Die Stunden ziehen sich, aber Adil ist völlig entspannt. Wir beobachten, wie zwei Männer im schwarzen Honda ankommen, an der Polizeistation ungefragt zahlen und, ohne die Polizeisperre zu passieren, umkehren und wegfahren. Nicht viel später kommt Adil und erzählt, er habe mit einem hohen Verwandten im Verkehrsministerium gesprochen und alles sei gut. Tatsächlich ruft uns kurz darauf der Chef der Polizeistation zusammen, erklärt, dies sei nur eine Warnung, und wir mögen uns bitte künftig an die erlaubten Tempolimits halten. Was bedeutet: Die nächsten 150 Kilometer 60 km/h fahren auf einer breiten, leeren, schlaglochlosen und so langweilig wie ermüdenden geraden Straße.

Wir halten uns tatsächlich an die Vorgabe. Auch wenn die einen oder anderen Teams die nächsten knapp drei Stunden mit dummen und klugen Sprüchen über Funk nicht hinterm Berg halten. Zum Glück besitzen die Autos Temporegelanlagen.

Es ist so schade wie gut, dass uns Adil in Golmud verlässt und das Zepter an Tenzin übergibt. Durch Adil – der, wie er kurz vor seiner Abreise zugibt, jeden Abend einen Report an unsere „Begleiter" über unsere Tagesetappen liefern muss – habe ich gelernt: In anderen Ländern (zum Beispiel in der westlichen Hemisphäre) wird man versteckt überwacht, hier macht man dagegen keinen Hehl daraus. Und wir haben uns hier keinen Moment lang unsicher gefühlt.

Normally, in addition to checking hotels and routes, the pre-scouts for all ten destinations have been used to find the guide to help (with language requirements, particular customs and traditions, potential problems not immediately apparent to a foreigner and customs formalities) and direct the convoy through the respective country. In this respect, China proved to be the exception. There, the government provided us with "assistants". One of these was Tenzin – a very candid insider who knew exactly how the country ticked and who managed to guide us through Tibet with all the political difficulties that this involved. For the greater part of China, we were assigned Adil – the weirdest individual I have ever had on any of the ten Experience Tour destinations, including the Silk Road.

We first met Adil at the second checkpoint on the way from Kyrgyzstan to China. He was three hours late, small, and thickset. He walked with a swaying gait, and his vase-like hand had only one function in life, and that was to hold a cigarette. His English was reasonable, his work ethic unfathomable. He was never there when and where he was needed yet always there where one least suspected him. Born in Kashgar, he was apparently allergic to Chinese food and would often disappear into the bushes, where we would see him having a quiet smoke. If he wasn't snoring coma-like in the back seat of the lead vehicle (no other guide allowed himself the luxury of even the briefest of naps during a working day), he would attempt to learn German or at least copy it phonetically, sing Turkish songs or speak so loudly on his phone that the team in his vehicle was neither able to listen to music or understand info over the CB radio. Once he surprised everyone at lunchtime by ordering a cold beer (the Chinese normally avoid cold drinks like the plague). On opening the semi-frozen bottle, half of its contents shot across the restaurant en masse – which wasn't really his fault. However, we had to give him this: he had friends in high and low places.

This was immediately apparent between Hotan and Qiemo. The never-ending journey across the 6,000-foot-high mountain region was strenuous in the extreme, particularly after we had noticed our "official inofficial" guides who, at regular intervals, would overtake the convoy in their limited-edition Toyota Land Cruisers. Our whole convoy, vehicle occupants included, was filmed and photographed – not that it was difficult, as speed limits on the well-built roads were limited to 50 mph and in some cases 40 mph.

The first five cars oversaw a 40 mph speed limit sign only once, along with the speed camera, which was hidden inside a tree. At the next police checkpoint (one of many), we were pulled over. Adil had to hand over all the specially manufactured Chinese number plates for the first five cars and the equally bespoke Chinese driving licences of the five German drivers. Then we played the waiting game. The result: a Chinese policeman demanded 8,000 yen, which was approximately 1,000 dollars.

This was a lot of money for us. As usual in such situations, I argued that this was impossible and that we wanted to see the photos, check the official list of penalties and generally stall for time. The police, however, had proof of the offence, thanks to pictures and speed data on their laptops. Okay, if we have messed up then we should admit our guilt – at home it is no different. I was about to pay the ransom money for our five drivers when Adil said, "Let me see if I can get a discount."

I admit I wouldn't have picked him myself, but the guy was worth his weight in gold. Time dragged on, but Adil remained totally relaxed. We watched as two fellows in a black Honda drove up, paid up at the police station and, without passing the police barrier, turned round and drove off again. Shortly afterwards, Adil returned and said he had spoken to a relative who was something important in the Ministry of Traffic, and that everything had been sorted out. Shortly after that, the police chief called us together, saying that this had been a warning and that we should stick to the speed limits in future. Which meant for the next 90 miles of wide, empty, straight and pothole-free road, we should stick to the sleep-inducing speed limit of 40 mph.

We did as we had been told, although one or the other team couldn't resist making the odd clever and less-clever comment over the radio. Fortunately, the vehicles were all fitted with cruise control.

With a tear in our eyes and a smile on our faces, we said goodbye to Adil in Golmud, where he passed the baton to Tenzin. Just before saying goodbye, Adil admitted that he had had to report to our accompanying vehicles on the road every night. I learnt that in other countries (such as those in the West), observation was carried out in secret. Here in China, they were completely open about such things. The fact is we felt safe the whole time.

*Von der kirgisischen Jurte durchs chinesische Hochland bis in die grünen Täler Nepals:
Wer so lange wie wir durch Asien fährt, lernt die exotischsten Menschen, die fremdesten
Bräuche und die einfallsreichsten Transportmöglichkeiten kennen.*

*From the Kyrgyz yurt across the Chinese highlands to the green valleys of Nepal: anyone
who spends as much time as we do travelling through Asia is confronted by the most
colourful people, the strangest customs and the most inventive forms of transport.*

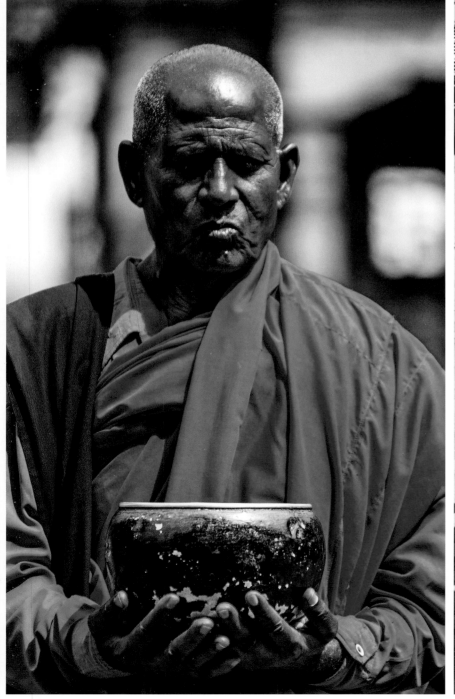

ROLAND LÖWISCH

geb. 26.9.1959
seit 1990 Autoredakteur (Auto Bild, Stern),
seit 2006 selbstständiger Journalist

born 26 September 1959
automotive journalist since 1990 (Auto Bild, Stern),
freelance journalist since 2006

Was fasziniert dich an den Land Rover Experience Touren?

Roland: Ganz einfach: Jede Tour führt eine Gruppe von Menschen, die das alle nicht alleine erfahren würden, an Orte auf dieser Welt, die keiner von ihnen normalerweise sehen würde. Denn solche Touren sind nur möglich, weil es durch den Einsatz vieler Fahrzeuge immer einen Ausweg gibt, selbst in technisch oder geologisch höchst problematischen Fällen.

Schon selbst technische Probleme erlebt?

Roland: Kleinere gibt es immer mal, aber selbst betroffen war ich durch einen Ausfall von einigen dringend benötigten elektrischen Bordsystemen in Bolivien. Wir – meine Beifahrerin Theresa und ich – waren in meinem Lieblings-Landy, dem Defender, auf dem Weg hoch zu einem 5 145 Meter hohen Pass. Natürlich mit offenen Fenstern, weil ich auf der Fahrt immer gerne die Luft schmecken und den Wind fühlen möchte. Plötzlich merkten wir, dass nicht mehr viel von der normalerweise zuverlässigen Elektrik funktionierte. Für uns relevant: Die elektrischen Scheibenheber verweigerten die Arbeit, die Scheibenwischer samt Scheibenwaschwasserpumpe auch. Aber alle Sicherungen waren okay – der Defekt konnte also nicht mal eben beseitigt werden.

Und dann?

Roland: In großer Höhe ist es kalt, und in Trockenheit staubt es. Gegen die Kälte gab es Klamotten, den Staub auf der Windschutzscheibe bekämpfte Theresa mit Wasser aus Trinkflaschen – seitlich während der Fahrt aus dem Auto heraushängend. Wirklich problematisch wurde es erst, als es dunkel wurde. Denn auch die gesamte Lichtanlage hatte den Geist aufgegeben. Das einzige Licht, das funktionierte, waren die Zusatzscheinwerfer auf dem Dachgepäckträger. Allerdings auch nur durch ständiges Ziehen am Blinkerhebel, also beim Dauer-Lichthupen. Der Hebel befindet sich aber bekanntermaßen rechts, wo man auch schalten muss. Ich habe mich wohl noch nie vorher und nachher so blind, frierend, arbeitend und müde in einem Auto mehrere Stunden lang durch unbekanntes, staubiges und bergiges Terrain getastet.

What do you find fascinating about the Land Rover Experience Tours?

Roland: It's very simple. Every tour takes a group – people who would not undertake such a trip on their own – to places they would normally not get to see. The tours work because vehicles travelling in a group can always overcome technical or geological obstacles.

Have you experienced any technical problems yourself?

Roland: Little things can always go wrong, but where I was directly affected was when an electrical component failed in Bolivia. We – that is my co-driver Theresa and myself – were driving my favourite Land Rover, the Defender, up a mountain pass at an altitude of 16,900 feet. We had the windows open because I always like to taste the air and feel the wind. Suddenly, we noticed an electrical problem, which was unusual as these days the electrics are pretty reliable. The electric windows had stopped working, the windscreen wipers and the screen wash fluid pump had also ceased to function. The fuses were all okay, and it looked like this was a problem that would take a little longer to solve.

What happened?

Roland: At that altitude, it is very cold, and in dry weather you create a lot of dust. To defeat the cold you have good clothing. For the dust on the windscreen we had another solution. Theresa hung out of the passenger-door window and poured water out of her drinking bottle over the screen. By nightfall, we had a serious problem. We had lost all the lights except the additional spotlights mounted on the roof rack and they only worked by constantly pulling the indicator stalk backwards, as if one were using full beam as opposed to main beam. The switch is also on the right-hand side, near the gear stick. I have never felt so blind, cold and tired while fumbling my way forwards in a vehicle for hours over unknown, dusty and mountainous terrain.

What was the cause of the problem in the final analysis?

Roland: That same night the Land Rover guys found a short circuit in the trailer coupling.

Ich bin ja schon durch ziemlich viele Länder gefahren, und bislang musste ich die Teilnehmer und Journalisten kaum auf besondere Verkehrsregeln hinweisen oder sie auffordern, auf der Straße vorsichtig zu fahren. Das ändert sich allerdings schlagartig in den letzten beiden Ländern der Seidenstraßentour: Nepal und Indien.

Es gibt nur zwei Regeln: Sei als erster an dem Flecken, der für dein Weiterkommen wichtig ist (das gilt außerstädtisch, zum Beispiel beim Überholen auf Landstraßen). Und: Nutze die Lücke, sonst nutzt sie jemand anders (innerstädtisch). Berücksichtigst du dies nicht und verhältst dich wie ein braver Europäer, stehst du noch übermorgen da, wo du losfahren wolltest.

Beispiel Landstraße. Nepal ist Himalaya und damit bergig, was die unendlich vielen altersschwachen und fast immer hoffnungslos überlasteten einheimischen Lkw mit Tempi von 10 bis 20 km/h bergauf quittieren. Meistens bewegt sich davor ein ebenso überladener Bus, hinten wuseln fünf untermotorisierte Motorräder (gerne mit bis zu vier oder fünf Personen besetzt) hin und her. Dadurch wird das Überholen ein Vabanquespiel und geht nur, wenn der Beifahrer mitschaut. Denn Nepal und Indien haben Linksverkehr, und wir das Steuer auf der linken Seite.

Damit nicht genug: Wer hier überholt, hat recht (zumindest aus Sicht des Überholenden). Das kann darin gipfeln, dass einem bei vielleicht mal kurzzeitig freier Bergabfahrt plötzlich zwei Laster auf den beiden Spuren entgegenkommen, wobei einer versucht, den anderen mit einem Überschusstempo von 2 km/h niederzuringen. In so einem Fall hilft es nur, weit weg anzuhalten, einen Drink zu nehmen und das Treiben zu beobachten, bis sie uns passiert haben.

Allerdings ist es auch nicht besser, einen dieser wunderbar bunt und freundlich angemalten Lastwagen hinter sich zu haben. Natürlich übersieht in Nepal einer eine Stauende, hat Bremsen im gleichen Zustand wie das restliche rollende Wrack und verbeult einem unserer Evoque sichtbar die Hecklappe. Mithilfe unseres Guides Rajeshwor fordere ich den armen Mann auf, mir all sein Geld zu geben. Er besitzt ganze 20 Dollar, die ich ihm – zunächst – abknöpfe. Dann rechne ich kurz durch: Schaden am Auto rund 2 000 Euro minus 20 Dollar, dazu einen jammernden Nepalesen, der nicht weiß, wovon er sich Essen kaufen soll. So gebe ich ihm das Geld zurück und hoffe, er nutzt wenigstens 10 Dollar, um einen halben neuen Bremsbelag anzuzahlen.

Aber nicht nur die Laster erfordern auf der Landstraße extreme Aufmerksamkeit. Da werden ganze Schafherden rübergetrieben, ein paar heilige Kühe machen es sich auf der Fahrbahn gemütlich, unzählige Schulkinder toben über den Asphalt, taube Opas schieben zweirädrige Karren, und dann noch die vielen dummen Hühner und langmütigen Hunde – alles, aber auch wirklich alles kann zum ungünstigsten Zeitpunkt die Fahrbahn benutzen. In Indien kommen noch Affenhorden und ein paar Transport-Elefanten hinzu. Ach, ich vergaß den Zustand der Straßen: Bodenschwellen an Brücken und vor Engstellen, Schlaglöcher mit einer beachtlichen Tiefe, von Grund auf fehlender Straßenbelag und hier und da ein auf dem Boden kauernder und nur von ein paar faustgroßen Steinen angekündigter Straßenmaler, der mit Hingabe einen Mittelstreifen pinselt – all das sind auch noch Kriterien, die das Autofahren zur Herausforderung und Prüfung werden lassen. Das bedeutet: Hier fährt jeder Schlangenlinie – bis zur Kante des Restasphalts auf der Gegenfahrbahn, wenn nötig. Und man sollte tunlichst auf der richtigen Seite sein, wenn Gegenverkehr kommt. Klappt das nicht, bleibt nur noch die oft verdreckte und verschlammte Kraterlandschaft. Wenn da nicht schon ein paar Kühe, Ziegen, Hunde, Menschen … siehe oben.

Die Landstraßen sind wirklich gefährlich, will man nicht zehn Stunden für 150 Kilometer benötigen (auch wenn man fast nie schneller als 70 oder 80 km/h fahren kann). Innerstädtisch allerdings kann man sich einen Spaß daraus machen, voranzukommen. Beispiel Kathmandu, Hauptstadt Nepals mit rund 1,5 Millionen Einwohnern. Die Hälfte davon scheint Autos, dreirädrige Tuk-Tuks oder Motorräder zu fahren, die andere Hälfte will zu Fuß dazwischen durch. Also geht der Fußgänger, wo er kann (nämlich da, wo gerade kein berädertes Vehikel steht), und alle anderen versuchen, ihn nicht umzufahren. Das funktioniert erstaunlich gut, hat aber zur Folge, dass auf diese Weise so ziemlich jeder Quadratzentimeter Straße besetzt ist. Will man hier vorankommen, muss man drängeln, Stoßstange an Stoßstange fahren und – ganz wichtig – hupen. Was Teammitglied Kerstin dazu bewegt, als sie die Trompetensymbole auf dem Lenkrad nicht gleich findet, ihren männlichen Beifahrer hektisch zu fragen: „Wo sind meine Hupen …?"

Ist es tagsüber in der scheinbar nicht enden wollenden City noch ein Spaß, ändert sich das schlagartig bei Dunkelheit. Den Einwohnern der beiden Länder ist es viel lieber, ihr Licht für warnende Lichthupe zu verwenden, als es bei Dauerabblendlicht zu verschwenden. Radfahrer haben sowieso kein Licht, Motorräder und -roller auch nicht und viele Lastwagen und Pkw ebenfalls nicht – im besten Falle vielleicht eines, was beim Überholen zur irrigen Annahme verleiten kann, ein Motorrad käme entgegen.

Aber es geht noch schlimmer: abends im Regen. Und es geht immer noch schlimmer: abends im Regen in einem Viertel, in dem gerade der Strom ausgefallen ist. Viel Beleuchtung gibt es sowieso nicht, aber es in stockdunklem Nass dank unserer „Tannenbäume" (eine geniale und hocheffektive Ansammlung von Zusatzleuchten an den Dachgepäckträgern) zu schaffen, kein Lebewesen und keines der abenteuerlich parkenden Vehikel zu berühren, macht uns bei Ankunft im Stadthotel stolz.

Ich behaupte: Wer hier unter allen Bedingungen gefahren (und auch vorangekommen) ist, den schreckt kein Verkehr mehr auf der Welt.

I have travelled through many countries and have hardly ever had to inform participants or journalists about peculiar traffic regulations or tell them to be careful. Yet the last two countries on the Silk Road Tour, Nepal and India, were most definitely the exception.

There are only two rules: be the first to reach the spot you need to reach to get ahead (this is particularly relevant out of town when overtaking on country roads). And: use the gap, because if you don't, someone else will (in town). If you fail to observe these rules and drive like a well-behaved European instead, then you will get nowhere fast.

Take the aforementioned country road, for example. Nepal is in the Himalayas, consequently mountainous and full of hopelessly overloaded local trucks crawling at between 6 and 12 mph. In front of the truck is usually an equally packed bus, and behind five underpowered motorbikes, each with their obligatory five locals on board. Overtaking is a gambling game and requires the full concentration of your co-driver, as traffic in Nepal and India drives on the left and our vehicles were left-hand-drive.

There was more: the overtaking vehicle has right of way (as far as the overtaking vehicle is concerned), meaning that just when you take advantage of the open road downhill, you could be faced by two trucks coming your way with one trying to outdo the other. With a difference in speed of barely 1 mph (in the case of the trucks). The healthy way to live is to park the vehicle and enjoy the spectacle from a safe distance while having a drink until they pass by.

That said, it isn't that much better when these beautifully painted, attractive trucks are behind you. One of them failed to notice the traffic jam in front, his brakes were in the same condition as the rest of his wreck on wheels, and the truck put a nice big dent in the rear hatch of one of our Evoques. With the assistance of our guide Rajeshwor, I persuaded the trucker to give me all the money he had – 20 dollars, which I pocketed. Then I started to do the maths on the damage to the Evoque. The bill would be around €2,000 minus the 20 dollars I had extracted from the driver. On top of that, I now had a moaning Nepalese driver who had no idea how he was going to eat that night. So I gave him his money back, hoping that he would at least use some of it to buy a new brake shoe.

It wasn't only the trucks that demanded our constant attention. Herds of sheep; some holy cows deciding to take a break in the middle of the road; scores of school-children racing here, there and everywhere over the tarmac; deaf grandads pushing two-wheel carts; and then a myriad of stupid hens or over-courageous dogs – all these can be sharing your bit of road with you when you least expect or need it In India, the list grew longer still, whether it was hordes of monkeys or elephants transporting goods. Oh, and I forgot to mention the state of the roads: speed bumps on bridges and before narrow passages, remarkably deep potholes, roads that simply hadn't been tarmacked and, every once in a while, a road worker bent double in the middle of the road, protected only by a couple of stones warning of his presence as he painted the dividing strip with gusto. All these put driving here in the category of challenge and driving test all in one. Weaving in and out of traffic was the norm (if need be, to the edge of the tarmac on the other side of the road), and woe betide you if you were on the wrong side of the road facing oncoming traffic. If you got it wrong, then the only alternative was the craterous, muddy moonscape at the side of the road along with the cows, goats, dogs, people…(see above).

The country roads were downright dangerous, especially if you needed to cover 90 odd miles in less than ten hours (even if your top speed was restricted to 40 or 50 mph.) In town, it could be quite fun. In Kathmandu, for example, Nepal's capital city with a population of around 1.5 million. Half of them were in cars or three-wheel tuk-tuks or on motorcycles. The other half was on foot. The pedestrian is, as a rule, forced to seize any opening in traffic. Everyone else on the road must simply try to avoid mowing them down. It seemed to work, but one side-effect was that the road surface was fully occupied, down to the last inch. If you wanted to make progress, you had to be pushy, drive bumper-to-bumper and – very important – use the horn.

What may have been a barrel of laughs during the daytime changed in an instant the moment the sun set. The inhabitants of both countries see headlamps as an extension of the horn, rather than as a means of being seen at night. As a rule, cyclists have no lights at all, and the same holds for motorcycles and mopeds. Many trucks and cars have one working lamp at best, making them easy to mistake for a motorcycle in the dark.

And it got worse. Rain at night. And then rain at night in a part of town where there had been a power outage. After that, we were grateful for our "Christmas trees" (a clever and extremely effective system of additional lights mounted on our roof racks) that enabled us to manoeuvre in the pitch black rain through streets that, even if lit, were a constant struggle – as we tried to avoid running people over or brushing optimistically parked cars. Arriving in our hotel that night without a scratch was indeed reason to celebrate.

For this reason to anyone who has driven in these conditions and arrived at his or her destination on time – I would say there is no need to worry about traffic anywhere else, ever again.

Richtung Indien wird es immer bunter: Frisches Obst gibt es überall, Märkte für Touristen nur in den großen Städten. Auf den Landstraßen regieren die von Hand bemalten Busse und Lastwagen, die von stolzen Truckern gelenkt werden. Ladeflächen und Dächer sind oft voll mit Reisenden.

The closer we get to India, the more colourful it becomes. Fresh fruit abounds; markets for tourists, however, can only be found in the bigger cities. On the country roads, hand-painted buses and trucks driven by their proud owners dominate the landscape. Their cargo bays and roofs are often crowded with passengers.

JORDANIEN

JORDAN
2000
4 DEFENDER, 1 FREELANDER, 1 DISCOVERY
STRECKE / DISTANCE: 850 KM / 530 MILES

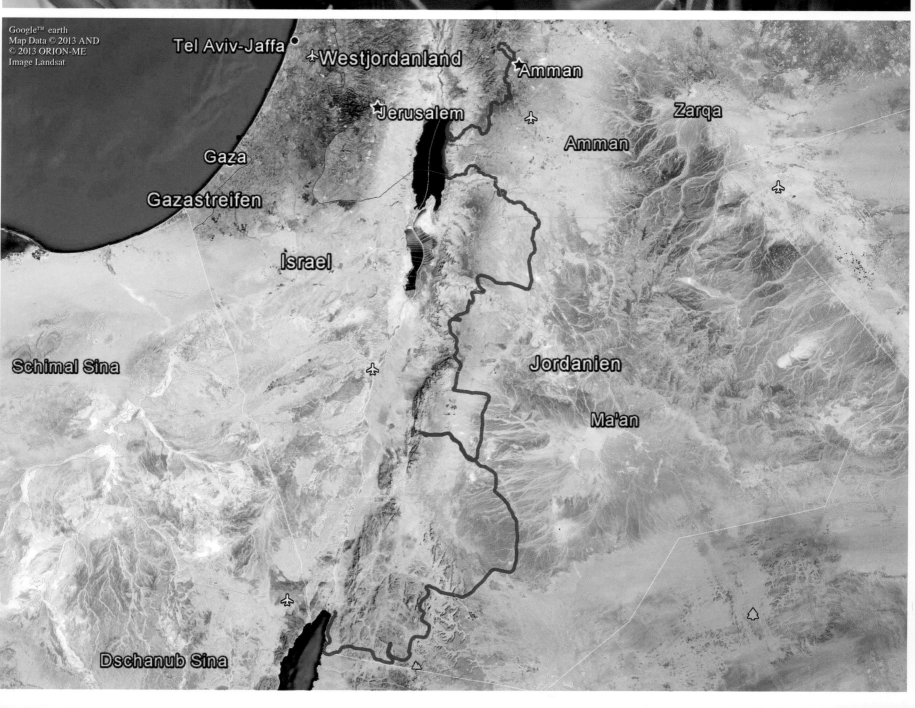

DAS ZIEL
THE DESTINATION

Der Anruf von BMW kommt unvermittelt, ist kurz und knochentrocken: Die erste Tour – sie heißt zunächst „Land Rover Entdecker-Tour" – startet in vier Monaten. Also hopphopp!

Es gibt kein verabschiedetes Gesamtkonzept, keine Kooperationspartner und keine geplanten Reisen nach der Tour. Das alles wird erst im Jahr 2001 passieren. Es gibt eigentlich gar nichts außer vier Monate Zeit. Für die Bekanntmachung, für Qualifikationscamps, für die Endqualifikation, für eine Vortour, für die gesamte Event-Organisation. Ich setze mich mit offenem Mund erst mal eine Weile hin und sage gar nichts. Auch wenn die Zeit drängt. Und wie. Wir haben kein definiertes Ziel. Aber die Infos für die Bewerbungen müssen raus. Wie, bitteschön, bewirbt man eine Tour, von der man nur weiß, dass sie stattfinden muss? Liebe Leute, Land Rover befindet sich gerade in einer Umbauphase, und die beginnt damit, dass wir mit euch irgendwohin touren wollen, wo es nett ist, was zu der Marke passt, was euch ein bisschen mehr abverlangt, als nur einem Reiseleiter zu folgen, und was ihr nie vergessen werdet – aber wir haben keine Ahnung, wohin? Na prima.

Mit insgesamt acht Festangestellten und ein paar Freelancern gilt es, so schnell wie möglich sechs verschiedene Standorte für die Qualicamps aus dem Boden zu stampfen. Das Areal für die Endqualifikation ist dagegen schnell definiert: unser Steinbruch in Wülfrath. Perfekt für Fahrübungen aller Art, ein guter Startpunkt für Navigationsaufgaben in den Kohlenpott, und bei Mondschein kann ich die Reiselustigen wunderbar aus den Zelten schmeißen für Nachtaufgaben, ohne dass sich meine Nachbarn nachhaltig über die Action im Revier beschweren.

Die Zeit rennt. Noch drei Monate Zeit. 6 000 Menschen bewerben sich in aller Schnelle, 2 400 laden wir zu den Qualifikationscamps ein. Wohin es letztlich geht, verschleiern wir so gut wie möglich. Was nicht schwer ist, weil wir es selbst noch nicht wissen. Dabei sein kann dagegen fast jeder: Wir achten ein bisschen auf das jeweilige Hobby, auf das Alter, natürlich auf die Gültigkeit des Führerscheines, aber auf mehr auch nicht. Auch wenn wir keine so dramatischen Abenteuer wie bei der Camel Trophy planen, so können wir doch nicht das Risiko eingehen, Fahranfänger mitzunehmen (was sich bis heute nicht geändert hat). Die Hoffnungsfrohen müssen zeigen, dass sie mit den Autos umgehen können, Grundzüge der Navigation lernen, Erste-Hilfe-Kenntnisse beweisen. Jeder Trainer macht Aufzeichnungen, schmeißt seine Prüflinge wie geplant (und mit großer Freude) auch mal nachts aus dem Zelt, um ihnen eine Aufgabe zu stellen. Und schnell sind sechs Menschen gefunden, die auf die erste Reise gehen dürfen.

Aber wohin? Die Zeit wird immer knapper, und wir müssen schnell entscheiden: Was kennen wir? Wo müssen wir nicht bei Null mit der Recherche anfangen? In Jordanien! Hans und ich hatten dort unseren bislang letzten Urlaub verbracht. Eine Endqualifikation für die Camel Trophy (mit Hans als Organisator) fand dort auch schon mal statt. Fast 90 000 Quadratkilometer steinige Spielwiese, heißes, trockenes Sommerklima, das Tote Meer als perfekter Swimmingpool und schließlich eine reichhaltige Natur – Planerherz, was willst du mehr? Und der Schwager von Hans namens Hussein ist auch noch gebürtiger Jordanier – einen besseren Guide können wir uns nicht vorstellen. Das Land ist sicher, ruhig und damit erfüllt es einen der wichtigsten Grundsätze der Land Rover Experience: „Es darf nie etwas Schlimmes passieren!"

The call from BMW came unexpectedly and was short and to the point: the first tour is to kick off in four months and is provisionally called the "Land Rover Entdecker (Discoverer) Tour". So get on with it!

There was no overall concept that had been approved, no co-op partners and no customer trips planned for after the tour. All that would have to wait until 2001. We had four months to organize the event, including the pre-event PR and call-to-action campaign, selection camps, final selections and a pre-scout recce. Somewhat dumbstruck, I sat down for a while and said nothing. And that with the clock ticking inexorably. We had no clearly defined destination but at the same time we had to go public with the application information. How does one market a tour when all you have to talk about is the fact that it is going to happen at all?

"Dear potential candidate, Land Rover is currently restructuring itself, and part of this process is to take you on a tour to a nice place that matches the brand, that requires a bit more from you than just following the guide, and that will remain unforgettable. One other thing: we don't know where we're going." Nice idea.

With a total of eight permanent staff and a few freelancers, we had to create six locations for the selection camps out of nothing. Final selections were clarified almost immediately and would take place in our quarry site in Wülfrath near Düsseldorf. A perfect place for all manner of driving exercises, a good location for navigational tasks spreading across the Ruhr area and, in the middle of the night, ideal for pulling would-be globetrotters out of their tents to complete a night task without waking up the neighbours at the same time.

We were on a mission. Three months to go. 6,000 people applied almost spontaneously. We invited 2,400 to the selection camps. We said as little as possible regarding the tour's final destination, which wasn't difficult as we still hadn't decided where we were actually going. Almost all of the candidates had what it takes to accompany us. Hobbies that fitted our requirements, age and of course a valid driving licence were pretty much the only criteria. That said, even though we weren't planning a Camel Trophy-style adventure assault, we still couldn't afford to risk taking learner drivers with us (a criterion upon which we still insist to this day.) Our hopeful candidates needed to show that they could operate the vehicles safely, and that they understood the basics of navigation and first aid. Each trainer observed each and every candidate, took notes and with considerable gusto threw his fledglings out of their tents at some ungodly hour to confront them with a special task. In no time at all, we had six candidates who had earned the right to accompany us.

Yet we still didn't know where we were going. Time was running out, and we needed to come to a decision. Where had we been before? Was there somewhere where we wouldn't be starting with an empty page? How about Jordan? Hans and I had spent our last holiday there, and Hans had organised Camel Trophy final selections there, too. 35,000 square miles of stony playground; a dry, hot climate; the Dead Sea as a perfect swimming pool; and, not least, a rich and diverse environment – a planner's dream! Hans' brother-in-law is a native Jordanian – we wouldn't find a better guide. Political and social unrest was unheard-of, which enabled us to tick one of our most important prerequisites: "We should always avoid getting into trouble!"

DAS PROBLEM
THE PROBLEM

Während noch die Teilnehmer gesucht werden, gilt es, sich so schnell wie möglich über Import-/Exportvorschriften schlau zu machen, die Autos nach Jordanien zu verschiffen und diverse Genehmigungen einzuholen. Wir sind auf einem guten Weg – bis wir an den Zollchef im Hafen von Akaba, dem einzigen jordanischen Seehafen, geraten. Der Mann ist so beleibt wie stur. Er kennt zwar die Prozedur, Autos ins Land zu lassen, die dort bleiben, aber nicht diejenige, Autos ins Land und dann wieder ausreisen zu lassen. Kurz: Er setzt unsere für die Vortour dringend benötigten Allradler im Zollbereich des Hafens fest.

Hussein muss uns retten. Uns ist schon ganz anders, weil der Zollchef von Akaba uns bei den vielen Besprechungen unablässig mit viel zu viel heißem, irrsinnig süßem Tee füttert (nicht ohne dabei ständig Solitaire zu spielen). So fliegen wir mit Hussein nach Amman, um eine Unterredung mit dem Tourismusminister von Jordanien zu erbitten. Der Einsatz von Hans' Schwager ist Gold wert, denn es klappt: Nach einer vollen Woche persönlicher Blockade muss der Zollchef die Wagen auf Weisung der Regierung freigeben. Und weil er nach wie vor keine Ahnung hat, was er da eigentlich tut, setzt er einen Stempel auf das Ausfuhrdokument, das fortan regierungsgenehmigt besagt, dass die Wagen ein volles Jahr im Land bleiben dürfen – damit hat er ungewollt die Grundlage für alle Land Rover Experience Reisen gelegt. Denn daraufhin können wir später Reisen für Journalisten und alle buchenden Land-Rover-Fans in dem wunderschönen Land anbieten, ohne uns Gedanken um die Autos machen zu müssen. Man kann eben auch mal Glück haben.

Nachteil der Hängepartie im jordanischen Hafen: Wir haben nur noch wenig Zeit, bis die Teilnehmer kommen. Und immer noch ist keine Vortour erledigt, um Hotels zu checken, interessante Trails zu suchen, Campsites vorzubereiten. So rasen Hans und ich „in letzter Minute" einen Tag und eine Nacht die Hauptstrecke ab und klären die wichtigsten offenen Fragen. Wir fallen zwar am Abend halbtot in die Betten, aber die Tour steht. Wie erwartet nach vier Monaten und keiner Stunde mehr.

While we were still selecting our participants, we needed to get to grips with the import/export regulations, ship the cars to Jordan and sort out numerous permits. We had made considerable progress until we made the acquaintance of the head of customs in Jordan's only port in Aqaba. Obese and obstinate in equal measure, he understood the procedure whereby vehicles are imported into the country to stay there. He had not, however, heard of any procedure facilitating the entry and exit of the same vehicles in and out of the country. In short, our four-wheel drive vehicles, which we urgently required for the pre-scout recce, were impounded and remained in the port's customs area under lock and key.

Hussein had to save our skins. We were at our wits' end, not least as a result of interminable conversations with the same customs chief who would serve us endless cups of unfathomably hot, extremely sweet tea while playing solitaire. We flew to Amman, taking Hussein along, with the intention of talking to Jordan's minister of tourism directly. Hans' brother-in-law's intervention was worth his weight in gold. For the plan worked. After a week of his personal blocking tactics, a government directive instructed the intransigent customs chief to release the vehicles. The moment he stamped the vehicle-release document, thereby putting a government seal of approval on the vehicles' staying in Jordan for a year, he unknowingly laid the foundations for all future Land Rover Experience Tours, as we were now able to offer a tour package to media and Land Rover fans willing to pay without having to worry about the vehicles. A little luck never hurts.

The long stalemate in the port of Aqaba left us with another problem, though – there was now very little time left before the participants' arrival. We still had to finish up a pre-scouting: We needed to find hotels and interesting routes, and we needed to prepare campsites. Hans and I shot off at the last minute to drive the main route in 24 hours and sort out the remaining issues. The following day, we were both exhausted, but the tour was ready to roll as instructed in four months and not a day longer.

HANS HERMANN RUTHE

geb. 6.2.1951
gelernter Maschinenbautechniker und Werkzeugmacher, überzeugter
Weltenbummler, rechte (und manchmal auch linke) Hand von Dag Rogge

born 6 February 1951
engineer and toolmaker, dedicated globetrotter,
Dag Rogge's right (and sometimes left) hand

Wie bist du zum Offroad- und Outdoor-Thema gekommen?

Hans Hermann: Ich habe mich 1990 für die Camel Trophy Sibirien beworben und auch gleich qualifiziert – nach der Tour war ich zweitbester Teilnehmer, was das Lösen von Aufgaben anging. Von da an arbeitete ich rund zwei bis drei Monate pro Jahr für die Trophy – das Projekt Tonga/Fidschi/Samoa sehe ich heute als meinen bestbezahlten Urlaub aller Zeiten.

Und seit wann bist du mit dem Land-Rover-Virus infiziert?

Hans Hermann: Schon ein bisschen früher – und zwar seit dem Auswahlcamp für die Sibirientour. Vorher fuhr ich ganz brav einen Opel Rekord Caravan, nach Sibirien aber ging es mit Defendern. Diese Autos haben mich sofort fasziniert und in ihren Bann gezogen. Da passte es, dass ich mit meiner Werkzeugfirma auch Bergsportartikel herstellte und Reinhold Messner mit meinen Produkten seine letzten 8000er erobert hatte. Ich hatte also schon vorher eine besondere Affinität zur extremen Natur – wie Land Rover auch.

Wie hast du Dag kennengelernt?

Hans Hermann: Seine Firma bekam 1994 den Auftrag, den Defender – der ja vorher in Deutschland nicht vermarktet wurde, der stand nicht mal auf der Preisliste – für Presse und Händler einzuführen. Die damaligen Verantwortlichen bei Rover in Neuss schlugen Dag vor, doch ein paar Camel-Trophy-Trainer mit ins Boot zu nehmen. Dazu gehörte ich.

Du bist seit Jordanien grundsätzlich bei den Planungen und soweit möglich bei den Vor- und Haupttouren der Land Rover Experience dabei. Wie lässt sich das mit einem Job vereinbaren?

Hans Hermann: Ich habe meine Firma im Jahre 2006 verkauft und toure seitdem etwa sechs bis sieben Monate im Jahr mit meiner Frau und meinem selbst umgebauten Defender 130 durch die Welt. Den Rest der Zeit widme ich der Experience.

Du fährst natürlich seit langem selber Defender. Wie hast du ihn verändert, um ihn an deine Ansprüche anzupassen?

Hans Hermann: Haha, meinen gibt es so kein zweites Mal. Bei meinem jüngsten Auto habe ich nur das Chassis gekauft und alles andere selbst gebaut. Zum Beispiel wollte ich aus Sicherheitsgründen eine isolierte Glasfaserkabine, die mit dem Fahrerhaus durch eine Schiebetür verbunden ist. Das funktioniert dank eines verlängerten Führerhauses und eines Stahlhilfsrahmen, der hinten gefedert aufgebaut ist. So kann sich der Defender-Rahmen planmäßig verwinden, ohne dass es die Kabine stört. Innen gibt es Alkoven, Dusche, Toilette, 90-Liter-Kühlschrank. Alles, was schwer ist, liegt unten: Statt erstem Auspufftopf ein 120-Liter-Frischwassertank, auch der Batteriekasten und ein Abwassertank liegen unterhalb des Schwerpunktes, ebenso 45-Kilo-Gas und 120-Liter-Dieseltank. Das Ersatzrad liegt auf der Fronthaube – auch als Schutz gegen Steinschlag. Ist natürlich alles vom TÜV abgenommen.

Wo reist du am liebsten?

Hans Hermann: Zum Beispiel in Brasilien, Bolivien, Peru, Argentinien. Mit Militärkarten findet man winzige Pisten zu Geysiren in den Bergen, von denen kein Mensch etwas weiß. So etwas fordert mich heraus.

Gibt es etwas, das sich auf jeder Experience Tour wiederholt?

Hans Hermann: Vieles. Routine ist einfach wichtig, wenn es jedes Mal so viel Neues zu bewältigen gilt. Aber mir fällt natürlich sofort unser Funkruf ein, je nachdem, wer ruft: „Dag, Dag, Hans Hans." „Hans, Hans, Dag, Dag."

How did you end up off-road and outdoors?

Hans Hermann: In 1990 I applied to go on the Camel Trophy to Siberia and qualified to go along. As far as solving special tasks was concerned, I was the second-best competitor that year. Thereafter I spent between two and three months every year working for the Trophy. I still think the Tonga/Fiji/Samoa event was the best-paid holiday I ever had.

When did the Land Rover virus infect you?

Hans Hermann: It's been a few years now – ever since selections for the Siberia Tour. Up until then, I had an Opel Rekord Caravan. After Siberia I started on Defenders. I was fascinated the moment I first encountered these vehicles, and I have been ever since. It seems appropriate that my tool company also produced the mountain-climbing equipment Reinhold Messner used on his last climbing expeditions. I've always had a thing for extremes in nature – a bit like Land Rover, I suppose.

How did you meet Dag?

Hans Hermann: His company won the contract from Land Rover to launch the Defender in Germany to both press and dealers. Up until that point, Defender hadn't been officially sold in Germany – it wasn't even on the price list. Rover management at the time in Neuss suggested he talk to a few Camel Trophy trainers. I was one of them.

Ever since Jordan, you have been involved in the planning and, whenever possible, in the pre-scout recces and main events. How do you manage to get the time off work?

Hans Hermann: I sold my company in 2006 and spend six or seven months a year with my wife touring the world in our converted Defender 130. I dedicate the rest of the time to the Experience.

You have been driving Defenders for a long time. What have you done to change your vehicle so it matches your specific requirements?

Hans Hermann: Ha-ha – my Defender is truly a one-off. For my most recent vehicle project, I literally just bought the chassis and built everything else myself. For safety I wanted an insulated fibreglass cabin that was connected to the driving compartment with a sliding door. This would only work with an extended driver's cabin and an additional steel sub-frame with its own suspension at the rear. This provides the torsional flexibility one expects from the Defender ladder frame without compromising the cabin. Inside the cabin, I have two sleeping alcoves, a shower, a toilet and a 90-litre refrigerator. Heavier items are underneath. Where normally the exhaust muffler would sit, there's a 120-litre freshwater tank. The battery rack as well as the wastewater tank are mounted below the vehicle's centre of gravity along with a 100-lbs. gas tank and a 120-litre diesel tank. The spare wheel is mounted on the bonnet – that protects against stone chips. The German Technical Inspection Agency (TÜV) has approved everything.

What are your favourite destinations?

Hans Hermann: Brazil, Bolivia, Peru and Argentina. Using old military maps, we found tiny routes to mountain geysers that nobody has ever seen. I love the challenge.

Is there some aspect of the Experience Tour that is always the same?

Hans Hermann: Lots. Routine is very important when there is always so much to discover that is new. Of course there is our classic radio call depending on who is calling who, "Dag, Dag, Hans Hans" "Hans, Hans, Dag, Dag".

DAS WADI
THE WADI

Es ist perfekt: traumhafte Landschaften, wilde Vegetation, malerische Camps unterm Himmelszelt. Und viel Sand – gut zum Festfahren. Man darf in weichem Sand nicht anhalten, aber die nicht so gewieften Teams kommen um die von uns durchaus gewollte Erfahrung des Ausgrabens nicht herum. Größte Fahrunwissenheit: Bei eingeschalteter Untersetzung geben die Fahrer im soften Untergrund oft zu viel Gas. So verdichtet sich das lockere Sediment beim Anfahren hinter dem Rad, aber davor baut sich ein kleiner Sandhügel auf – der Wagen bleibt erneut stecken. Das passiert selbst bei den Defendern, man muss sie eben zu bewegen wissen. Alle 4 bis 5 Kilometer bleibt ein Wagen stecken – nur ausgerechnet nicht der mitgenommene Freelander. Der ist viel leichter als das Urvieh aller Offroader und gehorcht dadurch anderen physikalischen Gesetzen. So fährt Christian Uhrig, unser Marketingchef, mit dem recht neuen kleinen Landy Kreise in den Sanddünen um die von nur halbkundigen Händen bewegten Defender, was alle erstaunt. Mich eingeschlossen.

Nach so vielen Fragezeichen in den Augen unserer Erstteilnehmer denke ich, die nächste Aufgabe sollte einfach gestrickt sein. Sie lautet schließlich: Findet von Punkt A, dem Standort, zum Punkt B, dem Einstieg ins Wadi Rum. Und zwar in einer Nacht-Task.

Wer das traumhafte ausgetrocknete Flussbett nicht kennt: Das Wadi Rum ist das größte Wadi in Jordanien mit einer Länge von rund 100 und einer Breite von 60 Kilometern. Als Schutzgebiet mit einer Fläche von 74 000 Hektar wurde es 2011 in die Welterbeliste der UNESCO aufgenommen. Nachts wird es hier um diese Jahreszeit um die 3 Grad kühl, tagsüber bis zu 26 Grad heiß. Dank GPS und topografischem Kartenmaterial sollte der etwa 40 Kilometer lange Weg dorthin nicht so schwer zu finden sein.

Sollte. Denn statt sich mit den Karten zu beschäftigen, geben alle Teams einfach den GPS-Punkt für den Wadi-Einstieg ein und fahren los. Dass dazwischen vielleicht eine Schlucht liegen könnte, die den direkten Weg versperrt, daran denken sie nicht. Die einen fahren strikt geradeaus, die anderen im Kreis, die dritten eiern durch die Gegend wie ein wild gewordener Lunar Rover durchs Mare Imbrium. Hans guckt mich an, ich gucke Hans an, und wir beschließen, einzugreifen, bevor auch nur ein Team zu weit weg ist und damit außerhalb unseres Funkbereichs. Oder sogar kopfüber in die Schlucht stürzt.

Bis wir die so ahnungs- wie orientierungslosen Teams wieder eingesammelt haben, vergeht eine ganze Weile. Und nach wilden Einfangmanövern bilden wir einen Kreis – inzwischen haben alle Teilnehmer ihre Fahrzeuge verlassen. Ich will gerade in tiefster jordanischer Nacht ohne jedwede Lichtverschmutzung mit meiner Standpauke loslegen, da erschrecken wir alle fürchterlich – neben mir steht plötzlich ein völlig in schwarz gekleideter Beduine. Der Mann macht allerdings ein genauso erschrockenes Gesicht wie wir, er zittert wie ein Turbodiesel bei falscher Leerlaufdrehzahl. Bis sich alles aufklärt: Der arme Jordanier dachte, die dunklen großen Autos seien von irgendeiner halbseidenen Behörde ausgesandt, um weiß der Geier was in dieser Wildnis anzustellen. Er führt uns zu einem großen Felsen – dahinter kauert ebenso zitternd sein Harem in einem kleinen Zeltdorf.

Aufgrund der sowieso schon überlangen Nacht leeren wir schließlich im Camp ein Outdoor-Case, füllen es mit Eis, kühlen den Champagner darin und feiern bis morgens um 4 Uhr.

Perfection: fantastic landscapes, wild vegetation, picturesque campsites under a painted sky. And sand in abundance – enough to get really stuck. Stopping in soft sand is ill-advised, but the teams are new to the experience and sooner or later they have to grab their shovels (which is what we wanted in the first place). It is perhaps the most common error in soft terrain: after having selected low-range, to then put your foot down on the gas, kicking the loose material to the rear, behind the wheel, whilst creating a mini sand escarpment in front of the wheel. As a result, the vehicle simply digs itself in again. Defenders are not exempt – the driver just needs to understand how to move the vehicle. Every 3 miles or so, one of our vehicles became stuck, with the exception of the Freelander. The latter is much lighter than Land Rover's iconic off-roader and interprets the rules of physics differently. Our head of marketing, Christian Uhrig, drove circles in the sand dunes around the Defenders that were admittedly being driven by relative newcomers to off-roading. The group was astounded. Myself included.

The questions on the faces of our first participants forced us to simplify the next task. And that was to drive from A (where we were) to B (the entrance to the Wadi Rum)…at night.

For those who do not know this wonderful dry riverbed, the Wadi Rum is the largest wadi in Jordan, approximately 62 miles long and 37 miles wide. The protected reserve, with a surface area of some 285 square miles, was awarded UNESCO World Heritage Site status in 2011. From a daytime high of 26 degrees Celsius (79 degrees Fahrenheit) at this time of year, the temperature can drop to 3 degrees Celsius (37 degrees Fahrenheit) at night. Thanks to GPS navigation and topographical maps, one might think that finding the 25-mile route to the wadi would not be too difficult.

One might think… But rather than consult maps, the teams simply tapped in the GPS coordinates for the entrance into the wadi. They failed to consider that a gorge might be in the way, blocking the route. The first team headed straight as a plank into the distance, the second drove around in circles, and the third was all over the place like an out-of-control Lunar Rover heading over the moon's Mare Imbrium. Hans and I looked at each other and decided to put a stop to it either before the teams were out of range of our CB radios or one of them disappeared head first into a gorge.

It took a while before we had gathered up our clueless and completely disoriented teams. After having reeled them in – and doing so took some rather reckless manoeuvring in the sand – we parked the vehicles in a circle and everybody climbed down. As I wound myself up to rant at everyone in the dark of the Jordanian night, suddenly everyone jumped in fright. Standing literally right next to me was a Bedouin bedecked from head to toe in black. I think he was just as frightened as we were and was shivering and shaking like a poorly idling diesel engine. And then came the explanation. He thought the big dark cars were from some dubious government agency planning something equally dubious out here in the wilderness and then he led us to a huge rock. Behind it, equally terrified, was his harem in a small tent village.

As it was already way past bedtime by then, we returned to camp, filled one of our outdoor travel cases with ice, bedded the champagne in it and partied till 4 in the morning.

DIE FLUCHT
THE ESCAPE

Nicht alle Treffen in Jordanien klären sich so vorteilhaft für die Beteiligten auf wie die Begegnung mit dem verunsicherten Beduinen. In der streng islamischen Stadt Ma'an müssen wir erfahren, wie groß die Kluft zwischen Religionen, Volksgruppen, ja Welten sein kann.

Nachdem wir auf dem Weg durch Jordanien Kraftstoff in alten Olivenöldosen erworben und getreu unserem Motto „Jeden Tag eine gute Tat" einen liegengebliebenen Jordanier mit seinem Auto abgeschleppt haben (wobei sich dann herausstellt, dass sein Auto doch noch fährt …), legen wir in Ma'an einen Stopp ein, um Brot und andere Lebensmittel zu kaufen. Die Teams und Hussein verschwinden im Supermarkt, wir anderen warten bei den Autos. Ich stehe oben auf dem Dachgepäckträger, um die Spannung der Sicherungsgurte zu überprüfen. Ein anscheinend ausgesprochen schlechter Standpunkt.

Dass auf den Straßen nur Männer spazieren, macht uns zunächst nicht misstrauisch. Ab und zu fliegt mal ein Steinchen gegen unsere Autos, es wird auch mal dagegen gespuckt, aber mit solchen Missfallenskundgebungen können wir leben. Plötzlich und völlig unvermittelt fängt allerdings ein Geistlicher an zu schimpfen und sich übermäßig aufzuregen. Immer mehr Männer versammeln sich wütend um unsere parkenden Autos. Immerhin sprechen die Männer noch mit uns, und mich fragt der aufgeregte Araber, was ich von „Saft" halten würde. Wahrheitsgemäß gebe ich an, dass ich Saft mag, und zwar sehr. Das regt den bärtigen Gottesmann nun erst recht auf, und auch die anderen Ma'anner scheinen eine Menge gegen „juice" zu haben. Und es dauert, bis wir alle begreifen, dass es den Jordaniern gar nicht um „juice" geht, sondern um „jews": Juden. Zur Deeskalation der Situation trägt zusätzlich nicht gerade bei, dass ich auf dem Defender-Dach stehe. Auf der anderen Straßenseite befindet sich eine Mädchenschule und ich werde beschuldigt, aufs Auto gestiegen zu sein, um über die hohe Mauer dort hineinzublicken. Leider kann ich kein Arabisch – so fällt mir zur Entspannung der Situation nur ein, die Flucht anzutreten.

Über Funk informieren wir Hussein, dass wir abhauen müssen. In aller Eile entern wir die Autos und rasen aus der Stadt – blinde Fährten legend und Finten schlagend, damit uns auch niemand verfolgt, denn der nächste Halt ist eine Campsite. Da möchte wohl niemand von religiösen Eiferern überrascht werden. Zum Glück folgt uns niemand.

Ausruhen von diesem Abenteuer – dafür ist die alte jordanische Felsenstadt Petra genau richtig. Mein persönlicher Held Indiana Jones war auch schon hier: Das muss ja ein magischer Ort sein! Die unglaubliche Stadt war früher Hauptstadt der Nabatäer, die Monumentalfassaden sind direkt aus dem Fels gemeißelt. Eigentlich kommt man nur zu Fuß durch einen engen Canyon des Wadis Musa dort hin, und so lassen wir die Teams auch zu Fuß laufen. Sie wissen nicht, dass wir eine Sondergenehmigung bekommen haben, mit zwei Wagen direkt vor das Weltkulturerbe zu fahren – hier vertraut man uns, so wie übrigens sonst auch in diesem grundsätzlich sehr gastfreundlichen Land. Nachdem wir dann noch eine Offroad-Strecke finden, die selbst die Polizei als „unfahrbar" bezeichnet, und diese bewältigen, und nachdem wir mit einer bestellten Kamel-Polizeipatrouille samt Krummsäbel unsere Teilnehmer necken, haben Hans und ich endlich das Gefühl: Ja, wir sind auf dem richtigen Weg für die Land Rover Entdecker-Tour. So ungefähr haben wir uns das vorgestellt.

Not all encounters in Jordan are sorted out as easily as our run-in with the nervous Bedouin. In the strictly Islamic town of Ma'an we experienced first-hand just how great the differences in religions, ethnic groups and our worlds really are. After having bought fuel in old olive oil tins and recovered a vehicle belonging to a Jordanian who had broken down (according to the maxim "a good deed every day") – though it later turned out that his vehicle could move under its own power – we stopped off in Ma'an to buy bread and food. Hussein and the three teams disappeared into the supermarket while the rest of us stayed by the vehicles. I climbed up on the roof rack to check the tension of the ratchet straps. Clearly this was a poor choice on my part.

The fact that only men were walking on the street hadn't rung any warning bells. Every once in a while, someone had thrown a stone at the vehicles, and they have been spat at, but frankly we can live with such expressions of disapproval. Suddenly, and without warning, an Islamic priest began to rant and appeared to be more than just upset. More and more angry men suddenly swarmed around our vehicles. Some were still talking to us, and the rather excited Arab asked what I thought about "juice". Now I am a fan of "juice" and I said so. This really got the bearded priest going and the other men seemed to have something against "juice" as well. After a few minutes it dawned on us that the Jordanians weren't talking about "juice" at all, rather they meant "Jews". It didn't help that I was still standing on the roof of the Defender while unbeknown to me on the other side of the street there was a girls' school. I was accused of having jumped on the roof in order to be able to see over the school's high wall. Unfortunately, I can't speak Arabic, so to defuse the situation down I did the most logical thing possible. I fled.

Over the radio, I told Hussein that we had to get out quickly. We jumped into the cars and left town immediately, setting the odd false trail here and there, so that no-one was able to follow us, as our next stop was camp and we didn't want to be surprised by a crowd of religious zealots. Fortunately, no one had taken up the chase.

The best way to recover from this little adventure was a trip to the ancient city of Petra. My own personal hero, Indiana Jones, had been a visitor as well. This must be a magical place. This amazing city was once the capital of the Nabataeans, and its monumental façades are carved directly out of the rock. Normally the only way to enter Petra is via the narrow Wadi Musa, and this is how we let the teams walk into the city. They didn't know that we had received permits for two vehicles to drive right into the World Heritage Site – the authorities trusted us completely, something we experienced almost everywhere in this extremely hospitable country. We found an off-road route, which the local police described as impassable – which we then proceeded to drive. After even managing to organise a genuine mounted police patrol on a camel, complete with scimitar, as a practical joke for the participants, Hans and I were beginning to think: this is how the Land Rover Discoverer Tour could work. This was pretty much how we'd always imagined it to be.

Ob auf Kamelen der Wüstenpolizei oder über abenteuerliche Pisten in rund 1000 Metern Höhe – die angesteuerten Ziele sind alle Strapazen wert. Zum Beispiel die Ruinen in Amman oder die Felsenstadt Petra im Tal der Nabatäer. Das Tal ist unvorstellbar groß und hat weitaus mehr zu bieten als die Erinnerung, dass Indiana Jones hier den Heiligen Gral suchte.

Whether enjoying the sight of camel-mounted police in the desert or driving adventurous tracks in the sand at over 3,000 feet, it is worth all the effort getting there. Take the ruins in Amman, for example, or the ancient city of Petra in the Valley of the Nabataeans. The valley is huge and has more to offer than Indiana Jones' search for the Holy Grail.

DIE RACHE
THE REVENGE

Oh Wunder: Die Teilnehmer sind etwas enttäuscht. Es ist der letzte Abend in freier Wildbahn der einwöchigen Tour, und allen ist zum Feiern zumute. Zuerst wird der Biervorrat geleert, dann geht's dem Whisky an den Flaschenhals. Als die Cola alle ist, strecken einige die Spirituose mit Wasser und Brausetabletten. Das lockert die Zungen, und so erklären uns alsbald die Teams in blendender Laune, wie toll die ganze Tour doch sei – aber eben doch ein bisschen touristisch, zu wenig Abenteuer. Der Begriff der geführten Pauschalreise fällt zwar nicht, aber wir bekommen unser Fett weg, weil wir sie zum Beispiel nie allein gelassen haben.

So eine Kritik perlt an Hans und mir nicht ohne Folgen ab. Also warten wir – zugegebenermaßen nicht mehr so ganz nüchtern – in der Nacht, bis alle Teilnehmer und Journalisten schlafen, entfernen aus allen Fahrzeugen (bis auf unseres) die GPS-Instrumente und alle anderen Navigationshilfsmittel, hinterlassen in jedem Auto einen Zettel mit den aufgezeichneten Himmelsrichtungen, schnappen uns Doc Gunnar Wasmus und verlassen mit ihm und insgesamt zwei Wagen klammheimlich das Camp.

Als die sechs Teilnehmer, Hussein und das Fernsehteam dann irgendwann aufwachen, sind sie einheitlich sauer. Wir hören über Funk ihre Sprüche und amüsieren uns restalkoholisiert königlich.

Die armen Kritiker müssen sich mit insgesamt neun Leuten, Kameraequipment und dem ganzen Camp-Zeug samt Müll in drei Defender quetschen und wissen nicht einmal, wohin der Rest der Reise gehen soll. Besonders das Fernsehteam kocht über: Im Auto von Hans, der sich neben mir im Sand krümmt vor Lachen, liegen die neuen Filmkassetten – sie können die ganze Aufregung nicht mal drehen. Wer uns kennt, kann sich vorstellen, wie köstlich wir unsere vorsichtige Schadenfreude genießen.

So rumpeln wir bis zur Hauptstraße, bis auch wir müde werden. Wir halten, hauen uns neben die Defender auf den Boden zum Schlafen. Nur Gunnar schafft es noch, in einem weißen Nachthemd aufs Auto zu klettern und dort zu pennen. Bis eine Polizeistreife mit angelegten Waffen kommt. Die beweisen zum Glück Humor, als Gunnar wie ein Gespenst in Weiß auf dem Auto steht und beteuert, nichts Unrechtes getan zu haben …

Surprise, surprise. The participants were a little disappointed. The last evening in the wild on our week-long tour, and everyone was up for a party. The beer was quickly finished off before we moved on to the whisky. The cola didn't last long either, and another mixer was found using water and fizzy tablets. Suitably relaxed, the teams then proceeded to tell us how much they had enjoyed the tour – with one reservation: there had been too much tourism and too little adventure. They didn't actually use the words "package tour", but the complaint was loud and clear and meant for us, as we had never left them to their own devices. Hans and I aren't ones to ignore criticism, and the whisky clearly played a part in our next response. We waited until the teams and journalists had all gone to sleep and then removed the GPS and any other navigational aids from every vehicle but our own, leaving a piece of paper showing the four cardinal directions. We grabbed the doctor, Gunnar Wasmus, and left camp as quietly as possible in two vehicles.

When the six participants, Hussein and the TV crew awoke, they were furious. We listened to them over the radio, and in spite of our own hangovers we enjoyed the spectacle from afar.

Our poor critics now had to organise nine people and pack the camera and all the campsite equipment, rubbish included, into the three remaining Defenders, yet without really knowing which way to go. As Hans lay in the sand next to me, his eyes filled with tears from all the laughter, the members of the TV crew were beside themselves with rage, as they couldn't film anything: the unused film cassettes were in Hans' car. Anybody who knows us also knows how much we were enjoying this.

We trundled on in the direction of the main road until exhaustion hit us, too, parked up the vehicles and fell asleep underneath. Gunnar managed to climb onto the roof rack in his white nightshirt and slept on top of the car. Fortunately for us, the police unit that turned up, guns drawn, had a sense of humour when Gunnar stood up, looking all the world like a ghost on top of the Defender and imploring that he hadn't done anything wrong…

ISLAND

ICELAND
2001
6 DISCOVERY, 2 DEFENDER
STRECKE / DISTANCE: 1400 KM / 870 MILES

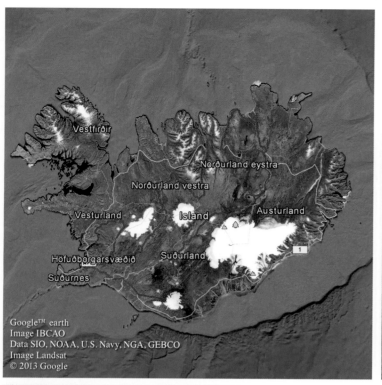

DER GEDANKE

THE THOUGHT

Jordanien war ein voller Erfolg – trotz diverser Anlaufschwächen und Zeitnöte. Das erkennt auch Reinhard Künstler, der von Ford inzwischen als neuer Geschäftsführer für Land Rover eingesetzt worden ist. Da sich die Autos auch nach der Tour noch in dem Land des Nahen Ostens befinden dürfen, haben wir eine Journalistenreise organisiert, die ein großes mediales Feedback nach sich zog.

So ein Feuer muss man am Kochen halten. Also gibt uns Künstler den Auftrag, fürs neue Jahr eine neue Tour auszuarbeiten. Und bitte nicht mehr unter dem etwas hemdsärmeligen Titel „Entdecker-Tour" – wir ersinnen „Experience Tour", das klingt wesentlich besser.

Und wieder ist die Zeit knapp – also suchen wir erneut ein Ziel, das uns nicht ganz unbekannt ist: Island. Mit einer Fläche von gut 100 000 Quadratkilometern wunderbar übersichtlich, als weltweit größte Vulkaninsel mit vielen tektonischen Spielarten voller Abenteuer und mit elf Prozent Gletscherfläche eine herrliche, eiskalte Glitsche. Hans hat dort bereits dreimal seinen Urlaub verlebt, auch ich war schon dort. Weitere Vorteile: ein kurzer Flug, ein sicheres Land, abenteuerliche Wetterbedingungen, beste Offroad-Möglichkeiten, sagenhafte heiße Wasserlöcher – und die Autos sind auch einfach zu importieren. Nur der Rotwein ist dort überproportional teuer, unser Budget dagegen übersichtlich … aber für solche Fälle gibt es ja Frischwasserkanister als Transportbehältnisse.

8 000 Bewerber registrieren wir; wie auch zur ersten Tour laden wir 2 400 von ihnen in die Qualifikationscamps ein, 60 in die Endausscheidung. Und machen uns mit den sechs Besten auf, längst vergessene Wege zu finden. Aber erst kommt die Vortour.

Jordan had been a complete success despite initial planning difficulties and the short notice. Reinhard Künstler, who in the meantime had been installed by Ford as Land Rover Germany's new CEO, recognised this. As the vehicles remained in this Middle Eastern country after the tour, we immediately organised a media trip that generated a lot of press coverage.

It is important to keep the fire burning bright, so Künstler commissioned a new tour for the new year. This time, we decided to drop the rather down-to-earth "Discoverer", choosing instead to call it the "Experience Tour", which we thought was so much better.

Once again, time was short, so we started considering a new destination, albeit one which we already knew well. Iceland. With a surface area of under 40,000 square miles, Iceland was a manageable size for the tour, and as the world's largest volcanic island, it provided us with a great deal of tectonic entertainment and pure adventure. With eleven percent of the island covered in glaciers, we had a wonderful mix of biting cold and difficult, slippery conditions. Hans had spent three holidays here, and I had also visited the island on a previous trip. Further advantages included the relatively short flight. Safety and security weren't an issue at all, the climate was challenging and thus perfect for an adventure tour, there were endless off-road opportunities and sensational hot springs, and importing our vehicles into the country would not be difficult. Unfortunately, red wine was ridiculously expensive, and our budget was modest. Fortunately, there are fresh water canisters that can be repurposed in just such eventualities.

8,000 applications flooded in, and, as with Jordan, we invited 2,400 to the selection camps and 60 to final selections. The plan was to take the six best with us to Iceland to find some long-forgotten trails. First of all, though, we had to complete the pre-scout recce.

VEGAGERÐIN

Vaðið krefst varúðar
- Hvar er vaðið?– Straumvötn breyta sér.
- Hjólför segja ekki alla söguna.
- Er vélin vatnsvarin?
- Fylgist einhver með þér?
- Kannið sjálf vaðið.
- Notið öryggislínu.
- Klæðist hlýjum fötum í áberandi lit.

Crossing requires caution
- Where is the crossing?– Rivers change.
- Tire tracks do not tell the entire story.
- Has your engine been waterproofed?
- Is somebody watching while you cross?
- Probe the crossing yourself.
- Use a safety line.
- Wear warm clothing in bright colours.

Mit einer erklecklichen Anzahl von Interessenten im Rücken satteln wir die Autos im Juli für die Vortour. Es gilt, abseits der Touristenwege anhand von topografischen Karten neue Herausforderungen zu finden. Und einen Einheimischen. Denn in Jordanien haben wir gelernt, wie wichtig es ist, einen Guide mitzunehmen, der sowohl die Sprache des Landes spricht als sich auch mit den Gegebenheiten und den Gewohnheiten der Einwohner, des Verkehrs und des Geländes auskennt. Wir fahren zum örtlichen BMW-Händler, der hat natürlich früher auch Land Rover vertrieben. Doch seine Vorschläge entsprechen nicht unseren Wünschen – wir wollen keine Touristenführer. Da fällt einem Verkäufer noch ein Defender-Fan ein, der von ihm einst einen 110er erworben hatte und ihn zum Bigfoot umbaute – also ihn mit riesigen Ballonreifen ausrüstete. Das war Ingo, ein Tänzer aus Reykjavík.

Mit ihm suchen wir nun zu fünft in zwei Defendern abenteuerliche Strecken – und finden sie ohne Probleme. Nur das Wetter haben wir unterschätzt: Es regnet. Ständig. Und wenn es in Island regnet, sollte man mehr als nur Gummistiefel dabeihaben.

Die erste Wasserdurchfahrt – und davon gibt es auf der Insel viele – schaffen wir noch recht problemlos: Ein paar große Steine zeigen, wo man den Fluss am besten queren kann. Bei der zweiten sind wir uns nicht sicher. Also schnappe ich mir einen Defender und probiere es ganz vorsichtig. Mit der Folge, dass der Wagen aufschwimmt und abzutreiben droht. Sofort stoppe ich den Wagen und rufe über Funk Hans um Hilfe. Er befestigt ein Sicherungsseil an seinem Auto und nach einem – mit Verlaub – schweinekalten Gang durchs knietiefe Schmelzwasser auch an meinem. So kann er mich zurückziehen. Wir beschließen, Island nicht weiter in dieser Richtung zu erkunden, sondern die 30 Kilometer zurück zur ersten Furt zu fahren und dort den Rückzug zu versuchen. Aber kaum angekommen, müssen wir erkennen: Die Steine sind nicht mehr sichtbar. Das Wasser ist auch hier rasant gestiegen.

Es nützt nichts – wir müssen es probieren. Hans rollt langsam mit seinem 130er Defender in den Fluss hinein, diesmal schon von Anfang an durch einen Bergegurt mit meinem 110er verbunden. Hans ist fast drüben, da kann er nicht weiter – weil der Gurt zu kurz ist. Also beginne ich, meinen Defender ebenfalls in das tosende Wasser zu manövrieren. Leider fahre ich mich fest.

Jetzt wird die Situation brenzlig. Denn der Bergegurt, etwa 5 Zentimeter breit, stellt sich in der Strömung quer. Das Wasser zerrt am Gurt, an den Defendern, an unseren Nerven – Ingo, der Tänzer, muss ran. Mit Wathose (ja, so etwas hat er tatsächlich vorausschauenderweise dabei) klettert er auf den Defender von Hans und versucht, den Gurt aus dem Befestigungshaken zu ziehen. Natürlich völlig ohne Erfolg: Tonnen von Wasser drücken auf die Verbindung. Inzwischen sackt mein Auto tiefer in den Kies. Es wird Zeit für härtere Maßnahmen. Ich schnappe mir meinen Leatherman, klettere auf meine Motorhaube und schneide – die bloßen Hände in dem eiskalten Gletscherwasser – den Gurt durch. So kann Hans auf die andere rettende Uferseite fahren. Ich schaffe es, meinen Defender zurück ans hiesige Ufer zu dirigieren.

Hans und Ingo dort, Christian, die Journalistin Inge und ich hier – keine gute Voraussetzung für eine weitere gemeinsame Erkundung der nordischen Insel. Also was tun? „Wenn du glaubst, es geht nicht mehr, kommt von irgendwo ein Lichtlein her …"

In diesem Falle gleich zwei, und zwar in Form von Scheinwerfern eines riesigen Traktors. Der steht inzwischen hinter mir und einem Jeep, der ebenfalls von den Wassermassen überrascht wurde und nicht weiß, wie es weitergehen soll.

Das einzige Fahrzeug, das nun noch problemlos durch den Fluss fahren kann, ist das Feldmonster. Wir bitten den Fahrer, meinen Defender an den Haken zu nehmen. Der freundliche Fahrer tut das, und drüben angekommen fragt Hans ihn, ob er auch noch unseren Discovery holt. Natürlich ersucht auch der Jeepfahrer um eine Passage. Der Traktorfahrer erweist sich als Superman: Wir seilen den Discovery an den Traktor und den Jeep an den Land Rover. So zieht uns das riesenrädrige Feldgerät durch das wilde Wasser.

Dabei entsteht ein Foto, dass ich heute noch liebe: Wie der Discovery den Jeep rettet. Natürlich nur rein zufällig ist der Traktor nicht auf dem Bild.

Interest in the tour was enormous as we set about preparing the vehicles for the pre-scout in July. Using topographical maps, we needed to find challenging routes off the well-beaten tourist trails. We also needed a local. In Jordan we had learnt the importance of having someone on board who not only spoke the language but was also familiar with local traits and traditions, traffic and terrain. We drove to the local BMW dealer who had also sold Land Rovers in the past. His suggestions simply didn't match our requirements – we needed more than a tour guide. Fortunately, one of the sales staff recalled a Defender 110 customer who had converted his vehicle into a "Bigfoot" – i.e. equipped the vehicle with oversize balloon tyres. This was Ingo, a dancer from Reykjavík.

So now we were five people in two Defenders on the hunt for challenging and adventurous routes. We were more than successful. However, we underestimated the weather. It rains all the time. Wellington boots alone are not enough to defeat Icelandic rain.

Our first water crossing – and there are many on the island – succeeded without incident. A pair of large rocks indicated where the river was shallow enough to wade across. The second was a bit more difficult. I grabbed a Defender and carefully started driving across until the vehicle suddenly started floating and threatened to drift away downstream. I immediately stopped and radioed Hans for help. He attached a safety rope to his vehicle, waded through the icy cold glacial water and attached the other end to mine, thus enabling him to pull me back out of the river. Straight away, we decided to abandon this route and drove the 19 miles back to the first crossing. On arrival, at once we noticed that the rocks were no longer visible. The water level had risen dramatically.

We had no choice – we had to attempt the crossing. Hans slowly entered the river with his Defender 130, though this time his and my vehicle were joined via a snatch strap. Hans had almost made it to the other riverbank when he was forced to stop – the recovery strap was too short. I proceeded to enter the roaring torrent of water with my Defender and bogged down almost immediately.

That's when things got a little hairy. The raging current had picked up the two-inch-wide snatch strap and was slowly pulling it at right angles to the vehicles. The strap, the Defenders and our nerves all began to suffer from the strain. It was time for our Icelandic dancer, Ingo, to do his stuff. In his wading trousers (which he had prudently packed), he climbed on top of Hans' Defender and attempted to release the strap from the retaining hook. Naturally, the plan was doomed. The strap was weighted down by tons of water. Meanwhile, my vehicle was sinking deeper and deeper into the gravel. The time had come for a more radical solution. I grabbed my Leatherman, jumped on the bonnet, plunged my hands into the ice-cold water and cut the strap in two. Hans could then drive onto the opposite riverbank, and I could drive back onto the riverbank on my side of the river.

Hans and Ingo were now on one side of the river, with Christian, the journalist Inge and myself on the other. Not the best point of departure for pre-scouting this island. Yet just when it looked as though things had hit rock bottom, there was light at the end of the tunnel…or, more precisely, two headlights mounted on an enormous tractor, which was now parked behind me, and a Jeep which had also been caught unawares by the surge of water.

The only vehicle capable of crossing the river was this monstrous piece of farm machinery. We asked the driver to take the Defender in tow, which he did without a murmur of complaint. On the other side of the river, Hans asked him if he could bring the Discovery over as well. The Jeep driver seized his moment and asked for a tow, too. Our friendly tractor driver was obviously from the planet Krypton – the Discovery was hooked up to the tractor, and the Jeep to the Land Rover, and the huge caravan was dragged through the churning maelstrom.

We took a photo at the time, and it is still one of my all-time favourites. It shows the Discovery pulling the Jeep to safety. As chance would have it, the tractor is nowhere to be seen.

DIE TROLLE
THE TROLLS

Ich bin kein ängstlicher Mensch, sonst könnte ich solche Touren wohl weder organisieren noch durchführen oder gar leiten. Doch hier auf Island beginne ich erstmals, an mir selbst zu zweifeln.

Auch mir sind die Geschichten von Elfen und Trollen bekannt, die in großen Felsen wohnen, weswegen die Isländer ihre Straßen kurvig drumherum bauen anstatt die Felsen zu eliminieren. Ach, Humbug – oder doch nicht?

Wir sind in Islands Norden, es ist der 9. Juli, und es schneit, als wolle uns die Insel zeigen, wer der Stärkere ist (obwohl ich das nie angezweifelt habe). Wir erkunden die Gegend um Gæsavatn und suchen – wie so oft – Wege als Herausforderung. Was wir finden, ist ein Straßenschild: „Askja 120 Kilometer". Prima – nur leider ist die Straße gesperrt. Aber wir wären nicht die Land Rover Experience Tour, würden wir nicht genau diese Tatsache als Einladung ansehen, es zu versuchen. Also machen wir uns auf den Weg zum Vulkan Askja.

Allerdings schneit es schnell immer stärker, die Sicht wird schlecht und schlechter, teilweise zieht Nebel auf, der über einer langsam unwirklich erscheinenden Landschaft wabert. Es wird dunkel, Schmelzwasser gluckert überall um uns herum. Und in diesem Moment denke ich: Ja, sie existieren – die Trolle, die eigentlichen Herrscher Islands, die mit uns machen können, was sie wollen. Es gibt Momente, in denen ich, der scheinbar mit allen Wassern gewaschene, weltreisende Offroad-Spezialist, nicht aussteigen will. Mir ist tatsächlich unheimlich zumute.

Was die Trolle nicht im Geringsten besänftigt. Im Gegenteil: Sie lassen mit weißen Gewändern die Straße verschwinden. Der Schnee hat sämtliche Markierungen überdeckt. Mit dem Fernglas suche ich irgendwelche Anhaltspunkte, meist vergebens. Wir bleiben andauernd in Schneefeldern stecken, müssen die Autos ausgraben, uns neu orientieren. Die Trolle haben überhaupt kein Einsehen mit den mutigen Menschen aus Deutschland und ihren englischen Autos, und die Nacht will nicht enden. Wahrscheinlich ist auch sie trollgesteuert.

Nach 13 Stunden Blindfahrt, Schneewühlen und Kampf gegen trollistische Windmühlenflügel sind wir restlos alle. In dieser Zeit haben wir gerade mal 30 Kilometer geschafft. Und dann muss der Obertroll selber müde geworden sein oder ein Einsehen mit uns gehabt haben – wir entdecken eine einsame Berghütte, die offen ist für hungrige Wanderer. Genau als solche fühlen wir uns, lassen die Autos stehen, entern die real existierende Nothütte und fallen in einen unruhigen Schlaf.

Natürlich baue ich später die Troll-Strecke in die Haupttour ein. Denn das ist Experience Tour pur.

I am neither anxious nor nervous – for were that the case I wouldn't be able to organise these tours, let alone manage or lead them in the first place. However, here on Iceland and for the first time ever, I began having second thoughts about my abilities.

I had also read about the elves and trolls which lived in large rocks and which were the reason why the Icelanders built the roads around the rocks instead of simply dynamiting the stone. Just fairy tales, right?

We were on the northern half of Iceland. It was the 9th of July, and it was snowing as if the island were bent on demonstrating which one of us was the stronger (not that I ever had my doubts). We were exploring the region around Gæsavatn, and, as usual, looking for challenging routes. We found a road sign reading "Askja 120 Kilometer (75 miles)", which was helpful – except that the road was blocked. That said, for the Land Rover Experience Tour a blocked road is just another obstacle to be overcome. So off we headed towards the Askja volcano.

Meanwhile, the snowstorm had moved up a gear, and visibility was worsening by the minute. Added to that, there was fog hanging over the ground, making the countryside look somehow unreal. It had grown very dark, and all you could hear was the gurgling of glacial water around us. At that moment I thought to myself: the real rulers of this island, the trolls, had us in their grip. I, the globetrotting off-road expert who had seen and done it all, was unwilling to get out of the vehicle. It all felt a little weird.

Not that the trolls were in any way motivated to calm down. Quite the opposite in fact. By now the road had disappeared under a white wall of snow. Whatever road signs and markings there had been were now completely covered in snow. I struggled to find any points of reference at all with the binoculars. We repeatedly bogged down in the deep snow. Again and again, we had to dig the vehicles out and figure out where we were. The trolls had no sympathy whatsoever for these courageous Germans with their English cars in this seemingly eternal night that itself seemed to be in the hands of the trolls.

After 13 hours of driving blind, shovelling snow and facing off against trolls bent on blowing us into the ground, we were absolutely exhausted. We had covered a paltry 19 miles. Either the head troll himself had had enough or had seen fit to grant us respite. Out of nowhere, we discovered a lonely mountain hut open for hungry travellers, which is of course what we were. We parked the cars and crawled into the rescue shelter, where we collapsed into a fitful sleep.

Naturally, we added the troll route to the main tour. The Experience Tour doesn't get any better than this.

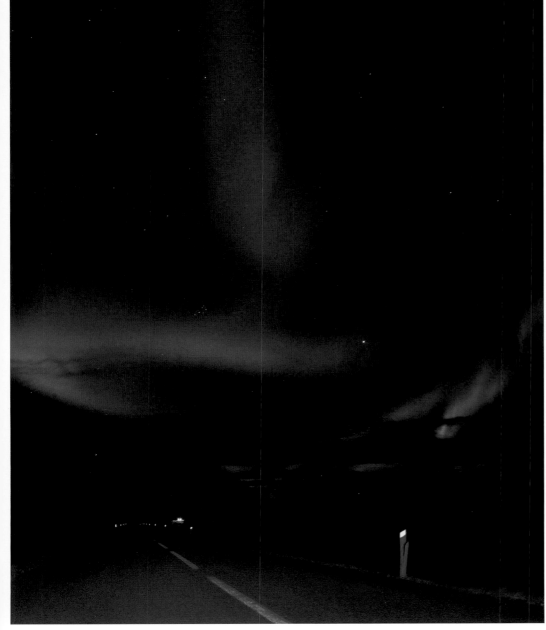

Die Farbwelten, die Island bestimmen, können Fotos kaum wiedergeben. Pechschwarz, Neongrün, Schneeweiß und Azurblau sind nur einige der Farben, die uns begegnet sind. Die Fahrt geht über riesige Sander und Aschefelder, geformt durch Vulkane, Wind, Schnee und Wasser. Am Rande dieser Welt sehen die Land Rover aus wie Modellautos.

Photography can't do justice to the landscape portrait that is Iceland. Inky black, neon green, snow white and azure blue are just a few of the colours we encountered. The expedition crossed huge outwash plains and ash and lava fields created by volcanoes, wind, snow and water. In this landscape the Land Rovers look like toy cars.

DIE JAGD
THE HUNT

Die Haupttour beginnt Anfang August, eigentlich die optimale Reise-
zeit für Island. Wir schocken die sechs Teilnehmer anfangs gleich
mal mit der Straße von der viertgrößten isländischen Stadt Akureyri
zum Geothermalgebiet Hveravellir, einer der anspruchsvollsten
Strecken für Offroader. Kenwood als neuer Sponsor hat uns mit
leistungsstarkem Funk ausgerüstet. Die Geräte besitzen zwei Kanäle,
die wir als Teilnehmerkanal und als Organisationskanal einrichten.
Die Teams müssen ja nicht unbedingt mithören, was Hans und ich uns
während der Fahrt für sie als kleine Gemeinheiten ausdenken. Ich liebe
es, mit Funk herumzuspielen. Das ist mein Steckenpferd und stammt
wahrscheinlich aus meiner Zeit als Fernmeldetechniker.
Leider kennt sich auch einer der Teilnehmer bestens mit solchen
Geräten aus, und es dauert nicht lange, da hat er entdeckt, dass wir uns
als Organisatoren auf einem anderen Kanal über sie und ihre neuen
Aufgaben unterhalten. Wir wundern uns bald, dass alle Teilnehmer
alle neu gestellten Tasks so problemlos und fehlerfrei lösen – bis wir
ihnen auf die Schliche kommen. Jetzt beginnt eine so unterhaltsame
wie unausgesprochene Jagd nach der richtigen Frequenz. Wir wechseln
unsere ständig, plappern Blödsinn über den Orga-Draht, ein bisschen
Unfug über den offiziellen Kanal, um dann wieder Schwachsinn über
die Orga-Frequenz zum Besten zu geben. So versuchen wir ständig, sie
in die Irre zu führen. Die Teilnehmer wissen bald nicht mehr, welche
Infos sie für bare Münze nehmen dürfen, und wir wissen bald nicht
mehr, wie wir uns inhaltlich wichtige Dinge zurufen können, ohne
dass die Teilnehmer wissen, wovon wir sprechen. Wir denken uns sogar
sogar Codewörter aus, damit wenigstens wir wissen, welche Frequenz
für uns gilt.
Aber schließlich greifen wir zu klassischen Mitteln: Der persönlichen und mündlichen Absprache zwischen Hans und mir ist kein
Frequenzhacker gewachsen.

The main tour began in August, which is the best time to visit Iceland.
The six participants are thrust right into one of the most challenging
off-road routes on the island: the road from the fourth-largest Icelandic
town of Akureyri to the Hveravellir geothermal region. Our new
sponsor, Kenwood, had outfitted us with powerful CB radios with two
channels – one for the participants and one for the organisers. The teams
didn't need to hear what we had up our sleeves for them. I love playing
with radios; it has always been something of a hobby of mine – probably
dating back to my work as a telecommunications specialist.
Unfortunately, one of the participants was also well-versed in
communications technology and in no time at all had discovered that
we were using the other channel to discuss the teams and the tasks to
come. We were surprised to see how well the teams solved the new
tasks without a single mistake until we caught onto the scam. What
ensued was an entertaining if unspoken hunt between the teams
and the organisation crew for the right frequency. We hopped from
one frequency to the next, talked complete and utter rubbish on the
organisation channel, only then to talk riddles on the participants'
channel before switching back to our own channel with more complete
nonsense. The plan to confuse the participants worked: after a while,
they no longer knew what to believe. It was a struggle communicating
the organisational aspects to one another while keeping the
participants in the dark. We even began using code words relating to
specific frequencies for organisational matters.
Finally, we reverted back to the classic method which is impervious
to radio hacking. Hans and I agreed on everything personally and
exclusively by word of mouth.

Eine solche Furt wie unten ist mit Vorsicht zu genießen. Das schnell strömende Wasser zerrt am Fahrzeug; Untiefen und Steine sind im aufgewühlten Fluss nicht zu sehen. Am Heck erkennt man den als Sicherung befestigten Bergegurt. Trotzdem beunruhigt den Fahrer das reißende Wasser – eine Flussquerung im Grenzbereich.

A ford like this has to be approached with care. The fast flowing water literally tears at the vehicle; irregularities in the riverbed and huge rocks are invisible in the foaming maelstrom. At the rear of the vehicle you can just make out the recovery strap as a safety measure. Nevertheless, the driver was concerned about the torrential stream – this was a river crossing on the limit.

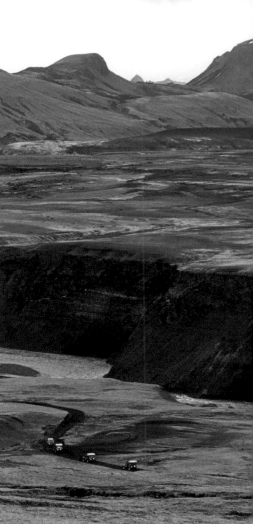

DER SCHLAUCH
THE HOSE

Zugegeben: Wenn wir die Teams durch deren Fehler mal auf falsche Fährten locken können, freuen wir uns wie die Kinder. Einmal lassen wir die Teilnehmer, als sie eine Abzweigung verpassen, tatsächlich durchs wilde Island irren. Als sie geknickt zurückkommen, steht das gesamte Orga-Team grinsend am Straßenrand und vollführt die La-Ola-Welle. So viel Spaß muss sein.

Just in dem Moment, als uns der letzte Discovery passiert, knallt es aus dessen Motorraum, weißer Rauch qualmt unter der Haube hervor. Ich denke nur: Motorplatzer. Sofort nehmen wir das Autoherz unter die Lupe: Öl okay, Wasser okay, Motor? Okay. Wir starten ihn – er läuft rund. Wir geben im Leerlauf Gas bis etwa 2 500 Umdrehungen – ein Knall, der Motor streikt, weißer Rauch …

Neuerdings mit Satellitentelefon ausgestattet, rufe ich in der Zentrale in Wülfrath an, wo Harry Hemmann sitzt, der Leiter der Pressewerkstatt. Der Mann kennt einen Land Rover besser als Maurice Wilks den Grund, so ein Auto erfunden zu haben. Ferndiagnosen sind zwar immer so eine Sache, aber letztlich noch besser als in Island mit qualmendem Motor dumm herumzustehen. Harry erklärt, welche Ursachen infrage kommen können, und wir steigen tief in die Ersatzteilkisten hinab – wir haben so ziemlich alles dabei. Wir bauen, wir schrauben, wir hämmern, und das einzige Ergebnis ist, dass uns die Zeit davonläuft. Denn so frei und abenteuerlich unsere Reisen auch sind, sie unterliegen einem festen Zeitplan.

So lasse ich den großen Teil des Experience-Konvois ziehen, nur die beiden Teilnehmer, die zu dem Problemauto gehören, sowie mein Kollege Lutz Hertel, genannt „Lutz Lutz", und ich bleiben an Ort und Stelle. Es wird dunkel, Nebel zieht auf, und wir schrauben bereits geschlagene fünf Stunden an dem Havaristen. Noch einmal wagen wir einen Startversuch. Ich schaue dabei in den Motorraum, und zwar auf den Schlauch des Turboladers. Und siehe: Bei höheren Drehzahlen beginnt er, sich zusammenzuziehen, worauf weißer Rauch und das Absterben des Motors folgen. Sofort baue ich den Übeltäter aus und finde in seinem Inneren einen Produktionsfehler. Bei höherer Beanspruchung bildet sich eine Gummiblase, die den Luftdurchlass behindert. Ich schneide die Blase heraus – das Problem ist gelöst.

Nicht aber das der Müdigkeit. Im Schritttempo, bei Nebel und in tiefster Dunkelheit tasten sich Lutz Lutz und ich mit den zwei Wagen Richtung Arnarvatn. Um 3 Uhr haben die anderen die Campsite in Húsavík erreicht – wir sind morgens um 8 Uhr dort. Und ich muss gestehen: Auf dieser Fahrt glaube ich Kurven zu sehen, wo keine sind – wir alle sind nah dran an Halluzinationen. Aber vielleicht haben sich auch nur die Trolle neue Spielchen ausgedacht.

This much I will admit: When teams make the wrong decision, it can be hilariously funny. We watched them take a wrong turn and then sat back to enjoy the spectacle that unfolded before us as they scooted here, there and everywhere through the Icelandic wilderness. When they returned looking somewhat dejected, a grinning organisation team greeted them from the side of the road with a Mexican wave. At the end of the day, all one could do was laugh.

As the last Discovery drove past us, there was a bang from the engine, and white smoke started pouring out from underneath the bonnet. My first thought was: engine failure. Upon closer inspection, we established that the oil and water levels were normal. The engine appeared to be good. We started it up and it ticked over as normal. Leaving the car in neutral, we increased the throttle to about 2,500 rpm, and there it was again. A huge bang, the engine cut out and white smoke billowed out…

We were equipped with satellite telephones on this tour, so I phoned back to the office in Wülfrath to talk to Harry Hemmann, the press fleet workshop manager. Now Harry's knowledge of Land Rovers knows no bounds – and while there are limitations to remote diagnostic analysis, even this was better than standing around looking stupidly at an engine spewing white smoke. Harry went through all the possible scenarios, and we dug deep into the spares box – we weren't short on parts. Still, the only result of our banging, hammering and extensive use of a ratchet screwdriver was that we were running out of time. For all the freedom and adventure that constitutes the spirit of the tour, the event has to run on a strict schedule.

I decided to let the majority of the convoy carry on to the next stop while the team members whose car was in trouble, my colleague Lutz Hertel – nicknamed "Lutz Lutz" – and I stayed put. It was getting dark, the fog was closing in and we had already spent five full hours working on the stranded Discovery. We tried starting it again, and I kept my eye on the engine bay, and in particular the hose leading to the turbocharger. Lo and behold, the instant the revs picked up, the hose started to contract, producing the white smoke and stalling the engine. I immediately removed the offending part and discovered a production error on the interior of the hose – under pressure, the rubber had begun to bubble, preventing the through-flow of air. Removing the bubble by literally excising it solved the problem.

It was no cure for our exhaustion, though. In the fog and in the dark, Lutz Lutz and I led our two vehicles at a walking pace towards Arnarvatn. The others had reached the campsite in Húsavík at 3 in the morning – we finally turned up at 8 am. I swear that I had seen curves in the track where there certainly weren't any. Perhaps we were just hallucinating, or perhaps it was the trolls dreaming up some other way to toy with us.

DER UNFALL
THE ACCIDENT

René Linke päppelt uns schnell wieder auf. Wir haben erstmals unseren Haus- und Hofkoch aus Wülfrath mit, der fast seine gesamte Küche dabeihat und uns mit Fleisch vom Grill, Reis und Sauce zu alter Stärke verhilft.

Nach dem Chaos mit dem Discovery läuft tatsächlich alles nach Plan. Bis zum vorletzten Tag der Tour. Wir sind auf dem Weg zurück nach Reykjavík, die Luft ist klar, der Regen macht Pause. Die Schotterpiste, deren Oberfläche konvex verläuft und die von flachen Felsen begrenzt ist, scheint gut ausgebaut. Die Teilnehmer halten sich an meine Tempovorgabe von maximal 60 km/h. Die Autos vor mir verschwinden hinter einer Kuppe, wie so oft in dieser Gegend.

Als ich den Zenit des Hügels erreiche, scheint mein Herz auszusetzen: Das Damenteam-Auto, das eben noch direkt vor mir fuhr, befindet sich nicht mehr auf der Straße. Ich registriere noch die großen Augen von Doc Gunnar, der neben mir sitzt, als ich nach rechts blicke und den Discovery durch das Seitenfenster über die Felsen wirbeln sehe. Der schwere Wagen bleibt etwa 20 Meter neben der Piste auf dem Dach zwischen großen Steinen liegen. „Es darf nie etwas passieren" ist unser Credo, und jetzt liegt ein Land Rover mit Teilnehmerinnen darin arg zertrümmert in der isländischen Wildnis.

Sofort stoppe ich den Konvoi per Funk und eile mit dem Doc zum zerstörten Auto. A-, B- und C-Säulen sind gestaucht, aber es gibt genug Überlebensraum in dem umgestürzten Offroader. Wir rufen irgendetwas in den Wagen hinein, dumme Sätze wie „Wie geht's euch?", und zum Glück erschallt sofort von innen: „Keine Sorge, alles okay." Die Damen krabbeln eigenständig aus den zerstörten Seitenfenstern heraus – Schock ja, leichte Schnittverletzungen auch, aber das ist alles. Gunnar setzt Infusionen und ist auch unersetzlich im psychischen Beistand, den er den beiden immer noch erschrockenen Fahrerinnen leistet.

Es stellt sich heraus, dass ein einfacher Fahrfehler zu der Beinahe-Katastrophe geführt hat. Die Fahrerin wollte einem großen Stein ausweichen, den sie aufgrund der Kuppe erst sehr spät am Rand gesehen hatte, verriss das Lenkrad, und wegen der konvexen Form des Untergrundes hob der schwere Wagen seitlich ab und flog in die Felsen. Am folgenden Abend feiern wir alle zusammen zwei zweite Geburtstage. Und ich schwöre, keine Tour mehr ohne Arzt zu absolvieren.

René Linke soon had us fighting fit again. We had decided to bring our Wülfrath chef - mobile kitchen and all - along with us on the tour for the first time, and his combination of barbecued meat, rice and gravy hit the right spot.

After the nightmare with the Discovery, things were actually running according to schedule. Until the penultimate day of the tour, that is. We were heading back to Reykjavík, visibility was good, and even the rain had let up. The well-constructed gravel roads have a convex surface structure and are bordered on both sides by relatively low rock faces. The participants were sticking to our set speed of maximum 40 mph. Ahead of me, the vehicles briefly disappeared from view as they drove over a slight crest.

As I reached the top of the crest, my heart sank. The ladies team car, directly in front of us just two seconds before, was now no longer on the road. I can remember seeing my co-driver Doc Gunnar's eyes widen as we both looked right, just in time to see the Discovery literally somersault over the low rock face. The heavy vehicle landed on its roof between larger rocks about 60 feet from the road. Our mantra, "Keep out of trouble", was ringing in my ears as I looked at a wrecked Land Rover with two participants on board in the middle of the Icelandic wilderness.

I immediately radioed ahead to the convoy, instructing them to stop, and the doc and I rushed over to the severely damaged vehicle. The A-, B- and C-pillars were all badly bent, but there was enough space in the upended off-roader for the team to survive. The rather stupid sounding question "How are you?" was all we managed to ask, and fortunately from the inside of the vehicle the answer was an immediate "Don't worry, we're okay." The ladies crawled out through the smashed side windows themselves, but aside from shock and minor cuts, they were okay. Gunnar put both on drips and was quick to administer psychological help as both ladies were still suffering from severe shock.

It turned out that the cause of the near catastrophe was simple driver error. The driver had turned sharply to avoid hitting a larger rock, which she only saw at the last minute as she came over the hill, and because of the convex shape of the gravel road, the heavy vehicle tilted to one side and flew into the rock face. The following night, everyone celebrated two second birthdays, and that night I swore that there would be no more tours without a doctor on board.

GUNNAR WASMUS

geboren am 04.01.1959
Orthopäde und Notfallarzt auf den ersten Touren

born 4 January 1959
orthopaedist and emergency doctor on the early tours

Bei welchen Touren warst du dabei?

Gunnar: In Jordanien, Island, Namibia, Mundo Maya, Kanada, Schottland sowie auf der Vortour von Argentinien/Chile. Dann musste ich aufhören – aus beruflichen und familiären Gründen.

Hattest du viel zu tun auf den Reisen?

Gunnar: Zum Glück gab es nie schlimme Verletzungen, aber etwas zu tun gab es trotzdem. Üblich waren Schnittverletzungen oder Abschürfungen, in Mexiko kümmerte ich mich um Magenprobleme bei den Teilnehmern. Auf der Vortour in Argentinien hat der begleitende Fotograf – ein starker Raucher – den plötzlichen Höhenunterschied von 1 500 auf etwa 4 000 Meter nicht vertragen. Er zeigte Anzeichen der gefährlichen Höhenkrankheit. Eine Messung bewies, dass er viel zu wenig Sauerstoff im Blut hatte – weniger als 70 Prozent. Wir beschlossen, ihn sofort in tiefere Regionen zu bringen. Dag saß am Steuer, ich war hinten beim Patienten. Dem Journalisten ging es unten sofort besser, nur mir war – wegen der Schaukelei im Auto und meiner Position quer zur Fahrtrichtung – speiübel.

Stammt aus dieser Zeit dein Spitzname „Speiing Doctor"?

Gunnar: Haha, nein – der wurde mir bei der Island-Tour verpasst. Wir saßen in einem sogenannten „Hot Pot". Von unten wurde das Wasser in dem natürlichen Badeloch durch die Erdwärme erhitzt, oben floss kaltes Gletscherschmelzwasser hinein. Nach einem langen Reisetag erholten wir uns dort von den Strapazen. Zuerst gab es Bier, dann aus Infusionsflaschen Southern Comfort – frag mich nicht, warum. Und ich wusste nicht, was das für ein Zeug in den Flaschen ist. Die Nacht war noch okay, aber ich hielt den Konvoi am nächsten Tag dann doch noch etwas auf ...

Du sollst auch einmal völlig nüchtern für eine explosive Stimmung gesorgt haben?

Gunnar: Stimmt. Das war bei der Argentinien/Chile-Tour. Ich hatte eine schwierige private Situation zu überstehen und war manchmal gedanklich nicht ganz auf der Höhe. Wir hielten ganz oben auf dem Socompa-Pass, weil die Fotografen und TV-Leute ihre Aufnahmen machen wollten. Denn hier, genau an der Grenze zwischen Peru und Argentinien, gab es ein Minenfeld, von den Argentiniern während des Falkland-krieges errichtet. Links und rechts Absperrbänder, dahinter ein zerstörter Land Rover, in der Mitte ein schmaler Sandpfad zum Passieren. Und während die Fotografen ihre Arbeit taten, riefen alle plötzlich laut meinen Namen und ob ich völlig verrückt geworden sei: Ich habe wohl ein paar dicke Steine ins Minenfeld geworfen. Diese blödsinnige Aktion hat mir aber eine meiner schönsten Erinnerungen an diese Reise eingebracht: Der Fotograf Reinhard schenkte mir später eine Schatzkiste, in der er die gesamte Situation detailgetreu mit Mini-Menschen und Wiking-Autos nachgebaut hatte.

Abgesehen von den Teilnehmern der Tour – konntest du auch woanders helfen?

Gunnar: Natürlich – getreu dem Experience-Motto „Jeden Tag eine gute Tat". In Namibia zum Beispiel gab es richtig Arbeit: In einem Kral baten uns die Bewohner, ihnen zu helfen – sie hatten es bitter nötig. Eine Frau war schwerkrank, ein Kind war in die Feuerstelle gefallen und hatte Verbrennungen. Da konnten wir nachhaltig helfen. Dort bekam ich übrigens meinen zweiten Spitznamen: Onganga.

Und das bedeutet?

Gunnar: Wir dachten immer: „Doktor".
Doch später erfuhr ich die wahre Übersetzung: Perlhuhn.

Which tours did you participate in?

Gunnar: Jordan, Iceland, Namibia, Mundo Maya, Canada, Scotland and the pre-scout to Argentina/Chile. I had to stop because of work and family.

Were you busy on the tours?

Gunnar: Fortunately we never had any serious injuries, but I was busy nevertheless. The usual suspects were cuts and scrapes. In Mexico the participants suffered from severe stomach cramps. On the Argentina pre-scout, the photographer – a heavy smoker – couldn't cope with the sudden change in altitude from just under 5,000 feet to just over 13,000 feet. I recognised symptoms of altitude sickness, we examined him and discovered that he had too little oxygen in his blood (less than 70 percent). We immediately decided to drive him down to a lower altitude. Dag drove and I remained in the back of the ambulance with the patient. Lower down, the patient immediately felt a lot better. I just remember feeling as sick as a dog – the road was not the smoothest, and I sat at right angles to the direction in which we were travelling.

Is this how you achieved your nickname "The puking doctor"?

Gunnar: Ha-ha – no, I received that accolade in Iceland. We were sitting in one of the so-called "hot pots". The water in the natural spring was warmed by geo-thermal energy from below and cooled from above by glacial melt. We were recovering from a long day behind the wheel. First of all there was beer, and then Southern Comfort started making the rounds in a transfusion bottle – don't ask me why. I didn't recognise the taste at all. I survived the night well enough, but the following day I slowed the convoy down a little...

You don't need alcohol to generate an explosive situation – can you tell me more?

Gunnar: You're right there. That was on the Argentina/Chile tour. My private life at the time was a little complex, and there were a few moments where my mind just wandered. We parked up on the Socompa Pass as the TV crew and our photographer needed to get their shots. On the border here between Argentina and Peru there was a minefield that had been laid by the Argentineans during the Falklands War. To the left and right there was barrier tape, behind it a wrecked Land Rover, and in the middle a small path in order to be able to get through. While the photographers were busy at work, someone suddenly started shouting my name asking whether I had gone completely barmy. I had thrown some bigger stones into the minefield. My complete idiocy, however, resulted in one of the best souvenirs of the trip. Reinhard the photographer later gave me a present, which was a treasure box with the whole scene recreated as a diorama with mini figures and cars.

Were you able to treat others apart from the participants?

Gunnar: Of course – in keeping with the Experience motto, "a good deed every day". In Namibia, for example, we were really busy. In one Kral, the local community asked us to assist as they urgently needed help. A woman was seriously ill, and a small child had fallen into the campfire and suffered severe burns. We were able to make a difference. I also received a second nickname there: Onganga.

Meaning?

Gunnar: We always thought it meant "Doctor".
Later on I was told the correct translation: guinea fowl.

Island besitzt eine ganz eigene Energie, die sich den Reisenden auf atemberaubende Weise mitteilt: Überall hört man es im Boden arbeiten, es riecht nach Schwefel, Geysire stemmen sich in den Himmel. Hinzu kommen die zahlreichen Wasserfälle, die sich tosend in die Schluchten stürzen.

Iceland has its own unique aura, one communicated to the visitor in the most breathtaking fashion. The earth here is quite literally at work; the smell of sulphur is everywhere, and geysers launch themselves to the heavens. Added to that are numerous waterfalls cascading into dramatic canyons.

NAMIBIA
2002
5 DISCOVERY, 2 DEFENDER, 1 RANGE ROVER
STRECKE / DISTANCE: 2 100 KM / 1,300 MILES.

NAMIBIA

NAMIBIA
2002
5 DISCOVERY, 2 DEFENDER, 1 RANGE ROVER
STRECKE / DISTANCE: 2 100 KM / 1,300 MILES.

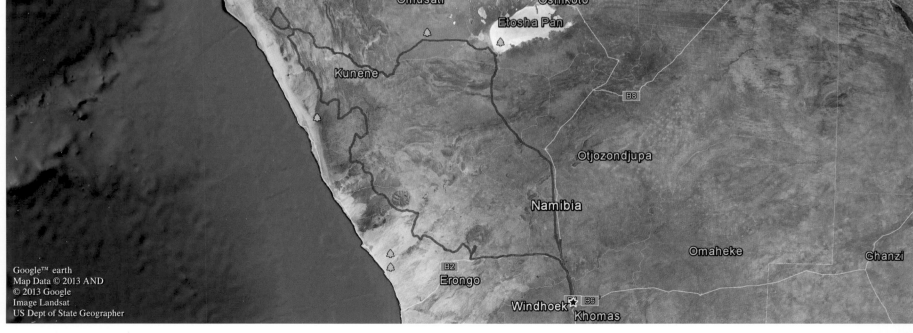

DAS KONDOM
THE CONDOM

Island ist kaum verdaut, da müssen wir schon die nächste Tour organisieren. Keine Zeit zum Verschnaufen. Aber wohin?

Nach dem abenteuerlichen, aber europäischen Island wird es Zeit, den Kontinent zu wechseln. Afrika ist traditionelles Land-Rover-Gebiet – da müssen wir jetzt unbedingt hin. Welches Land ist dort sicher? Was ist logistisch machbar? Klar: Namibia. Hans kennt das ehemalige Deutsch-Südwestafrika bereits, ich auch etwas. Es verspricht wilde Tiere, sandige Wüste, hohe Berge, unvergleichliches Licht. Kurz: Daktari-Feeling. Wer den legendären Buschdoktor nicht mehr kennt: „Daktari" (Doktor) hieß eine amerikanische Fernsehserie Ende der 60er Jahre, die die Arbeit eines afrikanischen Tierhospitals und deren Doktoren zeigte – mitsamt der frechen Schimpansin Judy und dem schielenden Löwen Clarence. Natürlich fuhren in der Serie alle beteiligten Zweibeiner Land Rover.

10 000 Bewerber goutieren unsere Wahl. Acht Tage soll die Tour diesmal dauern, wegen des Zehn-Stunden-Fluges zum Zielort. Ich halte mich inzwischen für einen absoluten Organisationsprofi, Land Rover feiert Erfolge und verströmt Aufbruchstimmung – die Welt gehört uns.

Gernot, ein weißbärtiger Namibianer, ist schnell gefunden und als Guide vereidigt. Wie sich herausstellt, kennt er zwar jeden Vogel beim Vornamen, doch mit uns lernt er Wege kennen, an die er noch nicht mal im Traum gedacht hatte. Wir wollen die Tour mit diversen Serienfahrzeugen absolvieren: Discovery für die Teilnehmer, Defender für den Support und einen Range Rover für Begleiter wie Christian Uhrig. So touren wir durch das Land auf der Suche nach Abenteuern. Zu den größten gehört, dass uns unsere Reifen wegen der vielen spitzen Steine nur so um die Ohren fliegen. Ersatz in 19 Zoll ist kaum aufzutreiben.

Gut gerüstet durch die Erfahrungen der Vortour kommen wir zur Haupttour mit massenhaft Reifen im Gepäck in Namibia an. Und wie wir vermuten, platzt das Gummi auch diesmal ständig. Bald kennen wir jeden „Flat Tire Repair" im Umkreis von 500 Kilometern. So ein Pneu-Gemetzel habe ich nie wieder erlebt: 30 platte Reifen auf 2 000 Kilometern bei zehn Autos durch Steine und Dornen. Manchmal reparieren wir erstmal die Elektrik der Vulkanisierbetriebe am Straßenrand, weil deren Kompressoren nicht funktionieren, bevor die sich um unsere Reifen kümmern können.

Aber es kommt natürlich so, wie es kommen muss: Ein Discovery erleidet einen Reifenschaden am Brandbergmassiv, nachdem wir sämtliche Ersatzreifen bereits aufgebraucht haben. Was tun? Anhand von GPS-Informationen weiß ich, dass in etwa 30 Kilometern ein weiterer Tire Repair firmiert. Also beschließe ich, den Konvoi aufzusplitten. Drei Autos sollen beim Havaristen bleiben, der Rest muss zur Reparaturwerkstatt eilen. Da kommt unser Fotograf Thomas auf eine Idee: Man könne das Dornenloch doch durch ein Kondom flicken. Zufällig habe er gerade eines dabei … Mit einem Holzstab drücken wir das Gummi ins Loch und pumpen den Reifen vorsichtig mit dem Kompressor auf.

Aber alle, die jetzt hoffen, eine neue Ausrede für ein (an)ständiges Kondom in der Leatherman-Tasche zu haben, muss ich enttäuschen: Es funktioniert nicht. Obwohl wir extrem vorsichtig waren.

It seemed like only yesterday that we had been on Iceland, yet it was already time to plan the next tour. As the saying goes, there's no rest for the wicked. The question was: Where to this time? After an adventurous but very European-feeling Iceland, it was time to jump continents. Since Africa has always been something of a second home for Land Rover, we decided we had to head there. Where was it safe? What were the logistics like? It was obvious: Namibia. Hans was already familiar with the former colony of German South-West Africa, and I had been there, too. Wild animals, sandy deserts, mountains – it was a photographer's dream. In short: Daktari. For those not in the know, "Daktari" (meaning Doctor) was a famous '60s American TV series about the work of an African animal hospital featuring a cheeky chimpanzee called Judy and a squinting lion called Clarence. The two-legged actors, of course, all drove Land Rovers.

10,000 applicants agreed wholeheartedly with our choice of location. A ten-hour flight meant that this time the tour would last for eight days. We were on a roll, Land Rover was striding from success to success, there was a real sense of optimism within the company, and I had become a logistics professional.

We quickly found Gernot, a white-bearded Namibian, and had him sworn in as our guide. Although he was on first-name terms with every bird in Namibia, in our company he would get to know routes that he had never dreamt even existed. We had three different Land Rover models on the tour: the participants were in Discoverys, the organisation team in Defenders, and we had a Range Rover for guests such as Christian Uhrig. Once again, we headed off into the bush on our hunt for adventure, and we found it immediately – in the form of numerous punctures, courtesy of the extremely sharp stones on the gravel roads. And 19-inch tyres were virtually unheard of in Namibia. After a pre-scout recce in which punctures featured far too prominently, we took plenty of spare tyres with us for the main event. As we suspected, history would repeat itself, with tyres blowing here, there and everywhere. Within a short space of time, we got to know every "flat-tyre repair" station within a 300-mile radius: 30 punctures on ten vehicles over 1,200 miles due to sharp stones and thorns remains a record in the annals of the Experience Tour. On some occasions, we first had to repair the electrical systems at the aforementioned repair shops before their compressors could be switched on to repair our tyres. Thankfully, we have not had tyre trouble like this on any tour since.

Naturally, the inevitable happened. With our supply of spares already spent, a Discovery suffered a puncture in the vicinity of the Brandberg Mountain. GPS data indicated another tyre repair station about 19 miles down the trail, so I decided to split the convoy up. Three cars were to stay with the stranded vehicle, while the rest were to head on to the repair station. It was then that Thomas, our photographer, suggested using a condom to seal the hole created by the thorn, as, by chance, he happened to have one (a condom) on him… Using a piece of wood, we forced the condom into the hole in the tyre and carefully pumped up the tyre using the compressor.

I regret to inform those in search of new and respectable reasons to carry a condom around that it didn't work – and this despite the fact that we were very careful.

Das afrikanische Land bietet viel Sehenswertes – aber etwas ganz Besonderes sind die Farbenspiele der Sonne, wenn sie auf- oder untergeht.

This country in Africa has a great deal to offer – of particular and spectacular note is the explosion of colour that accompanies sunrise and sunset.

DER ELEFANT
THE ELEPHANT

Es ist phantastisch – alles das, was wir auf der zeitlich engen Vortour nicht gesehen haben, wird uns nun geboten: Natur satt, Zeit zum Genießen, und vor allem wilde Tiere zum Beobachten. Das entschädigt dafür, dass die fahrerische Herausforderung in Namibia nicht so extrem ist, wie wir uns das erhofft haben. Zwar gibt es wenig asphaltierte Piste, aber die Schotterwege sind breit, und es existieren kaum Strecken, die einen Loop erlauben. Und um in eine Sackgasse zu manövrieren und den gleichen Weg wieder zurückfahren zu müssen, ist uns unsere Zeit zu schade. Deshalb sind wir für ein völlig ungeplantes Highlight ausgesprochen dankbar: eine Elefantenkuh und ihr Kalb. Die beiden stehen auf der anderen Seite eines etwa 40 Meter breiten, ausgetrockneten Flussbettes und schauen uns an.
Natürlich glotzen wir fasziniert zurück. Denn das ist so ein erhoffter Afrika-Moment für jeden Fotografen und für jedes Filmteam. Wir robben uns langsam im Flussbett vorwärts, um gute Bilder zu schießen – da trötet jemand rechts von uns und viel zu nah: Es ist der dazugehörige Bulle. Wir haben ihn nicht bemerkt. Er stampft mit den Vorderbeinen und ist sichtlich erregt. Und er steht auf unserer Seite des Flussbettes.
Nur Fotograf Thomas und Kameramann Franky wollen nicht gleich fliehen – werden dann aber ziemlich schnell eines Besseren belehrt, als das tonnenschwere Tier beginnt, in ihre Richtung zu laufen. Dass unsere Knipser so schnell rennen können, habe ich ihnen vorher gar nicht zugetraut.
Wir schaffen es in die Autos, somit gelingt uns die Flucht, aber wir haben wieder etwas dazugelernt: Rechne noch mehr als bisher mit dem Unberechenbaren.

It was just amazing – everything we had missed during the tightly scheduled pre-scout recce was now laid out before us: nature as far as the eye could see, time to enjoy it and, best of all, wild animals. To some extent, this compensated for the fact that the driving wasn't quite as challenging as we had hoped. While very few roads were tarmacked, the gravel roads were wide, and there were all too few routes that allowed us to drive a loop. Because our time was too precious to drive the same route in and back out again, we were particularly fortunate that the attractions should leap before our eyepieces: an elephant and her calf. The pair stood on the opposite bank of a dry riverbed approximately 130 feet wide and watched us.
Obviously, we stared back – we were fascinated. It was the perfect Africa moment for every photographer and film team. We were crawling our way up the riverbed for better camera position when suddenly there was a loud trumpet to the right of and in worryingly close proximity to our position. It was none other than the third family member – the bull – and we had failed to notice him before. Stamping his front legs on the ground, he was visibly upset. To make matters worse, he was on our side of the riverbed.
Thomas the photographer and Franky the cameraman were the only ones not to get up and make a break for it. As the mighty bull began running towards them, though, they too rapidly changed their minds. I would never have imagined beforehand that our picture snappers could run so fast.
We made it to the cars and managed to escape, but we learned something that day: more than ever, expect the unexpected.

Lieber zusammenbleiben: Das Lagerfeuer hält am Abend warm, der massive Land-Rover-Auftritt unliebsame Gäste fern. Elefanten gehören zu den sogenannten „Big Five" und haben jederzeit Vorfahrt. Und damit die Land Rover immer einsatzbereit bleiben, müssen die Luftfilter ständig von dem teilweise sehr feinen Staub befreit werden.

Better to stay together: the campfire keeps you warm, and the dominating presence of the Land Rover keeps unwelcome guests at a distance. Elephants rank among the so-called "big five" and have automatic right of way. And to ensure that the Land Rovers are always ready for action, the air filters need to be cleaned constantly.

Im Etosha-Nationalpark: Der Konvoi verteilt sich zur Beobachtung auf verschiedene Wasserlöcher – bis zur Nachricht: „Löwe am Olifantsbad …"

In the Etosha National Park – the convoy divided up to observe numerous watering holes until the message came over the radio: "Lion sighted at the Olifantsbad!"

DER SCHADEN
THE DAMAGE

Ich sage es unseren Teams und selbst unseren Experience-Kollegen immer wieder: Fahrt im Konvoi nicht so dicht auf. Und zwar allein wegen der möglichen Steinschläge in den Scheiben der nachfolgenden Autos. Aber es ist ja so lustig, dicht hintereinander durch die Lande zu touren, und der Fotograf verlangt ja auch oft wenig Abstand, damit das Foto mit mindestens sechs staubenden, dynamisch wirkenden Wagen perfekt gelingt. Sorry, wir können viel an Ersatzteilen mitführen, aber große Frontscheiben gehören nicht dazu.

Natürlich rede auch ich manchmal gegen Windmühlen, oder aber ein besonders aufmüpfiger Stein fliegt extrem weit. Aber in Namibia unterläuft mir selber ein Kardinalfehler in Sachen Konvoifahren.

Selbstverständlich haben wir auch hier Probleme mit von Reifen aufgewirbelten Steinen – das bösartigste Teil fliegt allerdings nicht in die Scheibe, sondern in den Kühler eines Discovery und zerstört ihn nachhaltig. Neue Kühler führen wir üblicherweise nicht mit – können aber zu Hause in Schwalbach einen bestellen. Die Lodge in Palmwag besitzt einen Landeplatz, wo eine neue Gruppe begleitender Journalisten erwartet wird. Die sollen den Kühler aus Deutschland mitbringen. Nichtsdestotrotz muss der malträtierte Wagen irgendwie zur Lodge gebracht werden. Was bleibt uns übrig außer Abschleppen? So nehmen wir den Discovery ans Seil und ziehen ihn nach Hause.

Das hätten wir lieber nicht machen sollen. Denn als wir ihn endlich abnabeln, fällt mir die Kinnlade herunter: An der Front des Autos ist so gut wie nichts mehr heil. Die Scheinwerfer zerschossen, der Lack ramponiert, die Nebelleuchten zerstört. Wir sind einfach unser normales Experience-Tempo gefahren und haben ein zu kurzes Seil verwendet. Der feine Sand und die Pistensteine haben nun auch noch den Rest der Front nachhaltig zerstört. Das nächste Mal bin ich schlauer.

It is something I repeat to teams, and even our own Experience colleagues, on a regular basis. When in convoy, don't bunch up; and I say this for one very good reason – the danger of stone impact damage for the following vehicles. That said, it is more fun in close convoy, and the photographers often demand that people stick together, as the image of six vehicles in their own dust is far more dynamic. Still, while we had all manner of spares on board, our problem was that window screens weren't among them.

Sometimes I feel as though the others are to blame, and that I am talking to a brick wall. And there are times when no one is to blame and e.g. a particularly obstreperous stone flies a great distance. In Namibia, though, I was to blame: I had made a cardinal error whilst driving in convoy.

It goes without saying that we had our problems with stones being thrown up by the tyres. The most dangerous incident saw a stone flying not into the windscreen but into the radiator, where it caused significant damage. We had no spare radiators on board but were able to order one from the Land Rover headquarters in Schwalbach, Germany. Our overnight lodge in Palmwag included a landing strip and was where we were expecting our second group of journalists to arrive, so we simply asked them to bring the replacement radiator with them. But because we had to get the Discovery back to the lodge first, we towed it home.

That was a mistake. For when we arrived at the lodge and unhooked the towline, my jaw dropped. The front end of the vehicle looked dreadful. Virtually nothing was intact. Both headlights and fog lamps had been destroyed, and the paint was scratched to hell. We had driven at normal Experience Tour speed, and the towline was far too short. Sand and gravel had finished off the front of the vehicle. It wouldn't happen again.

Das Matterhorn Namibias heißt Spitzkoppe – ein wunderschönes Landschaftsmerkmal in jedem Licht. Hier gibt es jahrtausendealte Felsmalereien.

Namibia's own Matterhorn is the Spitzkoppe. A wonderful feature of the landscape regardless of the light. It is also home to 1,000-year-old rock paintings.

CHRISTINE HÖFER-COLLINS

geb. 26.3.1973
Diplom-Geologin, als Projektleiterin bei Land Rover Experience von 2002 bis 2004 angestellt,
jetzt Mitinhaberin einer Agentur für Extremsport und Outdoor-Events in Südafrika

born 26 March 1973
geologist, project manager at Land Rover Experience from 2002 to 2004,
co-owner of an extreme sports and outdoor events agency in South Africa

Kannst du dir ein Leben ohne extreme Outdoor-Aktivitäten vorstellen?

Christine: Nein. Ich habe dem normalen Leben immer das Abenteuer vorgezogen, und das ist auch heute noch so. Mein Geo-Studium hat mich schon früh abseits der normalen Reiseziele gebracht. Zunächst arbeitete ich in Südamerika und in den Northwest Territories, dann gehörte ich zum Support Staff der Camel Trophy, ebenso bei der G4 Challenge, und dann kam die Land Rover Experience Tour. Übrigens gehöre ich wohl weltweit zur Familie mit den meisten Camel-Trophy-Teilnehmern. Nicht nur ich, sondern auch mein Mann und sein Bruder waren dabei und ebenso die Frau meines Schwagers.

Was war deine Aufgabe bei der Experience Tour?

Christine: Ich habe das Büro München der Experience Tour betreut. In Namibia war ich bei fast allen Touren dabei, also auch bei den Kundenreisen. Darunter auch eine Tour mit National Geographic in den äußersten Nordosten des Landes. Bei der Mundo-Maya-Tour war ich als eine der Hauptverantwortlichen dabei, weil ich fließend Spanisch spreche. Und einmal Island hab ich auch mitgemacht.

Hattest du jemals Angst?

Christine: Ja, na klar. Zum Beispiel, als Hans in Belize im Dschungel verloren ging. Aber auch in Namibia. Da wurden Hans und ich einmal überfallen – dunkle Gestalten mit langen Messern nahmen uns alles ab. Es gab noch mehr Momente, aber mit solchen kompetenten und phantastischen Menschen wie Dag und Hans im Team kam oft einfach keine Angst auf. Allerdings gab es auch Zeiten, da war ich wohl etwas zu sorglos. In Namibia schlief ich etliche Nächte direkt am Lagerfeuer; am folgenden Morgen fanden wir einmal frische Löwenspuren rund ums Camp …

Hattest du jemals das Gefühl, als Frau mit den Männern nicht mithalten zu können?

Christine: Natürlich gibt es Unterschiede in Sachen Ausdauer und vielleicht auch Leidensfähigkeit, aber ich habe immer genug Willensstärke besessen. Ich hatte übrigens auch nie das Gefühl, weniger Anerkennung als die Männer zu bekommen – im Gegenteil: Ich wurde eher hofiert und verwöhnt. Mit einer Ausnahme: Gernot, der Guide in Namibia, war ein echter Bure mit Haut wie Elefantenleder, und er hatte ziemliche Probleme mit der damals noch nicht mal 30 Jahre alten, kleinen, blonden Entscheidungsträgerin aus Deutschland.

Can you imagine your life without extreme outdoor activities?

Christine: No. I have always put adventure before everyday life, and I am no different today. My geography degree took me well off the beaten track, and initially I worked in South America and in the Northwest Territories. Then I was part of the support team on the Camel Trophy, and on the G4 Challenge before the Land Rover Experience Tour was born. By the way, I probably belong to the family with the greatest number of Camel Trophy participants. My husband and I, his brother and his wife have all taken part.

What was your job on the Experience Tour?

Christine: I ran the Experience Tour's Munich office. In Namibia, I accompanied almost all of the tours, including the customer trips and a tour we did with National Geographic in the far northeast corner of the country. On Mundo Maya I had more responsibility, because I speak fluent Spanish. I also did one tour to Iceland.

Were you ever afraid?

Christine: Oh yes, without a doubt. When Hans went missing in the Belizean jungle but also in Namibia. Hans and I were robbed. Guys with huge knives took everything. There were other moments, but working with such fantastic people as Dag and Hans in the team left no room for fear. There were other moments when I was a little reckless, such as in Namibia when I slept for a few nights right next to the campfire. Once we found lion tracks all around the campsite the following morning.

Did you ever feel that as a woman you couldn't keep up with the men?

Christine: There are obvious differences as far as stamina and one's ability to suffer are concerned but I have always been very strong-willed. I never felt that I received less recognition than the men – far from it: I was courted and spoiled, with one exception. Gernot, our guide in Namibia, was a true Boer, had skin like an elephant and problems with being told what to do by a little blond thing from Germany who hadn't even hit 30 at the time.

Die Himba leben auch heute noch vergleichsweise unberührt von der Zivilisation als Volk von Viehzüchtern, Jägern und Sammlern, vor allem im Kaokoland. Ein Zusammentreffen – nach unglaublich staubiger Tour durch Namibias Natur – ist auch immer ein kultureller Austausch und für beide Seiten gleich interessant und lehrreich.

To this day, the Himba people still live relatively unaffected by modern civilisation, herding cattle, hunting and gathering from the ground, particularly in Kaokoland. Meeting them is a cultural exchange, fascinating and educational for both parties.

DIE HILFE
THE AID

Die Land Rover Experience Tour fährt nicht nur durch die Gegend, um menschenleere Weiten kennenzulernen – im Gegenteil: Wir wollen ausdrücklich auch die Menschen und ihre Kultur besuchen, uns damit beschäftigen, ihre Botschaften weitertragen.

Das ist ein Grund, warum wir einen Kral aufsuchen, das Dorf eines traditionell lebenden Stammes. Der Dorfoberste hat eine Bitte: Der Doc möge sich um ein paar Einwohner kümmern. Einige Fälle kann Gunnar mit kleinen Pflastern und etwas Medizin heilen, aber zwei wirklich Kranke fordern sein ganzes Können. Eine Frau ist schwerkrank, sie benötigt dringend Erste Hilfe. Der zweite Fall betrifft ein Kind, das in die Feuerstelle gefallen war. Der Doc behandelt die verbrannte Haut so gut er kann. Wobei hundertprozentige Hilfe nicht an seinem Wissen scheitert, sondern an den begrenzten Hilfsmitteln, die wir mitführen.

Es ist schon immer ein Anliegen der Land Rover Experience Tour, nicht nur mit Freude am Abenteuer Teile der Welt zu erkunden, sondern auch zu helfen. Mit allem, was wir bieten können und was gebraucht wird.

The Land Rover Experience Tour is not just about discovering landscapes devoid of people – quite the opposite, in fact. We want to get to know people, the way they live their lives, and communicate their culture to others.

That is why we visited a Kraal (a South African word meaning "dispersed homestead"). Before agreeing to the visit, though, the village chief had one stipulation: that our doctor attend to several of the villagers. Some of them required nothing more than a plaster and medication. Two others demanded considerably more of Doc Gunnar's medical skills. One woman was seriously ill and required immediate first aid. Another patient was a child who had fallen into the campfire. The doc treated the burns as best he could, but it wasn't possible to provide all the help needed, as we simply lacked adequate supplies of the medical equipment needed to treat an injury of that nature.

The Land Rover Experience Tour has always been about more than just the joy of adventure while exploring the world. It is also about giving something back. And that means doing whatever we can to help people.

MUNDO
MAYA

MUNDO MAYA
2003
GUATEMALA, MEXICO, BELIZE
5 DISCOVERY, 2 DEFENDER
STRECKE / DISTANCE: 1850 KM / 1,150 MILES

DER HINTERGRUND
THE BACKGROUND

Jawohl, diesmal lassen wir es krachen. Drei Experience-Touren sind sehr erfolgreich absolviert, und jetzt wollen wir einen drauflegen. Zum ersten Mal durch mehrere Länder, genau gesagt: drei. Eine neue Herausforderung, wieder ein anderer Kontinent – Land Rover und ich haben inzwischen gelernt, mit dem Event umzugehen. Aufkommende Routine erleichtert die Organisation. So schocken uns auch nicht die 12 000 Bewerber, die ein neues Abenteuer mit uns erleben wollen. Und natürlich die Kultur: Wir ziehen los, um auf den Spuren der Maya zu wandeln.

Naja, zunächst nur Hans, Christine Höfer-Collins, Lutz Rathmann und Claudia Lütolf. Denn meine vielen Aktivitäten fordern ihren Tribut: operative Eingriffe in die Knie. So kann ich nur von Wülfrath aus unterstützend helfen – die Vortour leitet Hans.

Yes, indeed – it's time to let loose. We have completed three very successful Experience Tours and now we want to up the ante. This time with a tour through more than one country – three to be exact. A new challenge, another continent. Both Land Rover and I have learnt how to deal with such an event. The routine makes organisation simpler. We weren't even shocked by the 12,000 applicants who wanted to come with us, keen to catch the adventure buzz and to experience new cultures. We were heading off to follow in the footsteps of the Maya.

When I write "we", I mean Hans, Christine Höfer-Collins, Lutz Rathmann and Claudia Lütolf, for I had finally paid the price for being Mr 24/7: I had to have a knee operation, and that would keep me tied to my desk in Wülfrath. This time, Hans ran the pre-scout.

LUTZ RATHMANN

geb. 11.10.1975
Diplom-Ingenieur der Elektrotechnik, Land Rover Lead Instructor

born 11 October 1975
graduate electrical engineer, Land Rover Lead Instructor

Du bist schon als Schüler mit dem Outdoor-Virus angesteckt worden – wie kam es dazu?

Lutz: Ich kenne Hans Hermann Ruthe bereits sehr lange, und deshalb habe ich schon als 16-Jähriger Orientierungsläufe für die Camel Trophy organisiert. Als Hans anfing, für die Land Rover Experience zu arbeiten, ging ich mit. Dort gehörte es zu einer meiner ersten Tätigkeiten, die Fahrzeuge für die Jordanien-Tour in den Nahen Osten zu bringen. Aber diese scheinbar leichte Task hatte ihre Tücken, und zwar schon in Europa: Damals haben Trucker in den Niederlanden die Grenzen zugestellt, um gegen die Benzinpreis-Politik zu demonstrieren. Wir mussten nach Antwerpen, um die Defender zu verschiffen – das ging zu dem Zeitpunkt nur über grüne Grenzen …

Was ist jetzt deine Aufgabe?

Lutz: Seit dem Jahr 2006 kümmere ich mich um die Kundenreisen nach den Experience Touren, wie die nach Island, Namibia, Argentinien und Kanada. Außerdem bin ich zuständig für die Events, die wir hier im Land Rover Experience Center Wülfrath durchführen. Der Steinbruch bietet einen 120 000 Quadratmeter großen Offroad-Spielplatz, auf dem wir jährlich etwa 7 000 bis 8 000 Kunden umweltgerechtes Offroad-Fahren beibringen sowie Presse- und Händlerveranstaltungen durchführen. Darüber hinaus leite ich das Eventprogramm für den Rest von Deutschland. Wir bringen jährlich etwa 25 000 Menschen mit Land Rover in Berührung, bei Lifestyle-Programmen wie den Schlösser-Touren, Fahrmöglichkeiten bei Messen, Fahrzeugeinführungen und so weiter. Langweilig wird's nie.

Ist schon mal etwas Außergewöhnliches geschehen auf solchen Schulungsveranstaltungen?

Lutz: Ein Erlebnis werde ich nie vergessen. Vor einiger Zeit rief mich ein Fahrlehrer an und sagte: Hier ist etwas passiert, aber ich kann es nicht erklären. Du musst kommen. Ich wohne sehr nah am Steinbruch in Wülfrath, war also sofort vor Ort. Da sah ich einen Discovery, der mit allen vier Rädern in der Luft hing. Er lag allerdings nicht auf dem Kopf, sondern balancierte mit dem mittig verbauten Getriebe auf einem großen Stein. Der Grund: Eine zierliche Teilnehmerin sollte an der Stelle einfach nur wenden, aber sie gab zu viel Gas. Von anderen Steinen aufgestiegen landete der Disco mittig auf dem Felsblock. Das sah aus wie eine Kunstinstallation. Der Wagen hatte keine Schramme, nur das Getriebe war hin. Ganz nebenbei: Die Veranstaltung war ein Incentive für Rechtsanwälte für Verkehrsrecht.

The outdoor bug bit you while you were still a school kid – how did that happen?

Lutz: I've known Hans Hermann Ruthe for a very long time, so even as a 16-year-old, I was organising orienteering exercises for Camel Trophy. When Hans started to work for Land Rover Experience, I joined him. One of my first tasks was to organise shipping the Jordan tour vehicles to the Middle East. However, what appeared to be a relatively straightforward task had a few worms in it – before the vehicles left Europe. At the time, Dutch truck drivers, protesting against the price of fuel, chose to block the borders, and we had to get our Defenders to Antwerp. We ended up having to go across country.

What do you do these days?

Lutz: Since 2006 I have been responsible for the customer holidays to destinations such as Iceland, Namibia, Argentina and Canada. I am also responsible for all the events we put on in our Experience Centre in Wülfrath. Our quarry is a 30-acre, off-road playground that we use to teach responsible off-roading to between 7,000 and 8,000 customers per year as well as hosting numerous press and dealer events. Additionally, I coordinate our complete event programme in Germany, with the result that approximately 25,000 people get to know Land Rover every year via lifestyle events such as the "Castle Tour", test drives at Trade Fairs, vehicle launches and so much more. The job is never boring.

Has anything really unusual happened at a training event?

Lutz: There is something I will never forget. A while back, one of the instructors called me and said: "Something has happened but I can't explain how or why. You need to come down ASAP." I live pretty much next door to the quarry in Wülfrath and was there in next to no time. The Discovery was stuck with all four wheels in the air – however, it wasn't on its roof; rather, the central differential was stuck on a large rock. A participant had been given the instruction to turn the vehicle, had however put her foot down hard, the result being that the vehicle literally launched itself into the air and landed on the middle of a rock. It looked like a work of art. Other than a broken gearbox, the vehicle was without a scratch. Oh and by the way, the event was an incentive programme for lawyers specialising in traffic law.

DER FAHRER
THE DRIVER

Auch wenn Dag am liebsten mit mir fährt und ich am liebsten mit Dag – zur Not muss es auch ohne den anderen gehen. Außerdem sind die Leute aus Dags Büro ebenfalls schwer auf Draht. Also machen wir uns zu viert und ohne den Chef auf nach Cancún, Mexiko, um einen Guide für dieses Land zu suchen. Das ist bei jeder Tour das A und O – ohne Einheimische sind solche Reisen nicht zu machen. Aber wir treffen nicht auf die passenden Leute, also fliegen wir weiter nach Guatemala für gute Fotos, die wir für die mediale Vorbereitung zu Hause dringend mitbringen müssen.

Doch das Schicksal meint es nicht gut mit uns: Auch in dem Zwölf-Millionen-Einwohner-Land finden wir nicht den richtigen Mann. Wir seilen uns also ab in den Kleinstaat Belize, das frühere Britisch-Honduras. Belize ist ein im Vergleich zu Guatemala völlig anderes Land, fast westlich: sauberes Englisch als Landessprache, überall Land Rover (wegen der langen britischen Herrschaft). Und obwohl es der einzige Staat Mittelamerikas mit Englisch als Amtssprache ist, werden wir auch hier nicht fündig. Wir liegen zeitlich weit hinter dem selbst gesteckten Soll zurück.

Also schnell zurück nach Flores, Guatemala, mit einem abenteuerlichen Flugzeug. Wir sind ziemlich ratlos. Bis ein junger Kerl im Hotel Wind von unserer Suche bekommt und sich und seinen Vater in gutem Englisch als Guides anbietet. Der alte Herr kenne sich gut aus, und außerdem besitze man einen Land Rover, mit dem man die Gegend erkunden könne. Zudem hilft er uns, mit Kreditkarten sofort Bargeld zu besorgen – wir haben ja gar keine Landeswährung dabei, weil wir ursprünglich nur Mexiko im Visier hatten.

Am nächsten Tag zur Mittagszeit kommt der eifrige Guatemalteke namens Juan mit einem Serie-II-Landy zurück. Der sieht gar nicht mal so schlecht aus, nur der Eimer, der unter dem Wagen hängt und offensichtlich Öl auffängt, macht uns stutzig. Außerdem ist der Wagen eindeutig zu klein: Wir zählen insgesamt sechs Leute inklusive unseres neuen Guides samt Vater und – natürlich – muss unser gesamtes Gepäck mit. Juan sieht das ein und kommt nach einer halben Stunde mit einem anderen Auto zurück: einem Toyota Hilux Pick-up. Was für ein Vehikel, um die Land Rover Experience Tour vorzubereiten.

Even if Dag preferred travelling with me, and I with him, if need be then we had to be able to go it alone. Besides, the people in his team are just as sharp as he is. So the four of us got together and headed off to Cancún, Mexico, in search of a guide. The common denominator to every successful tour is a local guide. Unable to find the right person, we headed on to Guatemala to acquire images urgently required for the pre-tour media campaign.

Clearly, luck wasn't on our side. In spite of a population just shy of 12 million, we still couldn't find a guide. We hopped over the border into Belize (formerly known as British Honduras). Compared to Guatemala, Belize was a very different cup of tea. Very western, the official language there was British English, and Land Rovers were literally all over the place (in part due to its status as a former British colony). Despite its being the only country in Latin America where English was officially spoken, we still were unable to find our guide. Up to that point, we were far behind our own targets.

Aboard an aircraft that had clearly seen better days, we returned to Flores, Guatemala, at a loss as to what to do. There, we were approached by a younger fellow who had heard we were looking for help. In good English, he offered himself and his father as guides. The older man knew a lot about the region, and they actually had a Land Rover, which we could use to explore the area. Additionally, he helped us get cash using our credit cards, as we had no money in the local currency.

At lunch time the following day, the eager Guatemalan whose name was Juan showed up with a Series II Land Rover. The vehicle looked to be in reasonable shape, apart from the bucket hanging underneath which was clearly intended to catch oil leaking from somewhere. And it was too small for six people (including the guide, his father and our luggage). Juan realised his mistake and came back half an hour later with a different vehicle: a Toyota Hilux pickup. What a car in which to prepare the Land Rover Experience Tour.

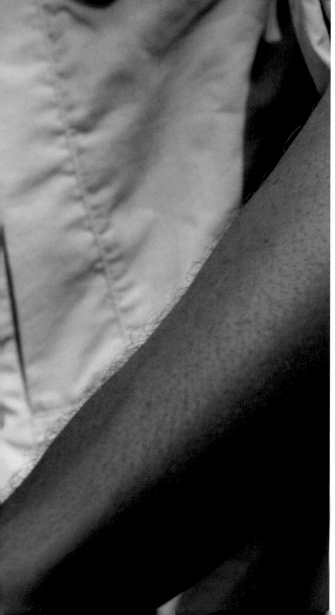

DIE LADEFLÄCHE
THE CARGO BED

In der Not frisst der Teufel bekanntlich Fliegen – also steigen wir tatsächlich in einen Toyota. Nein, nicht in, sondern auf. Vater und Sohn entern das zweisitzige Fahrerhaus, die vierköpfige Landy-Mannschaft okkupiert die Ladefläche, das Gepäck als Polster zwischen Blech- und Hosenboden. Ab in den Dschungel.
Zur Erinnerung: Eigentlich wollten wir in Mexiko einen Guide suchen, jetzt finden wir uns wieder zwischen Ameisen, Würmern, Fliegen, Moskitos und Spinnen, die auf den Toyota prasseln, während wir durch den Dschungel jagen. Denn um die Zeit zu nutzen, wollen wir jetzt neue, eventuell fahrbare Dschungelpfade kennenlernen. Mit Akribie durchpflügen unsere Fahrer mögliche und unmögliche Pisten. Die Tipps, wo es diese Pfade gibt, haben sie sich vorher bei Pflanzensammlern geholt. Das sind die einzigen Menschen, die sich noch hierher wagen.
Das bedeutet, dass die Trails mindestens zu drei Viertel zugewachsen und schon lange keine Straßen mehr sind. Das bedeutet aber auch: Äste und Blätter hängen ins Auto hinein, und beim Vorbeifahren streifen wir von Rinde und Blättern ab, was sich dort befindet und eigentlich auch dort bleiben wollte. Mit spitzen Fingern klauben wir die Fauna vom Toyota. Nie vergessen werde ich zum Beispiel die vogelspinnengroßen Achtbeiner (vielleicht waren es ja Vogelspinnen). Und während wir hinten tapfer mit fiesem Getier kämpfen, steht vorne unser junger Guide mit der Kupplung im Clinch. Besorgt lauschen wir den metallischen Geräuschen in den alten japanischen Eingeweiden. In dieser unwirtlichen Gegend hätten wir gerne ein zuverlässiges Gefährt gehabt. Egal von welchem Hersteller.
Irgendwann will der Hilux aber tatsächlich nicht mehr: Die Dichtung des Kupplungsdruckgebers ist hin. Wir schmieren das Ding voller Maschinenfett, dann geht's erst mal weiter. Tikal ist unser Ziel, und es sind noch 500 Kilometer bis dorthin. Uns tun inzwischen die Rücken weh, die Hintern, die Arme – von den ganzen Stichen der Insekten, die wir zum Glück nicht alle namentlich kennen, mal abgesehen. Noch zweimal bekommt die Toyota-Kupplung ihr Fett weg, dann sind wir endlich im Ort. Und die Kupplung ist restlos platt. Wir glauben nicht, dass hier im tiefsten und dschungeligsten Maya-Land Ersatz für das marode Toyota-Bauteil zu finden ist und gehen schon mal die gar nicht guten Möglichkeiten durch, diesen Ort im grünen Niemandsland irgendwie und irgendwann wieder verlassen zu können.
Aber Juan, unser Fahrer, ist hoffnungsfroh. Ich weiß nicht, wie er das macht, aber er findet hier in der absoluten Regenwald-Pampa tatsächlich Neuteile für den Japaner.
Und während die eingebaut werden, können wir uns derweil etwas mit Tikal beschäftigen: Erste Siedlungsspuren wurden auf das 1. Jahrtausend v. Chr. datiert, der Höhepunkt der städtischen Entwicklung wurde im 5. Jahrhundert erreicht. Etwa im 10. Jahrhundert haben die Maya die Stadt verlassen, ihre eindrucksvollen Stufentempel blieben zurück. Ganz Tikal erstreckt sich über eine Fläche von rund 65 Quadratkilometern, das Zentrum umfasst etwa 16 Quadratkilometer. Der Ort ist eine der am besten erforschten Maya-Städte, obwohl viele Bauten der Stadt, in der einst zwischen 50 000 und 200 000 Menschen wohnten, noch gar nicht ausgegraben worden sind.
So gern wir auch bleiben würden – sobald der Wagen repariert ist, müssen wir weiter. Die Zeit drängt. Es dämmert bereits, und wir haben noch viele Kilometer bis zur Grenze vor uns.

Beggars can't be choosers (or so the saying goes), so we climbed inside the Toyota. Actually, we jumped onto it – father and son climbed into the two-man cabin, while the Land Rover team occupied the cargo bed, using our luggage as cushions. Then we headed into the jungle.
Just to recap: The original plan was to find a guide in Mexico. Now we were sat between ants, worms, flies, mosquitoes and spiders racing through the jungle in the back of a Toyota pickup. To make the best of our time here, we decided to search for new jungle trails that we would drive on the tour. With meticulous dedication, our drivers ploughed through trails that ranged from driveable to impassable. The route suggestions came from plant collectors in the region, who are the only people who use them.
Three quarters of these trails are so overgrown that they can barely be described as roads at all. As we rode along them, in the back of the pickup we involuntarily collected much of what hangs from the trees, including all manner of insects that probably would just as soon have stayed home. We carefully removed as much of the fauna from the Toyota as possible. I certainly won't forget the arachnids the size of tarantulas (which they may actually have been!) that we combated in the back of the truck while the younger guide up front had his own personal struggle with the Toyota's clutch. It was disturbing to hear the sound of metal on metal deep inside the old Japanese four-wheeler. In this particularly inhospitable region, we would have been happier with a more reliable set of wheels – irrespective of its country of origin.
Eventually the Hilux just refused to go any further. The seal on the clutch pressure plate had gone. We packed it full of machine grease, which got it working again. We were heading for Tikal, still over 310 miles away, and besides the bites of insects – which, fortunately for our peace of mind, we were unable to identify – we had sore backs, backsides and arms. The Toyota clutch required two more helpings of grease before we finally arrived at our destination. By then, however, the clutch had finally died. The chances of finding a replacement Toyota part here in the deepest part of the Mayan jungle looked slim, and we began considering our options for leaving this green no-man's-land. Our driver's optimism was rewarded, however, and he actually managed to source the spares for the Toyo in the middle of this rain forest.
While they repaired the clutch, we got on with the business of exploring Tikal. The first evidence of civilisation there dates to 1000 B.C., and the city reached its zenith during the 5th century. The Mayans abandoned the city, with its impressive stepped temples or ziggurats, in or around the 10th century. The whole of Tikal extends over 25 square miles, with the city centre covering some 6 square miles. Tikal is one of the best-documented Mayan cities in existence, although many of the buildings in the city that was once home to between 50,000 and 200,000 inhabitants have yet to be excavated.
As much as we wanted to stay, as soon as the truck was repaired we had to make tracks. Time was tight, it was already getting dark and we still had a long drive to the border ahead of us.

DER DSCHUNGEL
THE JUNGLE

So zugewuchert wie viele der Maya-Stätten von der Flora des Dschungels sind, so muss man sich auch die Pisten vorstellen, die schon seit langem keine Straßen mehr sind. Optimal für eine Abenteuertour mit Teilnehmern, aber suboptimal, um Kilometer zu fressen. Wir vier Deutschen hängen wieder auf der Ladefläche des Toyota, und der beste Service besteht darin, dass uns unser Fahrerduo im geschützten Führerhaus des Hilux Brote schmiert und sie aus dem Fenster auf die Ladefläche reicht. Zeit verlieren geht nicht – die Einhaltung von Zeitplänen ist eine der ganz wichtigen Grundlagen für solche Expeditionen, wie sie die Land Rover Experience ausheckt.

Trotzdem, der Weg ist zu problematisch, zu dicht bewachsen, zu unübersichtlich, um ihn im Dunkeln bewältigen zu können. Wir müssen ein Nachtcamp einrichten.

Mit eindrucksvollen Macheten hacken Papa und Sohn ein Stück Dschungel an der Straße frei. Wo es geht, spannen wir Hängematten, schützen sie und damit auch uns mit Moskitonetzen. Auf dem lange nicht benutzten Weg machen wir Feuer, sehen ein paar Skorpione herumkriechen ... und tatsächlich, nach einiger Zeit schlafen wir ein. Juan und sein Vater direkt auf dem Boden. Zum Glück, wie sich herausstellen soll.

Denn nach viel zu wenigen Stunden Schlaf wecken sie uns aufgeregt: „Weg hier, bloß weg hier!", rufen sie. Und wenn Einheimische so zur Action auffordern, folgt man lieber, ohne überflüssige westeuropäische Fragen zu stellen. Sie werden ihre Gründe haben.

In diesem Fall ist es nur ein Grund, und der heißt „Bedford" und klingt gefährlich. Ein fetter Truck mit Pflanzensammlern auf der Ladefläche donnert über den selten befahrenen Weg und mäht alles nieder, was im Weg steht – also fast auch unser Nachtlager, den Toyota und uns selbst. Juan ist als erster aufgewacht von den Vibrationen im Boden, die der schwere Laster vorausschickte.

Da es bereits Morgen wird und wir unsere Ruhestätte zwangsweise in aller Eile zerstören mussten, können wir auch weiterfahren. Obwohl „fahren" nicht ganz der Wahrheit entspricht: Mit Macheten und einer Motorsäge kämpfen wir uns voran. Der Truck muss irgendwo abgebogen sein, jedenfalls befuhr sicher lange niemand mehr die Strecke, die wir jetzt erforschen.

Das Vorankommen ist zeitweise extrem mühsam. Anders ausgedrückt: 200 Meter in einer Stunde. Das größte Frischegefühl genießen wir, wenn wir das getragene T-Shirt alle paar Stunden auf links drehen. Das Gepäck ist bald völlig verschlammt, der Dreck findet zusätzlich jeden Weg ins Innere. Unsere Klamotten und wir machen den Eindruck von frisch ausgegrabenen Maya.

Irgendwie schaffen wir es tatsächlich zum Grenzübergang Chetumal, wo wir uns wenig später dank Dusche und Hotel schon wieder fühlen wie zivilisierte Menschen. Dort findet uns Professor Ernesto Parra, ein Archäologe aus Mexiko, der sich bereit erklärt, in Mexiko unser Guide zu sein.

Just as many Mayan sites are completely covered by jungle, the same is true of the jungle tracks that have long since fallen into disuse. The tracks are perfect for an adventure tour with participants, but less than perfect when all that matters is getting from A to B. The four Germans were once again stuck in the back of the Toyota pickup, the only highlight being the sandwiches-to-go service provided by our driver team through the rear window of the cab. Once again, we had no time to lose, as keeping to a strict schedule is fundamental to the success of any expedition put together by Land Rover Experience.

Nevertheless, with the route too complicated, too overgrown and too difficult to drive at night, we made camp for the night.

Using impressive-looking machetes, the father-and-son team hacked clear a section of jungle next to the track, creating an area where we could hang our hammocks between the trees, making sure to protect themselves and us with mosquito nets. On the trail, which had not seen any traffic for a very long time, we got a campfire going, watching a few scorpions go about their business. After a while, we actually fell asleep. Fortunately for us – for reasons I shall explain – Juan and his son slept on the ground, for after what seemed like minutes rather than hours, they were waking us up in a panic saying, "We have to go now". When locals demand action in this fashion, it is better to acquiesce and not ask the usual European-style superfluous questions. After all, they probably had a very good reason.

The reason was a "Bedford", and it sounded terrifying. The large truck full of plant collectors was thundering down the trail, crushing everything in its path and threatening to do the same to our campsite, the Toyota and our good selves. Juan had been woken up by the ground vibrations caused by the truck.

As it was already morning, and we had been forced to break camp in rather hurried fashion, we decided to continue driving where we had left off. Whereby "driving" was not quite accurate, as we had to chop our way through the trail with the machetes and a chain saw. The truck must have turned off the trail relatively quickly, as clearly no one had explored the section we then entered for a very, very long time.

Making progress was at times painstakingly difficult, or, to put it another way: 600 feet per hour. The most refreshing experience was turning one's t-shirt inside out every couple of hours. Our clothes were absolutely covered in mud, and the dirt clung everywhere. In our clothes we looked like freshly unearthed Mayans. Somehow we made it to the border crossing at Chetumal, where a hotel shower made us feel like civilised human beings again. There we met Professor Ernesto Parra, a Mexican archaeologist who offered to serve as our guide in Mexico.

DIE ANGST
THE FEAR

So eine umfangreiche Reise bedingt eine zweite Vortour – die kann ich dank heilendem Knie wieder mitfahren. Inzwischen sind auch die Autos angekommen.

Eine bestimmte Stelle, die meine Vorfahrer gefunden haben, weckt mein ganz besonderes Interesse: Abseilen in unterirdisches Gewässer. Hans und sein Team haben bei der ersten Vortour eine natürliche Höhle gefunden, durch die ein Fluss rauscht. Vom etwa 120 Meter hohen Hügel über dem Fluss kann man wunderbar als Task für die Teilnehmer eine Seilaktion einbauen, zumal wir im Qualifikationscamp extra eine Aufgabe mit Seilen und Klettern geübt haben. Die Fahrrouten stehen also fest, nur die Klettertour müssen wir noch ausprobieren.

Die Idee dahinter: Die Teams bekommen Koordinaten, von dort seilen sie sich etwa 90 Meter auf die Wasseroberfläche ab. Danach können alle entspannt in dem wunderbaren Flusswasser baden – was für ein Abenteuer!

Hans, Lutz, Christine, Claudia, unser Guide Professor Ernesto, der Allrad-Journalist Bernhard Weinbacher, Land-Rover-Pressechef Paul Entwistle und ich wollen das aber vorher noch ausprobieren. Es ist 8 Uhr morgens, wir sind an der richtigen Stelle angekommen. Christine, Lutz und Ernesto schlagen sich durch den Dschungel auf dem Hügel zum Test-Klettern. Die ganze Aktion dürfte nicht länger als eine Viertelstunde dauern.

Nach einer Stunde werde ich nervös. Wir hören nichts, und erst recht seilt sich niemand ab. Ich will schon hinterher, da sagt Hans: „Lass mich mal." Ich rate ihm noch, Bernhard mitzunehmen, und weg ist er.

Such a complex tour required a second pre-scout recce – which I was able to join, now that my knee had healed. Meanwhile, our vehicles had arrived as well.

One location that the team had discovered on the first pre-scout interested me in particular: abseiling into an underwater cavern. Hans and the team had found a natural cave with a river flowing through it. From the 400-feet-high mountain above the river, we could create a task for the participants that involved abseiling, as we had specifically practised rope climbing in the selection camps. The driving routes had been sorted, but we had yet to test the climbing task.

The underlying idea was that the teams would be given coordinates from which they would abseil 300 feet down to the river, where they could bathe in a beautiful stream – this was classic adventure stuff!

Hans, Lutz, Christine, Claudia, our guide Professor Ernesto, four-wheel-drive journalist Bernhard Weinbacher, Land Rover PR man Paul Entwistle and I needed to test it first. At 8 in the morning we arrived at the point where the task was due to start. Christine, Lutz and Ernesto started making their way up through the jungle to the top of the mountain to test the climbing section. We estimated this would take no longer than a quarter of an hour.

After an hour, I started to get nervous: We could hear no one, and nobody had abseiled down the hill. I wanted to head off up the hill, but Hans said, "I'll sort it out". I advised him to take Bernhard with him, but he had already disappeared.

HANS

Ich muss gestehen, ich habe Bernhard gar nicht gefragt. Ich nehme mein Bowie-Messer und ein Funkgerät – ich weiß ja, wo es langgeht. Immerhin war ich schon zweimal oben an dem Punkt, an dem die Teilnehmer starten sollen. Ich werde unsere drei Test-Kletterer schon finden. Kann ja nicht so schwer sein. Tatsächlich höre ich nach wenigen Minuten Fußmarsch Richtung bergauf Stimmen unserer Kollegen – die kommen aber von der falschen Seite des Berges. Ich versuche, mich durch das dicke Blattwerk zu schlagen, immer in Richtung Stimmen – aber plötzlich ist Stille. Es passiert nicht oft, aber jetzt lässt mich mein Orientierungssinn im Stich. Es ist 10 Uhr, es ist 42 Grad heiß, und es sieht überall gleich aus. Das Gezirpe von ein paar Grillen ist das einzige Geräusch, das ich wahrnehme. Kurz: Ich habe mich verlaufen und überhaupt keine Ahnung, wo ich hinmuss.

I admit that I didn't even ask Bernhard. I took my Bowie knife and a radio; I knew where I was going, as I had already been up to the jump-off point for the special task twice. Finding our three climbing guinea pigs couldn't be that difficult. After a few minutes' walk I could actually hear my colleagues' voices – albeit from the wrong side of the mountain. I started cutting my way through the thick undergrowth heading towards the voices – suddenly it went quiet. A rare occurrence for me, but I was completely disoriented. It was 10 am, 42 degrees Celsius (108 degrees Fahrenheit), and everything looked the same. All I heard was the chirping of a few crickets. In short, I was lost and had no idea in which direction to go.

HANS

Endlich: Stimmen. Ich gestehe, ich bin die vergangenen zwei Stunden ganz schön nervös gewesen. Aber jetzt höre ich sie, die drei Vorkletterer: Sie kommen vom anderen Ende des Tunnels. Lutz erzählt, wie sehr sich der Dschungel in den vergangenen Wochen verändert hat, man fände tatsächlich keinen der einst auserkorenen Orientierungspunkte wieder. Ich renne zum Funkgerät am Auto, um Hans und Bernhard die freudige Nachricht zu überbringen und ihnen zu sagen, sie können zurückkommen – da treffe ich Bernhard. Der weiß nichts von Hans' Alleingang.

„Hans, Hans, Dag, Dag?" Ich versuche ihn über Funk zu erreichen – keine Antwort. Ich weise alle Anwesenden an, zu den Autos zu gehen und zu hupen, Lärm als Orientierungshilfe. Keine Antwort. Jetzt weiß ich: Hans hat ein Problem. Ich habe ein Problem. Wir haben ein Problem: Hans Hermann Ruthe hat sich verlaufen. Mitten in Belize, und das ist alles andere als beruhigend.

At last: Voices. Admittedly, for the last two hours I had been pretty worried. Now, though, I could hear our three test climbers coming from the other end of the tunnel. Lutz explained how the jungle had changed in the last couple of weeks, and that they hadn't been able to identify any of the reference points we had set. I ran to the radio to tell Hans and Bernhard the good news, and that they could come back, when I met Bernhard, who was completely unaware that Hans had gone off on his own.

"Hans, Hans, Dag, Dag?" I tried to reach him on the radio, but there was no answer. I told the team to go back to the vehicles to sound the horns in the hope that the noise would help him with his orientation. No answer. Now I knew that Hans had a problem. I had a problem, and that meant we all had a problem. Hans Hermann Ruthe was lost in the middle of the Belizean jungle. This was not good.

HANS

Spätestens jetzt merke ich: Ich habe ein Problem – ich habe mich verlaufen. Aber wofür gibt es Funkgeräte: „Dag, Dag, Hans, Hans! Ich glaub, ich hab mich ver… krrrrrchhhchhch." Die Funke ist tot, kein Saft. Irgendjemand hat vergessen, dieses Funkgerät aufzuladen.

By now, I had realised I had a serious problem – I was completely lost. However I had a radio: "Dag, Dag, Hans, Hans! I think I am lo… Krrrrrrchhhchchch" The radio was dead. Somebody had forgotten to charge it.

„Ich hab mich ver…" krächzt es noch aus der Funke, dann ist Stille. Mit Verlaub: Scheiße. Funkloch? Akku alle? Oder ist Hans gerade Opfer einer Würgeschlange geworden? In so einem Moment gehen einem die wildesten Gedanken durch den Kopf. Als ich Hans heute das letzte Mal sah, trug er kurze Hosen – auch das noch. Hoffentlich hat er wenigstens Wasser mitgenommen. Ich muss etwas tun, warten ist nun überhaupt nicht mein Ding. Um 13 Uhr schicke ich eines unserer Autos zu dem großen Holzfällercamp in 10 Kilometer Entfernung. Dort muss es doch jemanden geben, der sich hier auskennt. Denn ich bin mir sicher: Wenn Hans sich verläuft und es merkt, macht er das einzig Richtige. Er bleibt an Ort und Stelle sitzen oder stehen.

"I think I'm lo…" there was a brief crackling from the radio, and then it went dead. Poor reception? Battery dead? Or had Hans just been attacked by a snake? I make no apologies for saying this, but it was a shitty mess and no mistake. In a situation like this, all manner of potential scenarios go through your mind. The last time I'd seen him that morning, he was wearing shorts – given the terrain, not good. Hopefully he had at least remembered to take some water with him. I had to do something. Sitting around waiting for something to happen is just not me. At 1 pm I sent one of our vehicles to a large logging camp about 6 miles down the trail, hoping there would be someone there who knew the terrain. Of one thing I was certain. If Hans had got lost, he would do the right thing and stay put.

Was macht man, wenn man die Orientierung verloren hat? Richtig: Man bleibt an Ort und Stelle. Ich zücke mein Messer und markiere einen Baum nach allen vier Himmelsrichtungen, die ich nach der Sonne bestimmen kann, indem ich einen Stock in den Boden ramme und mich nach dem Schatten richte. Ich weiß: Nach Westen existiert nichts anderes als 20 Kilometer dichter Dschungel bis zur Grenze nach Guatemala. Nach Osten sind es rund 15 Kilometer bis zur Hauptstraße – auch keine grandiose Aussicht. Und dann diese Hitze. Und wenn dieser Durst bloß nicht wäre.

Wir halten die Antennen hoch, rufen Hans immer wieder per Funk: nichts. In diesem Dickicht leben mindesten fünf Giftschlangenarten, ganz zu schweigen von den Skorpionen und den stechenden Insekten. Inzwischen ist ein Holzfäller vom Camp angekommen. Der zieht sich Gummistiefel an, schultert sein Gewehr und verschwindet im Dschungel. Nach einer halben Stunde kehrt er zurück mit der Nachricht, er finde Hans nicht. Wir sollten uns ans Militär wenden. Das würde die Chancen, Hans zu finden, erhöhen, weil das Gebiet Übungsgebiet der Soldaten sei. Ernesto telefoniert sofort über Satellitentelefon mit den zuständigen Soldaten, aber die winken ab: Heute nicht mehr. Erst morgen.
Es ist bereits 17 Uhr. Und es wird langsam dunkel. Ich habe Angst um Hans. Zum ersten Mal auf einer unserer Touren habe ich echte Angst.

Durst. Er kommt, und er geht nicht. Denk nach, denk an deine Camel-Trophy-Zeit. Was macht man bei Durst im Dschungel, wenn man nichts dabei hat? Man sucht eine Liane. Pro Meter Pflanze liefert sie ein halbes Glas Flüssigkeit. Ich suche und finde, sogar einige innerhalb des von mir selbst gesetzten Radius von 500 Metern um meinen Himmelsrichtungsbaum. Die Ausbeute ist nicht wirklich ergiebig, aber besser als nichts.
Wetterleuchten setzt ein, Donner grummelt in der Ferne. Unter anderen Bedingungen ein tolles Schauspiel. Ich zücke mein Messer, schnitze mir eine kleine Sitzbank, mache Feuer mit dem Feuerzeug, das ich in der Tasche habe, und warte. Inzwischen ist es 20 Uhr und stockdunkel. So etwas ist mir noch nie passiert.

Ich habe alle Journalisten und den Großteil der Experience-Mannschaft in die Lodge geschickt. Bei zwei Autos versagen inzwischen die Hupen, so sehr haben wir sie malträtiert. Ständig ist jemand am Funk, um Hans zu rufen – vielleicht kann er uns ja hören, aber nicht antworten. Dann schnappe ich mir die Landkarte: Wo ist Hans, geht es in meinem Schädel rund. Wo ist er hingegangen? Nein, er ist nicht weggegangen, er ist geblieben.
Wie sagen wir es seiner Frau?
Herrje, was war das denn eben für ein schräger Gedanke? Selbstverständlich finden wir ihn. Aber wenn nicht? Ich habe die Verantwortung, und ich habe meinen Freund „verloren". Das darf nicht passieren, das darf einfach nicht passieren. Jetzt geht noch einmal unser Guide mit dem Holzfäller los. Letzte Chance für heute.

Mein Zeitgefühl ist nicht mehr gut, meine Uhr aber immer noch genau: Es ist kurz vor halb zehn Uhr abends, da höre ich Stimmen. Ja, sie sind es, irgendwer von unserem Team, und als ich ihnen entgegenlaufen will, versagen mir die Beine. Ich bin dehydriert, habe Krämpfe, und die beiden müssen mich erst mal auf den Boden legen und meine Muskeln bearbeiten. Dann gehen wir zusammen lachend und weinend den Hügel hinunter.

Ja, auch harte Trophy- und Experience-Männer müssen, können und dürfen weinen. Hans ist zurück, und es ist wie Weihnachten im Sommer. Er war nur gut einen Kilometer von uns entfernt, aber der Dschungel schluckt alle Geräusche. Der Ärmste sieht ziemlich geschunden aus: Die Hornhaut der Augen verbrannt, voller Staub und Dreck von den Dschungelblättern, unzählige Zecken klammern sich an seinen Körper – aber er ist genauso glücklich wie wir.
Trotzdem möchte ich so etwas nie wieder erleben. Und nie wieder vergisst irgendjemand der Orga, die Funkgeräte aufzuladen.
Schlimmer kann es jetzt eigentlich nicht mehr kommen. Denke ich …

What is the right thing to do if you have lost your bearings? The right thing to do is to stay right where you are. I pulled out my knife and scored the four points of the compass into the bark of a tree using the sun as my point of reference, and then rammed a stick into the ground to see where the shadow was. I knew that to the west there was nothing but 12 miles of jungle to the Guatemalan border. Towards the east it was about 9 miles to the main road – not exactly motivating stuff, given the heat and the fact that I was thirsty.

We raised the antennas and repeatedly tried reaching Hans on the radio. But it was no use. At least five different varieties of poisonous snake lived in the undergrowth, not to mention scorpions and all manner of biting insects. In the meantime, a logger from the camp had shown up. He put his rubber boots on, shouldered his rifle and set off into the jungle. After half an hour, he returned saying that he was unable to find Hans and that we should get in touch with the army. Our chances of finding Hans would be greater because the region was a military training area. On the satellite phone, Ernesto talked to the military but was told they wouldn't be able to help that day. The earliest they could send a search party would be the following day.
By now it was 5 pm and beginning to turn dark. I was worried about Hans. For the first time on a tour, I was really afraid that something had happened.

Thirst. Once it's there, it never leaves. Think back to Camel Trophy. How do you deal with thirst in the jungle when you have no water? You look for a liana vine. A metre of vine produces approximately half a glass of fluid. Within a 1,600-foot radius of my compass tree, I found a few vines from which the yield of fluid was mediocre but better than nothing. Sheet lightning was visible in the sky, and in the distance I could hear thunder. Any other day, it would have been a marvellous spectacle. I pulled out my knife, made myself a chair, started a fire with the lighter I had in my pocket and waited. It was 8 pm and pitch black. This had never happened to me before.

I sent all the journalists and the majority of the Experience team back to the lodge. The horns on two of the vehicles were no longer working after we had sat on them all day. One of the team stayed on the radio in the hope that Hans could hear us but wasn't able to answer. I grabbed the map. My mind raced. Where had he gone? No – I decided he hadn't gone anywhere. Hans would stay put.
What would we say to his wife?
Good God – where did that come from? Of course we would find him, but what if we didn't? I was responsible, and I'd lost my mate. This just shouldn't happen. Our guide went off one last time with the logger. This was our last chance today.

My body clock was not functioning as well as before, but my watch was fine. It was 9.30 pm, and I could hear voices. Yes, it was someone from the team, and as I attempted to run towards them, my legs collapsed beneath me. I was dehydrated and had severe cramps. The two had to lay me out on the ground to massage my leg muscles before we returned, crying and laughing, back down the hill.

Hard-nosed Camel Trophy and Experience guys need to cry, too. Hans was back, and it felt like Christmas. He had been less than a mile away all this while, but the jungle absorbs all manner of sounds. Hans looked battered to say the least. Mildly sunblind, completely covered in dust and dirt from the jungle undergrowth, and his body a habitat for numerous ticks – but he was as happy as we were.
Nevertheless, I didn't want to experience this again. And no one in the team would forget to charge the radios in future, either.
It couldn't get any worse. Or so I thought.

DIE TRAGÖDIE
THE TRAGEDY

Eigentlich ist die Vortour vorüber. Wir müssen nur noch die Autos zurück nach Mexiko bringen. Die Straßen, die durch den Dschungel führen, sind eng und uneben, aber teilweise schnurgerade – ich habe endlich einen Moment Zeit zum Relaxen und dafür, die Strecke der Haupttour schon mal im Kopf abzufahren.

Plötzlich stockt der Verkehr, bis er völlig zum Erliegen kommt. Vor mir steht ein Lastwagen, der mir die Sicht nimmt. Ich steige aus, um nachzusehen, was los ist – und mir gefrieren trotz 30 Grad die Gesichtszüge. Etwa 40 Menschen sind aus ihren Autos ausgestiegen und stehen tatenlos um eine gespenstische Szenerie herum. Zwei Kleinwagen sind frontal zusammengekracht. Rauch steigt noch unter den verknitterten Motorhauben hervor, irgendwo wimmert jemand. Ich schnappe mir unseren Erste-Hilfe-Rucksack und renne zu den zerstörten Autos.

Wenn Nachdenken lähmen würde, dann in so einer Situation: In einem kleinen Seat sitzen drei Erwachsene. Ich greife instinktiv zu ihren Handgelenken, Nacken oder was auch sonst noch nach Mensch aussieht, um den Puls zu fühlen. Aber da ist keiner, nirgendwo. Im Unfallgegner, einem nicht viel größeren Fiat, kauern auch noch zwei Menschen. Der Mann am Steuer lebt, ist sogar bei vollem Bewusstsein, die Füße sind allerdings im Fußraum eingeklemmt. Neben ihm: seine Frau, mit schwachem Puls, leise röchelnd. „Helft ihr, helft ihr!", fleht der Mann auf Spanisch, Christine übersetzt für mich auf Deutsch. Sofort stabilisieren wir mit einem Beatmungsbalg ihre Atmung. Einen Arzt haben wir bei Vortouren bislang nicht mit.

Ihre Beine stecken im völlig zerstörten Fußraum fest. „Der Sitz muss raus!", brülle ich, und wir probieren, Schrauben zu lösen. Die rühren sich nicht. Wir versuchen, ihn mit Brechstangen auszuheben. Keine Chance. Wir legen das Seil der Defender-Winde über eine Umlenkrolle, um den Sitz herauszureißen. Aber wir ziehen nur den Fiat von der Unfallstelle. Wir befestigen die Winde eines zweiten Defender auf der anderen Seite. Doch so ziehen sich die schweren Wagen nur beidseitig an das Unfallauto heran. Inzwischen benötigen Lutz und der zweite Mundo-Maya-Guide Beto kurz unseren Rucksack. Sie haben im Wald einen Mann mit gebrochenem Bein gefunden. Er ist aus dem Seat herausgeschleudert worden. Wir machen uns an die letzte Möglichkeit, die mir einfällt: Mit Leatherman, Messern und Stangen zerkleinern wir den robusten Fiat-Sitz, schneiden Teile heraus, bis wir die Frau tatsächlich vorsichtig aus dem Wrack herauslösen können. Endlich gibt sich ein Arzt zu erkennen und legt Infusionen. Sie ist bei vollem Bewusstsein und fragt: „Wo sind die Kinder?"

Kinder? Was für Kinder? Wir haben keine gesehen. Hört das denn nicht auf? Sie sollen auf dem Rücksitz gesessen haben, erfahren wir. Gerade schreie ich – inzwischen auch an die Grenzen des Erträglichen gekommen – die Gaffenden an, sie sollen eine Kette bilden und die Unfallstelle absuchen, da erzählt ein Schaulustiger, dass direkt nach dem Unfall ein Mann beide Kinder in sein Auto verfrachtet habe, um sie ins nächste Hospital zu bringen. Ein schneller Helfer. Immerhin.

Aber jetzt bricht uns der Fahrer des Fiat zusammen. Nach der Bergung seiner Frau lässt seine Anspannung nach, der Kreislauf droht zu kollabieren. Wer in Mexiko so einen Unfall erleidet, hat meistens kaum Chancen, sagen uns die Gaffer. Krankenwagen seien offene Pritschenwagen, Helfer mit Blechscheren gäbe es gar nicht – der Mann habe einfach Pech gehabt.

Aber das akzeptiere ich nicht. Es klingt hart, aber es ist die einzige Chance: Mit der Brechstange brechen wir dem Fahrer beide Füße. Nur so lässt er sich aus dem Auto lösen. Wir vertäuen ihn auf unsere Sandbleche und heben ihn auf den offenen Toyota Pick-up-Krankenwagen, der endlich angekommen ist und auch die Frau auflädt. Dann wendet er und fährt Richtung Stadt.

Unser Erste-Hilfe-Rucksack ist leer, unsere Köpfe sind es auch. Die nächsten drei Stunden oder 70 Kilometer sagt keiner von uns auch nur ein Wort.

Mich hat die Geschichte erst richtig eingeholt, als ich mich später im Hospital nach den beiden Unfallopfern erkundige. Sie haben es beide geschafft, die Fußbrüche sind reparabel. Aber ihre Kinder waren tot.

Hätten wir früher am Unfallort ankommen können? Haben wir etwas falsch gemacht? Hätten die Kinder überlebt, wenn wir uns um sie hätten kümmern können? Ich weiß es nicht. Aber als Vater von zwei wunderbaren Töchtern denke ich noch heute darüber nach.

To all intents and purposes, the pre-scout recce was complete. All we had to do was get the vehicles back to Mexico. The roads that go through the jungle are narrow, uneven and at times as straight as a ruler. I finally had time to relax and to go through the route in my mind for the main event.

The traffic ahead of us suddenly slowed and then ground to a complete halt. A truck in front of us blocked our view of the road. I climbed down to see what had happened, and despite the heat my face froze at what I saw. Some 40 people had got out of their cars, staring as if paralyzed at the horrible scene. Two small cars had collided head-on; smoke billowed out of the crumpled bonnet of one of the cars, and somewhere I could hear someone whimpering. I grabbed our first aid pack and ran to the wrecked cars.

If ever there were a situation where reflection leads to a form of paralysis, then this was it. Three adults were inside a small Seat motorcar. I instinctively grabbed their wrists, necks or anything else that still looked human in hopes of finding a pulse. Nothing. In the other vehicle, a Fiat not much bigger than the first, there were two adults. The man behind the wheel was still alive; indeed, he was fully conscious, but his feet were trapped in the foot well. Next to him was his wife, groaning quietly with a very weak pulse. The man pleaded in Spanish, "Help her, help her." Christine translated it into German. We were able to stabilise her breathing with a ventilation bag almost immediately. Thus far, we had chosen not to take a doctor with us on the pre-scout recces.

Her feet were trapped in the foot well, which had been completely destroyed by the impact. I shouted, "We have to remove the seat!", and we attempted to loosen the screws. Nothing doing. We tried to lever the seat out using crowbars. Impossible. We attached the Defender winch cable via a return pulley to the seat but only ended up dragging the Fiat further away from the accident site. We attached the winch from a second Defender to the other side, but this only winched the two heavier vehicles closer to the damaged Fiat. In the meantime Lutz and our second guide, Beto, needed the first aid pack. They had found a man in the jungle who had been catapulted from the Seat in the crash, and his leg was broken.

Inside the Fiat, we started to hack at the solidly-built passenger seat, with Leatherman, knife and crowbars, removing it bit by bit until we could finally lift the lady carefully out of the wreckage. By now a doctor had turned up and was able to attach her to an intravenous drip. Fully conscious, she asked, "Where are the children?"

Children? What children? We hadn't seen any children. Where was this going to end? Then we were told that they had been sitting on the back seat. By now I was at the end of my tether, with people just standing around doing nothing, and screamed at them to form a chain to search the accident site for the children. That is when one of the onlookers explained that the children had been taken to hospital by another man immediately after the accident. At least there was one person who had shown some initiative.

The Fiat driver then collapsed – he had relaxed as soon as his wife was freed from the wreckage, and it was obvious he was about to fall into a coma. Onlookers commented that anyone involved in an accident like this in Mexico normally had no chance. The ambulance was usually nothing more than an open-top truck, and cutting gear was completely unheard of. The man had just been unlucky.

I was not prepared to accept this. While it may sound brutal, we used the crowbar to break both his feet. This was our only way of getting him out of the car. We lashed him to a sand channel and lifted him along with his wife onto the open-top Toyota ambulance that had finally just arrived. It then turned round and drove off to the next town.

Our first aid pack was empty, which was pretty much how we all felt. For the next three hours or 40 odd miles, nobody said a word.

The story really hit me when I went to the hospital to find out how the two accident victims were doing. They were fine, and the man's two broken feet would heal in time. Their children, however, hadn't survived.

Would it have made a difference if we had been able to get to the crash site sooner? Did we do something wrong? Would we have been able to save their lives if we had got to the children first? I don't know. As the father of two wonderful daughters, I still think about it to this day.

DER HURRIKAN
THE HURRICANE

Ich gestehe: Erstmals gehe ich nicht so locker auf eine Haupttour wie bislang. Sowohl die Suche nach Hans als auch der Verkehrsunfall haben mich auf brutale Art meine Verantwortung spüren lassen. Und jetzt kann Hans aus familiären Gründen nicht mit auf die Haupttour – mir fehlt mein Flügelmann an allen Ecken und Enden. Klar, die Vorbereitungen haben wir optimiert, aber trotzdem: Drei Länder, zehn Autos, dazu der Dschungel, der keine Fehler verzeiht, die unberechenbare Fauna und das ebenso launische Wetter – viel Ballast für ein paar Schultern.

Aber die Tour verläuft optimal. Es gibt keine Anzeichen von Dramen jedweder Art, eher Belustigendes. Wie den Zöllner in Belize, der nur mit Schiesser-Feinripp bekleidet handschriftlich die Fahrgestellnummern der Autos in die jeweiligen Pässe schreibt. Oder die dank stundenlangem Regen wunderbar aufgeweichten Matschpisten, die das genau richtige Land-Rover-Gefühl erzeugen. Sogar das Abseilen am Hans-Schicksalshügel, das wir trotz (oder vielleicht gerade wegen?) des unfreiwilligen Such-Abenteuers als Teamaufgabe in der Tour gelassen haben, klappt problemlos.

Nur das Wetter lässt sich nicht beeinflussen. Der Wind bläst schon ganz ordentlich, als wir unser Zeltcamp mit Genehmigung des Bürgermeisters auf dem Marktplatz von La Unión in Mexiko aufbauen. Wir sind gerade beim einfachen Essen in den Wellblechhütten, da verändert sich schlagartig die Farbe des Himmels. Der Wind wächst zum Sturm – ich habe überhaupt keine Lust zum Risiko. „Rein in die Autos!", brülle ich, und alle erkennen sofort, dass ich keinen Spaß mache. Kaum sind wir in den Landys, da wird aus dem Sturm ein Hurrikan. Er beginnt, die einfach zusammengenagelten Hütten um uns herum zu zerlegen. Fenster fliegen uns um die Windschutzscheiben, Wellbleche knallen gegen die Karosserien der Discovery und Defender. Aber die Stürme über den Produktionshallen in Solihull in der langen Land-Rover-Historie waren manchmal existenzbedrohender als dieser mexikanische Hurrikan. Da steht ein Land Rover wie eine Eins.

Admittedly, I wasn't as keen on the main event as I otherwise would have been. The search for Hans as well as the car accident had made it brutally clear to me what responsibility really felt like. And now, for family reasons, Hans couldn't come on the tour – my wingman was missing. Our planning had improved enormously, and yet: three countries, ten vehicles, a jungle uncompromising in the extreme, the difficult vegetation and the mercurial weather – all this was a great deal for one pair of shoulders.

That said, the tour ran perfectly. There no were no real dramas – quite the opposite, there was a great deal of laughter on the tour. How could I forget the customs official in Belize who jotted down the VIN numbers of the vehicles in our passports dressed in nothing but his underwear? Or the muddy tracks through the jungle that, thanks to the incessant rain, provided the perfect Land Rover Tour feeling. Even the abseiling team exercise on Hans' fateful mountain, which stayed in the programme despite the involuntary search and rescue operation (or perhaps because of it?), was a roaring success when the time came.

The only aspect we couldn't control was the weather. The wind was already starting to pick up when we made camp in the market square of the town of La Unión in Mexico (with permission of the local mayor). We had just sat down to dinner in one of the corrugated tin huts when, without warning, the colour of the sky changed dramatically. The wind had already turned into a gale – I wasn't prepared to take any risks – when I shouted at everyone, "Into the vehicles – now!", and everybody recognised I wasn't joking. Once inside the vehicles, we watched the gale transform itself into a full-fledged hurricane as the corrugated tin huts literally disintegrated before our very eyes, with windows thrown up against our windscreens and corrugated tin flying into the bodywork of our Defenders and Discoverys.

This Mexican hurricane, however, was nothing compared to the many economic storms that the Land Rover factory in Solihull had weathered over the years. And Land Rover had survived those without batting an eyelid.

Ein Baum quer über der Piste? Mit dem richtigen Equipment kein Problem. Schwieriger gestaltet sich da schon die Fahrt durch matschigen Dschungel mit tiefen Schlammlöchern und großen Pfützen. Schildkröten gehören da noch zu den angenehmen Reisebegleitern. Dreck und Stress fallen beim Tauchen in glasklarem Höhlenwasser sofort ab.

A tree straight across the track? With the right equipment, no problem. The drive through the jungle, with its huge mud holes and enormous ruts, was a little more challenging. The tortoise was one of the more popular companions. A plunge into the crystal clear water of an underground cave helped wash away the stress and the mud.

KANADA

CANADA
2004
4 RANGE ROVER,
3 FREELANDER, 2 DISCOVERY
STRECKE / DISTANCE: 2 000 KM / 1,240 MILES

Die Big Bar Ferry und ihr legendärer „Grumpy Old Man": So brummig ist er gar nicht.
Erst recht nicht, wenn man erzählt, wie wohl man sich fühlt in der typisch kanadischen Tyax-Lodge.

The Big Bar Ferry and its legendary "Grumpy Old Man" – who actually turned out to be not
so grumpy after all, especially after we told him how good it was to stay over in the classically
Canadian Tyax Lodge.

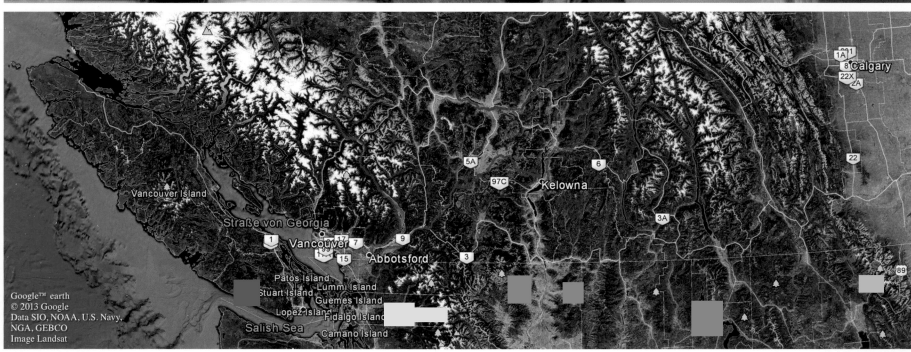

DIE AUTOS
THE VEHICLES

Viel zu schnell nach der aufregenden, traurigen und ereignis-reichen Dreiländertour sollen wir Land Rover wieder drei neue Ziele zur Auswahl vorlegen – Kanada ist eines davon. Aber erstmals bewerben sich weniger Menschen für die Tour als für die vorige, diesmal nur rund 8 000. Zieht Kanada nicht?

Dabei haben wir es uns wirklich nicht einfach gemacht mit der Wahl. Auf 10 Millionen Quadratkilometer Land in Kanada sollten doch wohl anspruchsvolle Offroad-Trassen abseits der rund 35 Millionen Einwohner zu finden sein? Auch Land Rover ist davon begeistert – wir entscheiden uns für British Columbia, die Provinz am Pazifischen Ozean. Im Winter herrscht hier arktisches Klima, im Sommer wird es im Binnenland manchmal bis zu 40 Grad heiß. Wälder dominieren und damit auch Holz-wirtschaft und Papierindustrie. Was aber Zivilisation bedeutet. Trotzdem – hoch motiviert starten wir zur Vortour. Dazu gehört, zu klären, wie wir unsere Autos ins Land schaffen können. Dass genau das zum großen Abenteuer werden soll, ist vorher nicht zu ahnen.

Defender wollen wir diesmal promoten. Was wir nicht bedenken: Der Defender besitzt in ganz Nordamerika keine Zulassung – sie ist nicht mal temporär zu bekommen. Aber auch der vorübergehende Import anderer Land Rover erweist sich als schwierig. Niemand will uns garantieren, dass wir die Autos auch wirklich aus dem Schiff ausladen dürfen, wenn wir sie in die Neue Welt schicken. Damit bricht eine unserer vier Säulen, auf die alle Touren aufbauen, weg: Hotels/Flüge, Genehmigungen, Wege und – Autos.

Was tun? Ein anderes Land aussuchen? Nein, wir laufen nicht weg vor Problemen – wir lösen sie. Idee: Wir vergessen die Defender, leasen ein paar Range Rover und ein paar Discovery beim örtlichen Land-Rover-Händler, rechnen mit 2 000 Kilometer pro Fahrzeug, zahlen dafür, und der Händler kann die Wagen hinterher als Geschäftsfahrzeuge verkaufen. Dazu hat der gute Mann aber überhaupt keine Lust. Lange verhandeln wir mit ihm und kommen nach harten Debatten zu folgendem Kompromiss: Wir kaufen die Autos komplett und er kauft sie nach der Tour zurück. Na prima.

In no time at all after the exciting, eventful but at the same time sad tour through three Central American countries we were already being tasked by Land Rover to present three new potential destinations. One of these was Canada. For the first time, the number of applications (this time around 8,000) was lower than for the previous tour. Was Canada perhaps not attractive enough?

We hadn't made things particularly easy on ourselves. About 4 million square miles should have been enough for us to find some challenging off-road routes in a country with a population of just 35 million people. Land Rover signed off on it, and we decided to focus on British Columbia, the province that borders the Pacific Ocean. It has an arctic climate in the winter, and in the summer the interior can experience temperatures of up to 40 degrees Celsius (104 degrees Fahrenheit). Dominated by forest – a fact reflected in the industries there (paper and logging) – the region's population levels were relatively high as well.

That aside, we were highly motivated as we set off on the pre-scout. First of all, we needed to find out how to ship our vehicles across the pond; little did we know that this would turn out to be a huge adventure in its own right.

This time we wanted to push Defender. We had forgotten, however, that the Defender no longer had type approval for the whole of the North American market, and that we wouldn't be able to secure temporary approval, either. There were difficulties involved in temporarily importing our other Land Rovers, too. No one could guarantee that we would be able to unload them from the ship once they had completed their journey to the "New World". Suddenly one of the four cornerstones upon which all our tours were based – hotels/flights, permits, routes and – vehicles – was looking very shaky indeed.

Now what? Head for another country? No. We don't run away from problems. We solve them. We chose to drop the Defenders, lease some Range Rovers and a few Discoverys from the local Land Rover dealer, put around 1,200 miles on them, pay the difference and let the dealer sell them on as company vehicles. Unfortunately, he simply wasn't interested. After long negotiations, we arrived at the following compromise: we would buy the vehicles outright, and he would buy them back from us after the tour. Easy.

Eigentlich gibt es nur zwei Straßentypen in Kanada: Holzfällerpfade und alle übrigen. Auf den Logging Roads gelten eigene Gesetze – hier haben die überlangen Holztrucks Vorfahrt. Man muss nur die Funkfrequenzen kennen, auf denen sie sich ankündigen. Auf allen anderen Pisten ist „Platz zum Atmen" – bei berauschenden Landschaften in unfassbaren Dimensionen.

There are only two kinds of road in Canada: logging roads and everything else. The logging roads have their own peculiar rules: the extra-long logging trucks have right of way. One only needs to know their CB radio frequencies which they use to tell you they're coming. Every other kind of road allows you space to breathe and enjoy the almost unbelievable dimensions of an intoxicating landscape.

DER LOOP
THE LOOP

Doch zur Vortour reicht uns die kleine Lösung. Wir leihen uns einen Disco, einen zweiten kaufen wir. Und suchen die herausfordernden Pisten. Und finden sie nicht. Es gibt unendlich viele Holzfällerorte, auch mit abenteuerlichen Wegen dorthin. Der Nachteil: Es handelt sich immer um Sackgassen. Mit jeder Menge Kartenmaterial setzen wir uns hin und suchen den passenden Loop – eine Schleife, die es sich zu fahren lohnt und die uns eine Woche lang in die wildesten Gebiete führt. Doch die wildesten Gebiete sind zunächst Waldbrandareale. An der Küste ist kein Durchkommen: Da hat vor kurzem der Feuerwehrchef die Dachrinne seines Hauses repariert und dabei eine brennende Kippe auf den Rasen geschnippt. Großer Fehler.

Trotz inzwischen bester Ausrüstung – Computer, GPS-Empfänger, digitalisiertes Kartenmaterial – sind wir nicht zufrieden mit den entdeckten Pisten. Es geht eben nichts über Menschen, die eine Gegend perfekt kennen. Am Straßenrand sprechen wir einen Mann an, der neue Pflanzen in die Asche setzt. Selbstverständlich hat er eine Karte in der Tasche, handgezeichnet, mit allen geographischen Daten. Geben will er uns das wertvolle Stück nicht, das auf alten Karten vor dem Feuer basiert. Aber kurz ausleihen ist okay. So breiten wir sie auf der Motorhaube aus und fotografieren sie Stück für Stück ab. Noch vor Ort geben wir die JPEG-Daten in den Computer ein und speichern sie mit meiner Touratech-Navigations-Software maßstabsgetreu ab. So finden wir ehemalige Schotterstraßen, die jetzt bedeckt von Asche sind, und es dauert nicht lange, da haben wir den von uns so verzweifelt gesuchten Loop entdeckt. Die Teams können kommen.

For the pre-scout, we were free to proceed as originally planned. We leased one Disco and bought a second. The next step was to find our challenging routes. It sounded straightforward enough, but there was one problem: there weren't any routes to be found.

There were numerous logging camps, many of them accessible only via difficult roads. The problem was that these roads were always dead ends. After purchasing every map available, we sat down and began hunting for a suitable loop that would be challenging to drive and would take us into the wilderness for a week. What wilderness there was, however, was also a high fire risk. The coast created a natural barrier. A local fire chief in the region had recently repaired the roof guttering of his house and had flicked a burning cigarette butt onto the grass. Big mistake.

While we had since upgraded our navigational equipment – route planning was now performed via computer, GPS receivers and digital maps – we were not yet happy with the routes we had found. At the end of the day, you can't beat local knowledge. At the side of the road, we got to talking with a guy planting new trees in the ash. Naturally, he had a handwritten map in his pocket, with all manner of geographical details. He wasn't prepared to give us the document, which was based on maps that pre-dated the fire, but he was prepared to lend it to us. We spread it out on the bonnet of the vehicle and photographed it bit by bit. We transferred the JPEG files straight to the computer, saving them in the original scale using my Touratech navigational software. We were now able to find the original gravel roads that had been covered in ash by the forest fire, and before long we had our loop. The teams could come.

DIE TRUCKS
THE TRUCKS

Zur Haupttour ein halbes Jahr später sieht die Geschichte schon viel entspannter aus. Die Brandschäden sind kaum mehr zu sehen, deshalb die Straßen erkennbar. Es wird eine softe Tour, die wir hier erleben (im Vergleich zu den Dschungelpisten Mexikos zum Beispiel). Wunderbare Bergpanoramen, Schneefelder, als Highlight auch mal eine weggespülte Brücke, die wir mit noch zu fällenden Bäumen ersetzen (wobei der gelernte Forstwirt Christian Uhrig einen Baum so geschickt absägt, dass er sofort in die richtige Position über den Bach kippt). Ein Blitzeinschlag in die Sandbleche neben einer Teilnehmerin, die kurz danach über Kribbeln in den Händen klagt, sorgt für Aufregung, aber nicht für Unruhe. Denn die größte Gefahr ist weder vom Wetter noch von den Wegen zu erwarten, sondern von Trucks.

Es sind riesige Holzlaster, die ständig und schnell mit Schwarz-, Weiß- und Sitka-Fichten, Ostamerikanischen Lärchen, Tannen und Douglasien über die Hauptstraßen donnern: den Trans-Canada Highway, Crowsnest Highway oder den Yellowhead Highway. Aber auch auf den Nebenstraßen, die alle Namen besitzen, die wir uns nicht merken können, sind sie unterwegs. Und meine Hauptaufgabe ist es, dafür zu sorgen, dass wir ihnen nicht in die Quere kommen. Denn die Trucker bremsen nicht – es würde auch nicht viel nützen bei dem langen Bremsweg, den die tonnenschweren Lastzüge benötigen. Zum Glück sind die jeweiligen Trucker-Funkfrequenzen auf Schildern am Straßenrand zu lesen, und ich werde zum Doppelfunker. Auf der einen Frequenz spreche ich mit den Truckern und frage ihren Standort ab, auf der anderen warne ich die Teams vor den rasenden Wandschränken und hoffe, dass die Trucker mithören: „Green Creek, Kilometer 105, zehn Fahrzeuge aufwärts … "

Tatsächlich rasen die manchmal aus mehreren Anhängern bestehenden Lastzüge nur zentimeterbreit an uns vorbei – aber keiner trifft uns. Das einzige, was uns wirklich betroffen macht, ist der Land-Rover-Händler in Vancouver, als er unsere Gebrauchtwagen wieder in Empfang nimmt: Akribisch rechnet er jede Schramme ab. Und ein paar sind auch ohne Baumlaster-Kontakt zusammengekommen.

Six months later, the time had come for the main event, but the region looked very different. There was very little evidence of the forest fire, and the roads were visible once again. Compared to the jungle tracks of Mexico, this would be a "soft" tour. Nevertheless, we had amazing mountain vistas, snowfields and a bridge we had to replace after a flash flood. Ex-forester Christian Uhrig was a dab hand with the chain saw and could fell trees so precisely that they bridged the gap exactly. The weather provided a brief moment of excitement, too, for one participant was standing right next to a sand channel when it was struck by lightning. She complained afterwards of pins and needles in her hands but other than that there had been no cause for alarm. Yet our greatest worry remained neither the weather nor the forest tracks – we constantly had to keep our eyes peeled for the trucks.

These were the logging trucks carrying black, white and Sitka spruce trees, the eastern larch, fir and Douglas fir along the main roads: the Trans-Canada Highway, Crowsnest Highway or Yellowhead Highway. The trucks travelled numerous secondary routes as well, the names of which none of us could remember, and it was my job to make sure we avoided any head-on collisions. As a rule, trucks don't stop for anything or anyone: with articulated units weighing many tons, the braking distance they required made any discussion of a sudden stop relatively academic. Fortunately, the truckers' CB radio frequencies were posted on the roadside, so I was able to talk to the truckers on one frequency to confirm their locations, while on another I could warn our teams about the multi-wheel nightmares coming our way: "Green Creek Kilometre 105, ten vehicles heading north…"

At times there was barely an inch between us and the road trains, often consisting of one artic unit with many trailers attached, that raced past us in the other direction. There was no damage, not that it made any difference to the Land Rover dealer in Vancouver, who meticulously noted every scratch when we returned the vehicles – yet not every blemish could be blamed on the trucks.

Wo der Weg verschwunden ist, stellt die Land Rover Experience ihn wieder her – zum Beispiel in Form einer Behelfsbrücke. Ein bisschen Flora nimmt der dringend benötigte Unterfahrschutz schon mal mit. Die Ernte wird nicht am Abend als Tee serviert, sondern macht sich für das Lagerfeuer als Zunder nützlich.

Where there was a way, Land Rover Experience has the will to put it back again – for example as a temporary bridge. Some undergrowth always falls victim to the very necessary under-body protection plates. The harvest isn't served up as tea at dinner; rather it serves perfectly as tinder for the campfire.

REINHARD KÜNSTLER

geb. 26.2.1949
von 2000 bis 2006 diverse Führungspositionen bei
Jaguar Land Rover, darunter Geschäftsführer Deutschland
von 2000 bis 2003

born 26 February 1949
numerous management positions at Jaguar Land Rover
from 2000 to 2006 including Managing Director of
Land Rover Germany from 2000 until 2003

In deiner Zeit als Geschäftsführer von Land Rover Deutschland fiel die Entscheidung, die LET, die Land Rover Experience Tour, aufzubauen.

Reinhard: Von Dr. Wolfgang Reitzle – damals Chef der Premier Automotive Group von Ford, zu der auch Land Rover ganz frisch gehörte – bekam ich im Jahr 2000 als Geschäftsführer die Aufgabe übertragen, Land Rover Deutschland zu einer funktionsfähigen, profitablen Gesellschaft aufzubauen. Stuart Daniels und ich mussten innerhalb von vier Monaten nach Auslauf der Unterstützung durch den vorherigen Eigentümer BMW eine neue Mannschaft aufstellen und Händler für zwei Drittel des Gesamtmarktvolumens finden, da die BMW-Niederlassungen das Verkaufs- und Servicegeschäft in den Ballungsgebieten zum 1. Januar 2001 einstellten. In dieser Zeit lernte ich Dag kennen, der vorschlug, Experience Touren mit Teilnehmern durchzuführen, die auf Basis nationaler Ausscheidungen als Gewinner mitfahren durften.

Welche Vorteile hast du darin gesehen?

Reinhard: Das war eine großartige Chance, um mehrere Dinge miteinander zu verbinden. Erstens: die Markenwerte von Land Rover nachhaltig beim Handel, insbesondere bei den neuen Händlern zu etablieren. Zweitens: die PR-Arbeit regional und national zu befeuern. Drittens: die Aktivierung von Neukundenpotential durch „Probefahrten" im Rahmen der Ausscheidungen sowie die Pflege der Bestandskunden. Viertens: eine positive Einbindung und damit „Infizierung" der neuen Land-Rover-Mannschaft. Und fünftens: dadurch, dass wir in die jeweiligen Touren-Länder von und mit Land Rover buchbare Reisen anboten, bauten wir dort eine weitere Kundenplattform auf – bei gleichzeitiger Teilabdeckung der anfallenden Kosten.

Bist du bei der Umsetzung auf Widerstände gestoßen?

Reinhard: Nein. Das Headoffice ließ mir am Anfang freie Hand, da niemand mit einem etwaigen Misserfolg bei der fragilen Situation von Land Rover Deutschland in Verbindung gebracht werden wollte. Budget-Diskussionen gab es erst später, als die Gesellschaft wieder erfolgreich war.

Was macht die LET so erfolgreich?

Reinhard: Der Erfolg basiert zum größten Teil auf der Professionalität von Dag und seinem Team sowie ihrer ansteckenden, nicht nachlassenden Begeisterung für die Marke und die Produkte. Ebenso wichtig ist natürlich die überwiegend äußerst positive Berichterstattung durch die begleitenden Journalisten. Um es betriebswirtschaftlich auszudrücken: Ich halte die Durchführung der Land Rover Experience nach wie vor für äußerst zielführend.

During your time as Managing Director of Land Rover Germany, the decision was taken to create the Land Rover Experience Tour.

Reinhard: In 2000 Dr. Wolfgang Reitzle, who at the time was head of Ford's Premier Automotive Group, appointed me to turn Land Rover Germany into a functioning and profitable company. Stuart Daniels and I had four months after the withdrawal of support by the previous owner BMW to put together a new team and find dealers who could supply two-thirds of the total market sales volume, as BMW franchised dealers had stopped selling and servicing Land Rovers in the major conurbations beginning 1 January 2001. It was during this time that I got to know Dag, who suggested running Experience Tours with participants who had been selected as winners on the basis of national selection camps.

What opportunities did you see here?

Reinhard: This was a wonderful opportunity to combine a number of things. First of all, we could establish Land Rover's brand values within the dealer network (particularly the newer dealers). Secondly, it gave us an opportunity to kick-start both regional and national PR. Thirdly, the "test drives" which were part of the selection camps process were both an opportunity to generate sales as well as keep existing customers in the family. Fourthly, they were the perfect way to motivate or "infect" the Land Rover Germany team. And lastly, as we intended to offer customer holidays in the tour destinations, organised by Land Rover with Land Rovers, this was an additional sales platform with at least partial coverage of the costs.

Did you face any resistance in putting the plan into operation?

Reinhard: No. In the early days I was given pretty much carte blanche, as no one wanted to be associated with any failures, given Land Rover Germany's fragile situation. Budget discussions became more intense once the company was back on its feet.

Why is the LET so successful?

Reinhard: Success is in part down to the professionalism of Dag and his team as well as their infective and constant enthusiasm for the brand and its products. Just as important is the largely positive PR effect, thanks to the accompanying journalists. To put it in a business context: I believe that the Land Rover Experience Tour makes good business sense.

Nach einem ordentlichen Regenguss sind die Pfützen wieder vollgelaufen und somit ein Lieblingsmotiv für die Film- und Kamerateams. Die Matsche fliegt planmäßig – Pech für die Fotografen, die ihren Standort zu nah am Wasser gebaut haben. Das Ergebnis: sensationelle Aufnahmen und einen Tag Kameras putzen.

After a severe downpour, all the ruts are full again and as such in great demand by photographers and film crews. As expected, mud flew in every direction, which was bad luck for photographers who had set up too close to the track. The result was sensational imagery and a day's cleaning for the cameras.

SCHOTTLAND

SCOTLAND
2005
8 DISCOVERY, 1 DEFENDER
STRECKE / DISTANCE: 1 400 KM / 870 MILES

Zugegeben, wer zum Balmoral Castle möchte, dem Sommersitz von Queen Elizabeth II., muss das nicht offroad tun. Aber es macht mehr Spaß – schließlich wollen die Land Rover auch in Schottland beweisen, was sie alles können.

It is true that if you want to visit Queen Elizabeth II's summer residence, Balmoral Castle, you don't require four-wheel drive. However, it is more fun, as the Land Rovers want to demonstrate what they can do in Scotland as well.

DER WHISKY

THE WHISKY

Wie wir in Kanada gesehen haben: Es geht auch auf die softe Tour. Die Teams, die Journalisten, die Land-Rover Verantwortlichen sind begeistert. Aber ist es jetzt nicht wieder Zeit für eine echte fahrerische Herausforderung? Für ein richtiges Abenteuer?

Land Rover möchte allerdings endlich mal ins Heimatland – da bietet sich in Großbritannien nur Schottland an. Knapp 80 000 Quadratkilometer groß, gut fünf Millionen Einwohner, viele Felder, grüne Wiesen, massenhaft Schafe sowie Singletrails, und Seen heißen grundsätzlich „Loch" – eigentlich gute Voraussetzungen für „Britishness on Wheels". Oder?

Ich habe da meine Bedenken. Denn nach meiner Meinung fehlt der Kick. Für mich ist es etwas wie ein Defender ohne Allradantrieb. Man ist von Deutschland aus in wenigen Stunden dort, jeder könnte auch alleine herumreisen, und wenn man sich in einem Bed & Breakfast einnistet, weiß man, dass einem nicht die Kakerlaken das Bett wegtragen werden. Wo also ist die Herausforderung? Das fragen sich wohl auch die Fans. Nur rund 4 000 Bewerber interessieren sich für die neue Tour. Für uns – Hans, Claudia, Land-Rover-Pressechef Paul Entwistle und mich – lautet die schwierigste Aufgabe auf der Vortour: Abenteuer finden.

Was wir finden, sind wunderbar asphaltierte einspurige Wege, sehr malerisch zwischen Hecken platziert, die man aber auch mit einem konventionellen Kleinwagen bezwingen kann. Klar gibt es jede Menge Grünland, aber auf Wiesen, Äckern und Blumenfeldern herumzufahren, entspricht nicht der Mentalität von Land Rover. Offroad ja, aber ohne Schäden zu hinterlassen.

Die hinterlassen wir lieber bei uns selber – und klappern zunächst leicht gefrustet, aber schon bald immer besser gelaunt, die Destillerien ab. Was bedeutet, sich mit dem wichtigsten Exportgut Schottlands zu beschäftigen. In jenem Jahr, 2005, führt dieser Teil Großbritanniens für 3,6 Milliarden Pfund hochgeistigen Whisky aus. Das Getränk belebt hier beim Highlander die Seele auf grandiose Art (nicht umsonst heiß Whisky auf Schottisch-Gälisch „uisge beatha", was „Lebenswasser" bedeutet), Aspirin übernimmt später ernährungstechnische Aufgaben.

Den Guide macht unser Presse-Paul, als „Native Speaker" können wir uns keinen besseren wünschen. Und neben dem Nationalgetränk in unendlich vielen verschiedenen Ausprägungen, Geschmacksrichtungen und Alter finden wir nebenbei auch stocknüchterne Bypass-Straßen, die meist über privates Gelände führen, und zu passender Zeit sorgen wir für alle Genehmigungen zur Durchfahrt.

Geht doch. Hicks.

As we had experienced in Canada, the soft tour option worked as well. Teams, journalists and the decision-makers at Land Rover – they were all very happy. But wasn't it time for a real drivers' challenge again, time for some proper adventure?

Land Rover wanted to take the tour to the home of the brand. In Great Britain, our only option was to go to Scotland. About 30,000 square miles, with a population of five million; rich, green countryside, thousands of sheep and endless trails, and the lakes there are called "lochs". Just perfect for the brand that almost defines itself as "Britishness on wheels", isn't it?

I had my reservations. I thought that we were missing a certain buzz. It felt like a Land Rover Defender without four wheel drive. Being but a few hours' drive from Germany, Scotland was easy for anyone to explore, and in your classical bed-and-breakfast you didn't run the risk of sharing your room with an army of cockroaches. So where was the challenge? The fans asked the same question. There were barely 4,000 applicants to join us on the tour. For us – meaning Hans, Claudia, Land Rover PR man Paul Entwistle and myself – the toughest task on the pre-scout was finding any adventure at all.

We found beautifully paved, single-track roads, pretty as a picture between rows of hedges – but requiring nothing more dynamic than a two-wheel-drive runabout. We were surrounded by greenery, but driving through peoples' gardens and ploughing up their fields is not the Land Rover way. Off-road was okay, but tread lightly and don't cause any damage.

Our frustration was soon a thing of the past, thanks to the joy of visiting a number of whisky distilleries. This acquainted us with Scotland's most significant export, which in 2005 generated a handsome 3.6 billion pounds sterling in revenue. Whisky, as any Scot will tell you, is vitality for the soul. The word "whisky" comes from the Gaelic "uisge beatha", which translates approximately as "water of life". But if life is to go on normally after the imbibing is through, one is well-advised to keep aspirin or something similar to hand…

Our PR man Paul took on the role of guide – as an almost (we were, after all, in Scotland) "native speaker", the Englishman was in his element and relished the task. Thus "informed" of the endless varieties, tastes and vintages of the Scottish national beverage, we could focus on the sober business of driving by-pass roads in search of private estates where, equipped with the necessary permits, we could continue the journey off-road. Though not always in a straight line. And with the aforementioned aspirin to hand.

Gut drei Viertel der Fläche Schottlands werden für die Landwirtschaft genutzt – da muss man geeignete Offroad-Strecken schon suchen. Die Wege sind zudem meistens in Privatbesitz: Mehr als 50 Prozent des gesamten Grund und Bodens gehören gerade mal 500 Familien.

Well over three-quarters of Scotland's surface area is given over to the agricultural economy – so you have to search long and hard for good off-road routes. The majority of them are privately owned. More than 50 percent of all land in Scotland is in the hands of 500 families.

ANDREA
LEITNER-GARNELL

geb. 21.4.1965
Pressechefin Jaguar Land Rover Deutschland seit 2003

born 21 April 1965
PR Manager Jaguar Land Rover Germany since 2003

Was macht den Umgang mit Allradautos so besonders?

Andrea: Man kann die Menschen unter ganz anderen Aspekten von Autos begeistern – eben nicht nur von Leistung und Design, sondern auch von Abenteuer und Freiheit. Ich habe 1990 bei Chrysler/Jeep angefangen und somit meine ganze berufliche Laufbahn mit den Kernmarken des 4x4-Geschäfts verbracht – und es lieben gelernt.

*Immer wieder bleiben Teilnehmer von Touren und Reisen
bei euch als Instruktoren. Warum?*

Andrea: Viele dieser Menschen wollen mit Autos arbeiten, aber nicht im Wettbewerb mit anderen Autos, wie zum Beispiel im Motorsport. Viel mehr Spaß haben sie an Autos, die in der Lage sind, Menschen zu Orten zu bringen, zu denen andere gar nicht hinfahren können. Und das gemeinsame Erlebnis, die vielen Eindrücke auf einer solchen Abenteuerreise schaffen ein unvergleichliches Gemeinschaftsgefühl, sodass sich die Teilnehmer einer Tour oder Reise auch danach immer wiedertreffen. Diese hohe Emotionalität ist auch für mich persönlich etwas, was mich an die Marke bindet.

Welche Außenwirkung haben die Experience Touren?

Andrea: Für die Medienarbeit sind sie ein echtes Juwel. Denn durch die Touren zeigen wir, was die Autos können. Die Medien vermitteln das Erlebnis dieser Tour, und die Kunden können sie als Reise nachfahren. Denn einzelne Touren können auch von jedem Interessenten gebucht werden. Aber auch wenn viele Menschen im Alltag ihre Land Rover nicht an deren Grenzen bringen – die Möglichkeit, ausbrechen zu können, wird von allen geschätzt. Viele Leute kaufen ja auch eine Uhr, die 200 Meter tief wasserdicht ist, ohne dass sie jemals so tief tauchen würden. Aber sie wissen, dass ein Extremsportler damit unten war. So ist es auch mit unseren Fahrzeugen: Wir fahren in den Dschungel oder auf hohe Berge, und die Land Rover meistern jede Situation. Dieses Abenteuer holen sich die Leute nach Hause. Und wenn sie von den Touren in den Medien lesen, freuen sie sich, dass sie so ein Auto besitzen, mit denen die Experience Tour gerade wieder die schwierigsten Passagen gemeistert hat.

Aber man muss trotzdem wissen, wie man mit den Autos umgeht?

Andrea: Selbstverständlich. Aber, um beim Beispiel zu bleiben: Man muss ja auch wissen, wie man taucht. Dafür gibt es unsere Land Rover Experience Trainings in Wülfrath, und bei den Reisen sind Guides dabei.

What makes four-wheel-drive vehicles so special?

Andrea: Instead of appealing to the senses with performance and design, as with ordinary cars, four-wheel drives appeal to people's sense of adventure and love of freedom. I started working in PR for Chrysler/Jeep in 1990 and have spent my entire career working with the original brands in the 4x4 business, and I love it.

Tour participants seem to end up working with Land Rover as instructors on a regular basis – why is that?

Andrea: Many of these individuals want to work with cars, but not in competition with other brands as one would in motor sports. They enjoy vehicles that are able to transport people to places that other vehicles can't get to. The common experience and the many impressions that an adventure trip leaves behind create an incomparable team spirit, and those who take part – whether on tour or on holiday – stay in contact with each other. This extremely emotional component is what ties me personally to the brand.

What is the impact of the Experience Tours in publicity terms?

Andrea: For PR purposes, they are an absolute gift. The tours demonstrate what the vehicles are capable of. The media can communicate the experience, and customers can follow in the footsteps of the tour. Many of the tours have been marketed also as customer events. Although many Land Rover owners never take their vehicles to the limit of their abilities, it is good to know that if they wanted to, they could. There are equally people who buy a watch that is waterproof to 700 feet below the surface without ever going diving but they know that an extreme sportsman or -woman would choose that piece of equipment. The same principle applies to our vehicles. We drive in the jungle or in the mountains, and the Land Rovers take it all in stride. It is this sense of adventure that people want to take home. When they read about a tour, then they bask a little in the glory, knowing that the same vehicle that sits in their garage just made it across the most difficult terrain known to man.

Nevertheless, you still need to know how to use the technology?

Andrea: Of course. But to stick with my previous analogy: you also have to know how to dive. We have Land Rover Experience training events in Wülfrath, and on the holidays there are always guides accompanying the customers.

DIE MÜCKEN
THE MIDGES

Sie heißen „Midges", die schottischen Hochlandmücken, und sie sind bekannt dafür, dass sie in riesigen Schwärmen vorkommen und einem das Leben zur Hölle machen können. Aber uns Outdoor-Spezialisten auch?

Es ist der 6. Juli, und das weiß ich so genau, weil ich an diesem Tag Geburtstag habe. Wir haben eine Campsite am See aufgebaut – nachträglich muss ich mich fragen, ob das eine so gute Idee war. Mit Mückennetzen über den Köpfen versuchen wir zu essen, nachdem die Teams am Tage zur Abwechslung mal eine echte fahrerische Aufgabe gelöst haben: einen Pass bezwingen, dessen Weg wirklich schweres Geläuf bot. Immer wieder mussten sie Felsbrocken beiseite räumen, einige gingen zu Fuß voraus und warnten vor Löchern und spitzen Steinen. Wir sind müde, wir sind hungrig. Und wir sind voller Mücken.

Abenteuer? Ja – speisen ohne unfreiwillige Fleischbeilage. Kaum haben wir den Löffel in die Suppe getunkt, sitzen Hunderte Mücken auf dem Besteck und machen uns die Mahlzeit streitig. Wer auch nur kurz irgendwo Haut zeigt, wird sofort gestochen. Mir geht so ein Geburtstag mächtig auf den Keks, und so beschließe ich, mich mit acht Vertrauten in einen Discovery zurückzuziehen, um den zum Ehrentage geschenkten Whisky zu genießen. Myriaden uneingeladener Mücken, die den Disco belagern, werden von Insektiziden aus Sprühdosen hinweggerafft. Mit jedem Schluck Lebenswasser nimmt mein Beileid ab, bis wir nahezu gesurrfrei im Auto endlich unsere Ruhe haben. Wozu so ein Land Rover alles gut ist …

Tatsächlich ist die Schottland-Tour letztlich fahrerisch keine große Herausforderung, trotzdem ein echter Erfolg. Erstmals berichten überwiegend Lifestyle-Magazine über die Tour – nicht zuletzt wegen der hochgeistigen Getränke. Und damit erfährt erstmals auch eine neue, nicht nur Offroad-affine Klientel, wohin einen ein Land Rover bringen kann. Aufgrund des Medieninteresses soll es als nächstes für internationale Journalisten ein Winter-Event auf Island geben – es den Schreiberlingen mal so richtig zeigen, was ein Landy kann und ist.

Noch mal in klaren Worten: Island im November.

Wie bekloppt muss man dafür eigentlich sein?

The mosquitoes in the Scottish highlands, commonly known as "midges", are notorious for their swarming characteristics and for generally making life hell for everyone who comes into contact with them. How would they affect the off-road specialists?

It was the 6th of July, and the only reason I remember the date was that it was and is my birthday. We had set up a camp at the side of a lake – in hindsight, of course, this wasn't a good idea. That day, with the teams for once having accomplished a genuine off-road challenge – a pass road that was technically very difficult to drive due to the many rocks that lay directly on the route – we were trying to dine with mosquito nets around our heads. During the drive, we had walked in front of the vehicles to check the terrain for large holes and particularly sharp stones. We were dog-tired, starving and slowly being eaten alive by the midges.

How about this for competition? – Try eating without swallowing a mouthful of insect flesh at the same time. The second I raised my spoon to my mouth, it was populated with hundreds of the little beasts, all of them keen to get my dinner before I could. Visible skin was immediately punished and punctured. This wasn't my idea of a birthday. So I retreated, joined by eight colleagues, to the safety of the nearest Discovery to enjoy my birthday present. The midges trying to crash our little party were annihilated in clouds of insect spray. Whatever sympathy I may have felt for the little creatures was rapidly vanishing with every sip of whisky, until finally the interior of the Disco was completely midge free. I'll take a Land Rover over a Scottish lakeside camp any day…

It must be noted that, in driving terms alone, the Scotland Tour wasn't the greatest of challenges. It was a roaring success nevertheless, with lifestyle publications writing about the tour – perhaps thanks to the influence of Scotland's greatest export. A different kind of clientele, one with interests ranging beyond mud-plugging, began to appreciate the breadth of the qualities that Solihull's finest had to offer. Due to so much interest from the media, the next event in the pipeline will be an international media drive to really hammer home to the scribes what a Landy was good for - in Iceland. In plain terms:

Iceland in November.

This was stupid. With a capital "S".

NICOLE LEHMANN

geboren 15.8.1967
Diplom-Ökonomin und von Anfang an
Assistentin der Geschäftsleitung von APS

born 15 August 1967
certified economist, assistant to the
management team at APS from day one

ANNA BAUNACH

geb. 10.5.1984
Bachelor in Internationalem Tourismus, bei APS seit 2008

born 10 May 1984
Bachelor's degree in international tourism,
who has worked at APS since 2008

Nicole, kannst du dich noch an die ersten Qualifikationscamps erinnern?

Nicole: Na klar. Beworben haben sich etwa 6 000 Leute, und hier haben sich höchstens fünf Festangestellte der Land Rover Experience Germany um die erste Tour kümmern können. Die 60 Glücklichen für die Endqualifikation haben wir alle noch persönlich angerufen.
Anna: Heute geht das alles übers Internet. Da ist es auch viel einfacher, Bewerber herauszufischen, die sich immer wieder bewerben. Trotzdem rutscht mal einer zum zweiten Mal bis zur Endqualifikation durch. Wer allerdings einmal eine Tour mitgemacht hat, kann das kein zweites Mal tun.

Und wie sieht heute die Aufgabenstellung aus?

Nicole: Ich kümmere mich jetzt um die Organisation und Planung von Veranstaltungen im Land Rover Experience Center und bundesweit sowie um die interne Büroorganisation. Inzwischen gibt es ja auch eine eigene Reiseabteilung. Und heutzutage bewerben sich bis zu 30 000 Interessierte für die Touren – das ist eine Menge Arbeit.

Anna, du hast die Jubiläumsreise, die Seidenstraßentour betreut. Wie viel Arbeit war das?

Anna: Das war logistisch die mit Abstand aufwendigste Tour, schon alleine wegen ihrer Länge im Vergleich zu den vorherigen Events. Aber trotz Stress und manchmal sehr langen Bürozeiten hat das richtig Spaß gemacht, weil es eine echte Herausforderung war. Denn die größte Aufgabe ist immer, den Überblick zu behalten.
Nicole: Es gibt eine Menge Herausforderungen, aber keine Probleme. Denn wir sind die Problemlöser.

Nicole, can you remember what the first selection camps were like?

Nicole: Absolutely. We had around 6,000 applications and only five full-time Land Rover Experience Germany staff to plan the first tour. I remember that we phoned the 60 happy finalists who had made it to final selections ourselves.
Anna: These days, the process is run via the Internet. It's much easier to pick out the applicants who apply again and again. Nevertheless, every once in a while one gets through to final selections. Anyone who has been on a tour once isn't allowed to apply for a second.

How is the work divided up today?

Nicole: I look after the organisation and planning of all the events we run in the Land Rover Experience Centre plus the events in Germany as well as managing the day-to-day running of the office. We now have our own holiday department, with up to 30,000 applications to go on the tour. That is a lot of work.

Anna, you oversaw the anniversary event – the Silk Road Tour.
How much work was involved?

Anna: Logistically it was by far the most complex tour, simply because of its sheer length compared to the previous events. However, despite the stress and long office hours sometimes it is a lot of fun, just because it is so challenging. The most important thing to remember is not to lose sight of the bigger picture.
Nicole: We have a lot of challenges and no problems, as it's our job to solve the problems.

LAND-ROVER EXPERIENCE CANADA 2004

Off-Road

ISLAND
WINTER
EXPERIENCE

ICELAND WINTER EXPERIENCE
2005
20 DISCOVERY, 1 DEFENDER
STRECKE / DISTANCE: 510 KM / 320 MILES

DER SCHNEESTURM

THE BLIZZARD

„Above and Beyond." Ja, und weiter, und jenseits, und überhaupt – dafür steht Land Rover, und es wäre doch gelacht, wenn wir nicht ein paar Journalisten damit beeindrucken könnten, wie wir den Winter an einem der zu dieser Jahreszeit ungemütlichsten Orte der Welt mit unseren Autos besiegen. Ich weiß: Im Hinterland ist das Wetter völlig unkalkulierbar. Aber es gibt Alternativstrecken – also wage ich das Abenteuer. Denn die Experience hat schon ganz andere Probleme gelöst. Schließlich sind wir die, die Unkalkulierbares kalkulieren. Zumindest, bis wir ins Kalkül ziehen müssen, dass auch wir Heißsporne kalt erwischt werden können.

Wir – das sind erstmals die englischen und die deutschen Experience-Kollegen gemeinsam – laden 120 Journalisten ein, die sich in Zwanzigergruppen 20 Autos teilen, allesamt Discovery mit Diesel- und V8-Motoren. Jeder kann, so der Plan, drei bis vier Tage nach Herzenslust in der weißen Wildnis kurven. Start ist in Reykjavík, eine Campsite samt Hütte mit Matratzenlager für die Zartbesaiteten befindet sich in Landmannalaugar. Dort gibt es heiße Quellen, in denen man sich – so man sich denn darauf einlässt und hinabtauchen mag in die Welt der unterirdisch erzeugten Hitze – lange ausgesprochen wohlfühlen kann.

Auch ich sitze dort drinnen, wohl wissend, dass ich in drei Stunden mit meinem britischen Kollegen Dougie vor dem Konvoi starten muss, um bei einer Flussdurchfahrt schon mal das zentimeterdicke Eis zu brechen, damit die schreibende Zunft später problemlos queren kann. Aber während ich da so im heißen Wasser sinniere, merke ich, dass sich das Wetter dramatisch ändert. Vielleicht habe ich als Pilot einen siebten Sinn dafür, vielleicht achte ich als Verantwortlicher auch nur etwas mehr auf die Zeichen der Natur – ich bin jedenfalls gewarnt.

Mein siebter Sinn ist es wohl auch, der mich frühmorgens um halb vier aufwachen und nach draußen gehen lässt. Kein Zweifel: Ein Schneesturm ist aufgezogen. Es schneit bereits heftig, der Wind fegt mit Böen von etwa 100 km/h um die Hütte. Die Situation ist brenzlig, zumal einige Journalisten zeitig zurück nach Reykjavík müssen, um ihren Flieger nach Hause zu erwischen, und neu angekommene auf die Autos und ihre Tour warten. Ich wecke alle vom Orga-Team relativ emotionsfrei und gebe eindeutig zu erkennen, dass für Waschen und Frühstücken überhaupt keine Zeit ist. Ich ordne unmissverständlich an, sofort die Gäste zu alarmieren und sich unverzüglich in die Autos zu werfen.

Es wird nicht so schlimm, wie ich befürchtet hatte – es wird viel schlimmer. Für die ersten 500 Meter aus dem Camp benötigen wir geschlagene zwei Stunden. Eine Straße, ein Weg oder auch nur eine Piste ist nicht mehr zu sehen. Keine Stangen, Bäume, Felsen begrenzen die Fahrbahn, es ist alles einfach nur weiß – nicht nur am Boden, sondern auch in der Luft. Wir müssen Schneeketten montieren, und das dauert. Die Hände werden kalt, die Körper auch, wir werden immer müder, und wir sind nur 12 Kilometer von der geräumten Hauptstraße entfernt.

Die ersten Journalisten werden unruhig, besonders die, die noch nach Amerika zurückfliegen müssen. Andere fangen tatsächlich an, Angst um ihr Leben zu bekommen. Gerechtfertigt ist das zwar nicht, denn noch haben wir diverse Möglichkeiten – aber nicht jeder Journalist mag die volle Härte der Natur. Dennoch muss ich zugeben, auch wir als Verantwortliche waren noch nie vorher in so einer Situation. Mithilfe von GPS-Daten tasten wir uns vorwärts, aber wir kommen nicht wirklich voran. Also übergebe ich als Leader meinen Defender meinem Kopiloten, nehme eine Stange und gehe zu Fuß voraus. Mit Stochern versuche ich, den Schotteruntergrund des Weges zu erfühlen. Das Wetter wird derweil immer schlimmer. Bei -8 Grad bleibt Schnee grundsätzlich an Scheibenwischern hängen; von den Höhenzügen mischt sich Lavaasche in den Schneesturm und peitscht schmerzhaft Körner ins Gesicht. Die Skibrille, die ich inzwischen aufgesetzt habe, bedeckt leider nicht mein ganzes Gesicht. Kurz: Es ist nicht nur ungemütlich, es ist wirklich beängstigend. Und es wird nicht besser. Als ich mich umdrehe, um nach dem mir folgenden Defender zu sehen, ist er nicht mehr da. In meinen Ohren tobt der Sturm, und tatsächlich hat mich der Fahrer verloren. Ich warte, und warte, und warte, und erst nach ein paar Minuten sehe ich seine Scheinwerfer. Damit das nicht wieder passierte, leine ich mich mit einem Abschleppseil an den mir folgenden Wagen an. Das sieht zwar bescheuert aus, ist aber sinnvoll. Und mich kann ja niemand sehen.

Die Zeit vergeht, und wir kommen nicht gut vorwärts. Hinten bleiben immer wieder Autos in Schneewehen stecken, und alle Mann müssen die Wagen ausgraben. Zwei Stunden, drei Stunden, vier Stunden gehe ich voraus, im Schlepp den ebenso unendlich langsamen Landy. Zwischendurch telefoniere ich über Satellitentelefon ab und zu mit Keflavík und frage, ob die dortige Wetterstation vielleicht baldige Entwarnung liefern kann. Aber ich werde ein ums andere Mal enttäuscht.

Ich gebe es nicht gerne zu, aber in diesem Moment muss ich einsehen, auf Hilfe angewiesen zu sein. Unser Guide, natürlich wieder „Ingo der Tänzer", mobilisiert sofort über Telefon ein paar Freunde. Die haben an ihren Autos Ballonreifen montiert, mit denen sie oben auf dem Schnee fahren können, weil sie nicht einsinken. Inzwischen habe ich den Konvoi halbiert: Überall, wo bislang zwei Leute in den Autos sitzen, werden jetzt vier platziert. Die leeren Autos lassen wir zurück, um sie später abzuholen. Das verkürzt den Konvoi. Ein weiterer Vorteil: Die Heizungen von Dieselautos versagen völlig bei der Kälte, denn durch das langsame Herumstochern im Schnee werden die Motoren und damit die Heizungen nicht warm. Aber vier Mann im Auto schaffen eine Menge Eigenwärme!

Endlich kommen die einheimischen Bigfoots, ziehen eine Spur, helfen uns heraus – wir hätten zwar nur noch 3 Kilometer bis zur Hauptstraße benötigt, aber tatsächlich haben wir insgesamt 23 Stunden für 12 Kilometer Nebenstraße gebraucht.

Kleiner Trost: Die Bigfoots basieren allesamt auf Defender-Konstruktionen.

"Above and Beyond". Onward and upward, and so on and so forth. This is what Land Rover was all about. And wouldn't it be amusing to impress a few journalists by defying winter in our vehicles in one of the most inhospitable places on the planet? Winter weather in Iceland is always hard to predict, but there are several navigable routes to choose from. For this reason, I agreed to support the venture. Over the years, we had managed to solve a number of equally problematic tasks, and, after all, we had become past masters at predicting the unpredictable. That said, even hotheads like us could be caught unawares.

We – and by this I meant, for the first time, the English and the German Experience Teams – jointly invited 120 journalists in six groups of 20, split among 20 Discoverys equipped with diesel and V8 petrol engines. The plan was to provide each journalist an opportunity to spend three to four days exploring the wilderness. Setting out in Reykjavík, our destination was Landmannalaugar, a campsite equipped with its own mountain hut with mattresses in a huge dormitory for the more fainthearted. The place is legendary for its hot thermal springs, guaranteeing the perfect wellness experience for those prepared to plunge into the hot water.

Which is why I sat in just such a spring, fully aware that, three hours later, I would have to set out in front of the convoy with my British colleague Dougie to clear any water crossings of the thick sheets of ice so that the scribes could wade across without getting their feet wet. As I sat musing in the thermal springs, I noticed that the weather had changed. Call it pilot's instinct; or perhaps I always have an eye on the weather because I am responsible for others. Either way, it was a warning.

It was probably the very same instinct that woke me up at 3:30 in the morning and saw me walk outside to take a look. There was no doubt. A weather front had closed in, and a blizzard was brewing. It had already started snowing quite heavily, and gusts of up to 62 mph were lashing the sides of the hut. The situation was critical, as some journalists needed to get back to Reykjavík to catch flights home, and new arrivals would be waiting for the vehicles to start their own tour. I woke up everyone in the organisation without getting too emotional but nevertheless making the point that there was no time to wash or eat breakfast. I made it clear that we needed to inform our guests immediately and get them in the vehicles.

It wasn't as bad as I had feared – it was a lot worse. We needed over two hours just to cover the first 1,600 feet out of the campsite. Roads, tracks, even footpaths had just disappeared in the blizzard. Poles, trees, even the rock face were no longer visible in the whiteout. We had to attach snow chains, and that took time. Our hands started to get cold – our bodies, too and we were getting tired. And all this just 7 miles from the main road, which had been cleared of snow.

Some of the journalists started to grumble, particularly those with flights to the USA. Others were actually afraid that they could freeze to death. At that point in time, their fears were unjustified, as we still had a number of options; but not every journalist is capable of dealing with extreme weather. Nevertheless, the situation was a first for the organisation as well. Using GPS data, we inched our way forwards but we simply weren't making enough progress. As the man in charge, I handed the wheel of my Defender to my co-driver, grabbed a crow bar, jumped out and made my way forward on foot, testing the ground as I went, in search of the gravel road beneath the snow.

The weather progressively worsened. At a temperature of -8 degrees Celsius (18 degrees Fahrenheit), the snow stuck to the wipers. The wind was also mixing up lava ash and tiny stones from the ground, and whipping this into my face. My ski goggles didn't cover my entire face. It wasn't just unpleasant – it was downright terrifying. Things weren't getting any better, either. As I turned around to check the Defender behind me, I noticed that it was no longer there. The roar of the storm was deafening in my ears, and my co-driver had actually lost me. I waited and waited, and after a few minutes I could make out his headlights. To prevent it from happening again, I attached a towrope to my belt and the other end to the Defender. It looked daft, but it made a lot of sense, for nobody could see me.

We were losing time and not making significant progress. Behind us, vehicles were stuck in snowdrifts, and everybody was helping dig them out. For two, three, four hours I was attached to the Landy, which was just as slow as I was. From time to time, I contacted Keflavík airport via satellite phone to find out whether the meteorological office had any news of a break in the weather. The news was disappointing.

I don't like having to admit this, but at that instant I realised I needed help. Our guide, naturally "dancing Ingo", organised a few of his friends on the phone. They had fitted balloon tyres to their vehicles to prevent them from sinking in the snow. By now, I had reduced the convoy by half. Vehicles that once held two people now held four. We left the empty cars behind, as we would be able to pick them up later. Another advantage was that the heaters in the diesel-engine Discoverys had failed to help combat the extreme cold – the reason being that driving at barely walking pace behind a man with a crowbar meant that the engines (and thereby the heating) weren't able to reach normal operating temperatures. Putting four people into the car, however, warmed it up no end!

Finally, the local "Bigfoots" turned up, created their own track and pulled us out. The main road was just 2 miles away, but we had required 23 hours for the 7 miles of track. The only compensation, and a little one at that: the Bigfoots were all modified Defenders.

ARGENTINIEN & CHILE

ARGENTINA & CHILE
2007
6 DEFENDER, 3 DISCOVERY,
1 AMBULANCE DISCOVERY
STRECKE / DISTANCE: 1600 KM / 1,000 MILES

DAS INTERNET
THE INTERNET

Auch wenn uns Schottland nicht so recht an die Grenzen unserer Leistungsfähigkeit getrieben hat – jedes Jahr so eine Tour zu stemmen, ist inzwischen nicht mehr machbar. Denn es kommen immer neue Aufgaben hinzu: buchbare Experience-Reisen nach Island, Namibia und Kanada und immer mehr Arbeit in Wülfrath, wo sich der Steinbruch zum Mittelpunkt sämtlicher deutscher Land-Rover-Fahraktivitäten entwickelt. Kurz: Land Rover beschließt – mit meinem vollen Einverständnis und fast mit meiner Dankbarkeit – nur noch alle zwei Jahre zu touren. Das bedeutet ein Jahr Zeit für die Camps, bis man die sechs Teilnehmer gefunden hat, im darauffolgenden Jahr die Vor- und die Haupttour. Das hat mehrere Vorteile: mehr Zeit zum Organisieren und dadurch weniger Stress, dazu zwei Jahresbudgets für eine Tour, die dadurch wieder aufwendiger werden kann. Prompt schlagen wir Land Rover Argentinien und Chile vor. Genauso prompt bekommen wir grünes Licht dafür.

Wir fliegen zuerst in die Stadt Salta, die wir wegen ihrer für uns strategisch günstigen Lage (im Nordwesten Argentiniens am Rand der Anden in gut 1 000 Metern Höhe) als Startpunkt wählen. Salta ist eine typische Kolonialstadt. Hier beginnt auch der „Zug über den Wolken", eine der berühmtesten Eisenbahnstrecken der Welt, die über die Anden bis zum Viadukt La Polvorilla führt. Tatsächlich waren weder Hans noch ich jemals zuvor hier, aber die Recherche im Internet ist inzwischen wesentlich einfacher geworden. Und damit auch die Suche nach Wegen, Hotels und Agenturen.

Denken wir. Tatsächlich finden wir einige Firmen, die sich nach allen Regeln der Kunst anbieten, bei Reisen durch das Land behilflich zu sein. Wir besuchen sie – und erfahren einmal mehr, dass sich die Vorstellungen solcher Einrichtungen von „Reisen" und unsere von „Touren" überhaupt nicht decken. Die inländischen „Spezialisten" sind eindeutig touristisch ausgerichtet. Was wir wollen, wird als „geht nicht, zu gefährlich, kommen wir nicht hoch" eingestuft. Die Verantwortlichen haben mehr Bedenken als Ideen, mehr Sorgen als Hirn – gefrustet gehen wir erst mal Kartenmaterial kaufen und Hotels inspizieren. Ausgerechnet dabei treffen wir auf Gerry – einen so österreichischen Österreicher, wie es ihn in Österreich nicht mehr gibt. Sein Credo: „Geht nicht gibt's nicht." Er ist als Guide genau der Richtige.

Zurück in Deutschland stellen wir die Tour dank Internet und der Touratech-Software komplett fertig. Damit können Straßen und Tracks auf hundert Meter genau bestimmt werden. Google Earth beginnt zu dieser Zeit mit seinem beeindruckenden Service, und über diverse Suchfunktionen finden wir im Netz eine Geschichte von Weltenbummlern, die im Krater Galán gewesen sein wollen.

Krater? So etwas ist unser Ding, da werden wir hellhörig. Von den Abenteurern wollen wir die Ein- und Ausstiegskoordinaten für den Krater erfahren – die sie uns aber nicht liefern können. Also Hochstapler? Prima! Wenn die nicht wirklich dort gewesen sind, ist es eine wunderbare Aufgabe für die Land Rover Experience Tour, ihnen zu zeigen, wo der Weg verläuft.

Kurz: Wir wollen genau dort hin.

Das weckt den Landy in uns …

Even if Scotland hadn't quite tested us to the limits of our abilities, organising and running a tour on an annual basis was no longer possible. More and more projects were landing on our desks. Customer Experience Tours to Iceland, Namibia and Canada, and more work in our Experience centre in Wülfrath, which had increasingly become the focus of all Land Rover's driving activities. In short, Land Rover decided to run the Experience Tour now only once every two years – I could see it made sense, and to be perfectly honest I was grateful for the respite it gave us. It meant we now had a whole year to plan and run the selection camps to find our six candidates before running the pre-scout and main event the following year. We had more time to organise the event with less stress involved. We could spread one tour over two years' budgets, permitting us to do so much more per tour. Within an instant, we suggested Argentina and Chile with a programme entitled the "Road to the Clouds", and almost immediately we received the go-ahead to start planning.

First we flew to Salta, which we had already chosen as our starting point because of its ideal position in the northwest of Argentina at the edge of the Andes mountain range and its altitude of 3,280 feet above sea level. Salta, a classical colonial town, is also the starting point of one of the world's most famous railway routes, the "Train to the Clouds", which heads into the Andes by way of the La Polvorilla viaduct. Neither Hans nor I had been here before, but researching a destination online – including routes, hotels and agencies – had improved tremendously over the last couple of years.

Or so we thought. We found numerous firms claiming to be the last thing in do-it-yourself tours, only to discover, upon visiting in person, that their interpretation of "tour" was nothing like ours. Quite clearly, these national and regional "specialists" catered to the package-tour segment. Invariably, the response to our plans was something along the lines of "that won't work, that's too dangerous, and that's too high." The people we spoke with spent more time expressing their reservations about what we wanted to do rather than helping us develop ideas. To combat our frustration, we went shopping for maps and explored hotels. Quite by chance, in one hotel we met an Austrian guy called Gerry – he was an original – one of a kind that has long since ceased to exist in Austria. His maxim was "nothing is impossible". He would turn out to be the perfect guide.

Once we had returned to Germany, and with the help of the Internet and our navigation software, we started to put the tour together. Roads and tracks can be identified to within just over 300 feet. Google Earth went live at around the same time, and using various search engines we discovered a story about a bunch of globetrotters who had driven in the Galán crater. Just the word "crater" got us going – this was just the kind of thing we were looking for. We contacted the adventure-seekers hoping to get the exact coordinates for entering and exiting the crater. They couldn't deliver – what kind of con trick was this? Fabulous! If that were the case, and they actually hadn't been to the crater, then it was the perfect opportunity for the Land Rover Experience Tour to show them the way.

This was exactly where we wanted to go.

And it woke the Land Rover in every one of us.

Was nach Bräunungshilfe aus den 70ern aussieht, hat einen ernsthaften Hintergrund: Teekochen mit Solarenergie. Regenerative Energien nutzt man hier schon lange, weil so gut wie kein Feuerholz existiert. Dafür gibt es unter der weißen Salzkruste, die wie ein Meer mit Wellen wirkt, braunen, zähen Schlamm. Autos auszugraben ist in der Höhenluft echte Schwerstarbeit.

It looks like a seventies-style tanning studio but has a more serious job: a solar-powered tea kettle. Regenerative energy has long featured here, as firewood is virtually unheard of. And underneath the white salty crust that has the appearance of a huge lake with waves is tenacious, brown mud. Digging cars out of this stuff at altitude is very hard work.

DIE AMBULANZ
THE AMBULANCE

Unsere Recherchen bringen zunächst eine Gewissheit: Das Abenteuer wird nicht ungefährlich für die körperliche Unversehrtheit der Teilnehmer und aller anderen Mitfahrer – und das allein wegen der großen Höhen, die in den Anden bewältigt werden müssen. Bei rund 30 Menschen, die insgesamt mitfahren sollen, ist die Chance, dass einen von ihnen die unberechenbare Höhenkrankheit trifft, groß. Ich überlege lange, ob wir uns in Sachen medizinische Notfälle noch ein bisschen mehr professionalisieren sollen und entscheide mich noch vor der Haupttour für ein Ja. Das bedeutet: Aufbau eines Ambulanzwagens.

Land Rover unterstützt die Idee sofort mit einem Discovery. Ich entwerfe den Innenraum, Doc Dominik Doerr sorgt für den Feinschliff. Auf engstem Raum gibt es seitdem – natürlich auch dank vieler Sponsoren – alle notfallmedizinischen Instrumente, um über Stunden jede Intensivbehandlung durchführen zu können. Trotzdem ist innen noch genug Platz, um jemanden liegend auf einer Trage zu transportieren. „Wo andere schon aufwendig geflogen werden, werden Sie bei uns noch bequem gefahren", fällt mir schnell als Spruch zu dem rund vier Tonnen schweren Disco ein. Wert des Autos: knapp 200 000 Euro. Wir sind stolz wie Bolle auf das neue, rollende Orga-Mitglied.

Allerdings bringt uns das Gefährt zunächst ganz schön in die Bredouille, gleich zu Anfang bei der Einreise nach Argentinien. Die Zöllner haben überhaupt keine Lust, die Drogen und Betäubungsmittel, mit denen eine gut gepackte Ambulanz nun mal ausgerüstet ist, ins Land zu lassen. Sie schließen den lebensrettenden Wagen weg und üben sich in Taubheit.

Natürlich gilt es wieder, sich etwas einfallen zu lassen. Mit etwas Geduld findet Hans einen bestechlichen Zollbeamten, der uns gegen ein paar Peso zum Sperrbereich im Zoll führt, wo die Ambulanz festsitzt. Unseren bezahlten Konfidenten lassen wir seinen Kollegen erklären, dass wir dringend einen Reifen am Notarztwagen wechseln müssen.

Um unsere Aktion zu tarnen, rollen wir einen dicken Gabelstapler vor die Ambulanz. Dann schlüpfen Gerry und Hans in den Wagen und stopfen alle auf dem Index stehenden Medikamente in blaue Müllsäcke, die sie in einem mitgebrachten Defender deponieren und so verstauen, dass sie nicht auffallen. Zur Sicherheit kleben wir den großen Blaulichtkasten auf dem Dach der Ambulanz noch vollständig ab. Nur die rote Außenfarbe, die können wir nicht ändern. Das macht aber auch nichts: Trotz des auffälligen Kastens auf dem Dach und unserer grinsenden Gesichter können wir mit der Ambulanz daraufhin problemlos den Zollbereich verlassen.

Und das ist gut so: Prompt muss eine Teilnehmerin bei der Haupttour in 4 900 Metern aufgrund von Höhenkrankheitssymptomen behandelt und unter Sauerstoffzugabe in ein niedriger gelegenes Tal gebracht werden. Sowohl unsere Findigkeit als auch die Ambulanz haben sich sofort bezahlt gemacht.

One thing was clear from our research work. Travelling at altitude in the Andes could have serious effects on the health of the participants and everyone else accompanying the tour. With approximately 30 people taking part, the chances were high that at least one of them would suffer from altitude sickness. I thought long and hard about improving our ability to respond to medical emergencies, and before the main event I decided to build an ambulance.

Support from Land Rover was immediately forthcoming, and they provided us with a Discovery. I designed the interior, and our doctor Dominik Doerr provided the final touch. For every subsequent tour, and thanks to the involvement of many sponsors, we now had a vehicle capable of dealing with all manner of medical emergencies, with a full range of intensive-care equipment on board, and which, thanks to good use of the stowage space, still had room for an injured person on a stretcher. "Costly and complicated medevac by plane, or cost-effective and comfortable by Discovery ambulance" is how we pitched the use of the four-ton vehicle valued at around €200,000. We were as pleased as punch with our new member of the organisation team.

That said, our new vehicle got us into trouble the moment we arrived in Argentina. Customs had no intention whatsoever of letting the drugs and other anaesthetics with which any self-respecting ambulance is equipped into the country. The ambulance was impounded lock and key, and customs officials went deaf in both ears.

Time again to tap our creative juices. Patient as ever, Hans found a customs official not averse to a little bribery and corruption who, for a handful of pesos, was prepared to take us to the restricted area where the ambulance was parked. Our inside man told his colleagues that we urgently had to change a wheel on the vehicle.

To camouflage what we were doing, we parked a huge forklift truck in front of the ambulance. Gerry and Hans crept into the Discovery and started removing all the blacklisted substances and packing them in blue bin bags that were then hidden in the Defender we had brought in with us. As an added precaution, using masking tape we completely concealed the blue flashing-light unit. The only thing we couldn't modify was the ambulance's red paint job. Not that it mattered anyway. Despite the obvious-looking box on the roof of the Discovery and our grinning faces we were able to leave customs with the ambulance.

And it was a good job, too – in no time at all, and at an altitude of 16,000 feet above sea level, a female participant had to be treated with oxygen for altitude sickness and was transported down to a lower altitude. Our creativity with customs and the decision to build the Discovery ambulance had both paid off.

DER KLEINKRIEG
THE BORDER INCIDENT

Zunächst läuft die Haupttour lange problemlos, aber natürlich steht uns noch eine ganz spezielle skurrile Situation bevor – so etwas können wir bei jeder Land Rover Experience Tour fast versprechen, ohne es zu planen.

Entlang der Strecke des „Zuges über den Wolken" geht es aus San Pedro de Atacama, Chile, zur Grenze nach Argentinien. Es ist stets einsam da oben, und wir bleiben selbstverständlich immer wieder in Schneefeldern stecken, aber gut gelaunt kommen wir letztlich am Socompa-Pass an. Es ist der höchste Pass für den Zug, auf immerhin 4 895 Metern Höhe, und links und rechts rosten vom Weg abgekommene Lokomotiven, Anhänger und Lastwagen in den Felsen. Hier fährt niemand außer uns freiwillig, und trotzdem halten hier je eine Handvoll Männer in zwei Zollhäuschen akribisch Wache: auf unserer Seite Chilenen, hundert Meter weiter Argentinier.

Für das Verständnis der folgenden Geschichte muss man wissen, dass sich die beiden Länder nicht gerade grün sind und strategisch auch jeden abgelegenen Posten wie diesen hier sehr ernst nehmen. Zur guten Laune der Zöllner trägt auch nicht unbedingt bei, dass eine Wachschicht hier zwei Monate dauert. Wenn sich da vier bis fünf Mann auf den Senkel gehen, und man dann auch noch böse Miene zum eigentlich friedvollen Volksfeind ein paar Meter weiter machen muss, ist klar, dass jede Abwechslung willkommen ist und ausgekostet werden will.

Wir sind – eindeutig – die erste Abwechslung seit langer Zeit.

Lassen uns die Chilenen ohne jegliche Schikanen ausreisen, stellen sich die Argentinier freundlich, aber mächtig quer. Das hat einen eindeutigen Hintergrund: Uns fehlen Stempel in den Pässen für die Autos. Die Zollchefin in Salta hat uns vor ein paar Tagen die Ausreise zwar verboten, aber wir waren trotzdem gefahren. In der Hoffnung, dass Provinzgrenzer nicht so genau in die Papiere schauen. Falsch gedacht.

Na klasse. Wir sind also auf 4 895 Metern Höhe irgendwo zwischen Chile und Argentinien und kommen nicht weiter. Die Chilenen sind sehr freundlich und bieten uns Asyl an, bis alles geklärt ist – wir mögen doch bitte bei ihnen schlafen. Ein eindeutiges Angebot, um den Argentiniern da drüben eins auszuwischen.

Das wollen die Argentinier – die uns ja gerne durchgelassen hätten, aber nicht dürfen – natürlich nicht auf sich sitzen lassen. Bitte, bitte, ob wir nicht bei ihnen schlafen wollten? Schließlich seien das da drüben ja Chilenen.

Um niemanden zu verärgern, teilen wir uns jetzt schon mal auf. Die Hälfte des so genervten wie amüsierten Teutonen-Trecks schlägt ihr Nachtlager bei den Chilenen auf, die andere Hälfte bei den Argentiniern.

Aber bis es ans Schlafen geht, ist der Abend noch lang. Koch Stefan spendiert deswegen Spaghetti für alle – aber wo zubereiten? Bei den Chilenen? Bei den Argentiniern? Wir wählen die Chilenen – nicht ohne die nach ihrer Meinung dubiosen Grenznachbarn auch einzuladen. Und: Es klappt! Leicht unsicher betreten die Argentinier seit weiß der Geier wie vielen Jahren (oder sogar erstmals) das chilenische Grenzerhäuschen, demontieren mit einem Rest von Pflichtbewusstsein ihre argentinischen Epauletten und sind bereit, mit Chilenen samt Deutschen zu essen. Als Nachtisch spielen wir Billard zusammen, gucken das Fußballspiel Chile gegen Kanada, und selbst die Argentinier freuen sich nach ein paar Bier mit den Chilenen, wenn deren Mannschaft ein guter Zug gelingt.

Die Zeit schreitet voran, und voller Euphorie schlachten die Chilenen morgens um 4 Uhr ein zeterndes Huftier in der irrigen Annahme, jemand hätte noch Hunger auf frische chilenische Hochlandziege. Durch diverse Touren diplomatisch geschult verspeisen wir trotz kugelrunder Bäuche noch ein paar Muskelstränge des behörnten Viehs, ehe wir uns zum viel zu kurzen Schlaf verabschieden.

Nach der ungewöhnlichen Nacht lassen uns die scheinbar mit leichten Kopfschmerzen kämpfenden Argentinier auch ohne Stempel ins Land. Dass wir nach der Tour erneut und noch mehr Probleme haben werden, die Autos aus dem Land zu schaffen (wegen inzwischen diverser fehlender Stempel), ist uns in diesem Moment relativ egal.

At first the tour ran like clockwork. Soon enough, however, we were to be faced with another of those bizarre moments which every tour has thrown up and for which you just can't plan. Following the route of the "Train to the Clouds", we headed from San Pedro de Atacama in Chile to the Argentinean border. It is a lonely part of the world, but despite frequent intermissions where we had to dig the vehicles out of the snow we arrived in fine fettle at the Socompa Pass. At an altitude of 16,060 feet, it is the highest mountain pass that the train crosses. Rusting in the rocks below are the remains of locomotives, trailers and trucks that couldn't complete the journey in one piece. With the exception of our convoy, privateers up here were unheard of, and yet on both sides of the border, in their respective customs buildings, a handful of soldiers guarded the border meticulously: on our side the Chileans, and a hundred yards further on, the Argentineans.

To understand why the following story played out as it did, one must recall that there is little love lost between these two countries, and even border crossing points in the back of beyond such as ours are of immense strategic significance. The mood of the customs officials was also not helped by the fact that, for them, a tour of duty in this part of the world lasts two months. Four or five guys cooped up in a hut together, making evil faces at the enemy (who is actually just minding his own business) down the road, were probably looking forward with more than a bit of relish to the break from the usual monotony that our arrival at the border signified. For we were – and this was patently obvious – the only thing to have happened here for a long time.

The Chileans let us exit without any hassle whatsoever. Unlike the Argentineans, who, despite putting on their broadest of smiles, were not going to be co-operative. The reason was simple. We lacked the necessary vehicle stamps in our passports. A few days prior, the head of customs in Salta had explicitly forbidden our leaving the country. We had nevertheless driven off in the hope that those working at the border wouldn't be quite as meticulous when it came to paperwork. Our mistake.

So here we were, at 16,060 feet above sea level, somewhere between Chile and Argentina, and we were stuck. The Chileans were very friendly and offered us asylum, saying we could sleep in their barracks. This was clearly an opportunity for them to poke fun at the "enemy" across the border. The Argentineans, who, as they pointed out, would have loved to let us pass but weren't allowed to, were equally unwilling to take the Chilean affront lying down and asked us whether we would like to stay on their side of the border – they wouldn't feel happy if we were forced to stay with the Chileans.

To maintain some semblance of peace and stability and not cause an international incident, we divided the team up. Half of the crew – who by now were not sure whether to laugh or cry at the whole spectacle – put up their tents on the Chilean side, while the other half went to the Argentineans.

Bedtime was still a while away, though, so our cook Stefan set about making spaghetti for everybody – there was still the question of where to cook the noodles – at the Chilean post, or would it be better to go Argentine…? We chose Chile, making sure that we invited the neighbours over, too, regardless of what the Chileans thought about them. And – it worked. For the first time in who knows how many years (or perhaps at all), the Argentineans warily walked over to the Chilean border-crossing station, prudently removing their Argentinean epaulettes, to sit down for dinner with the Chileans and the Germans. For dessert we hit the pool table, watched some football as Chile was playing against Canada, and after a few beers even the Argentineans were celebrating when the Chilean national team put some moves together against the Canadians.

Time passed rapidly, and by now completely euphoric, the Chileans slaughtered one of their animals, believing in some crazy way that at four in the morning people would not be averse to grilled Chilean mountain goat. Thanks to numerous tours, and despite our full stomachs, we were diplomatically wise enough to force some of the lean meat down before hitting the sacks for a very short night's sleep.

After such an unusual night, the Argentineans, clearly suffering from morning-after syndrome, let us enter their country. At that moment we didn't care a damn, but the missing stamps here and in Salta would cause us further problems later on when it came time to export the vehicles back out of the country.

Manchmal sind es die kleinen, einfachen Dinge, die einem noch lange im Gedächtnis bleiben. Wie zum Beispiel die Begegnung mit dem kleinen Mädchen, weitab von jeder Zivilisation. Man teilt sich einen Apfel, erzählt, wo man herkommt und was man noch alles vorhat auf der Tour. „Ihr seid ja verrückt", sagt sie. Wir können nicht voller Überzeugung widersprechen.

Sometimes it is the little things that stick in your memory. Miles from anywhere, we met this little girl. We gave her an apple, told her where we came from and what we planned to do on the tour. "You're crazy," was all she said. We couldn't disagree with her.

Nach dem 4 895 Meter hohen Socompa-Pass (festgehalten auf dem verwitterten Schild) und stundenlanger Hochland-Fahrt ist der örtliche Supermarkt ein weiteres echtes Highlight.

After the 16,000-foot Socompa Pass (which can be seen on the weather-beaten sign) and hours spent in the highlands, the local supermarket was another highlight.

DER KRATER
THE CRATER

Noch in Deutschland haben wir herausgefunden, wessen Grundstück wir passieren müssen, wenn wir durch den bislang offensichtlich von noch niemandem fahrenderweise bezwungenen Krater Galán rollen wollen. Es ist ein Franzose, der in Paris lebt. Die Dienstreise nach Paris ist erfreulich kurz: Der Mann hat nichts dagegen.

Es wird Zeit, vor Ort die Tour-Strecke zu testen. Die Autos für die Vortour werden nach Buenos Aires verschifft, im Konvoi fahren wir nach Salta – das sind mal eben 2 500 Kilometer. Die Tour steht bald fest: Von Salta Richtung Calama in die Atacamawüste, über San Pedro zum Socompa-Pass, von da aus zurück nach Salta. Das sind rund 1 600 Kilometer – perfekt für die neue Experience Tour. Und jetzt müssen wir nur noch den Krater einbauen.

Krater an sich sind faszinierend, dieser hier ist es auf besondere Weise. Vom Eingang bis zum Ausgang sind es etwa 30 Kilometer, wobei wir den Eingang aus dem Internet kennen, den Weg und den Ausgang allerdings nicht. Mit den Autos fahren wir über das endlos große Farmland des Franzosen, bis der Weg so eng wird, dass fast nur noch Eselskarren durchkommen. Allein die Anfahrt zum Krater dauert so lange, dass es schon Nachmittag ist, als wir den Eingang erreichen. Wir schnaufen bei der Höhe von 4 000 bis 5 000 Metern nicht schlecht, die Autos auch. Nur ganz langsam kriechen wir voran, weil wir versuchen – möglicherweise vom Höhenwahn ergriffen – die Auto-Elektronik zu überlisten. Die Höhensensoren in den Steuergeräten der Discovery verkleben wir mit Gießharz, sodass den Motoren vorgegaukelt wird, sie befänden sich auf 1 200 Metern Höhe. Das Ergebnis: Die Autos qualmen viel mehr, aber die Leistung ist trotzdem weg. Daraufhin befreien wir die Wagen wieder von dem sinnlosen Knebel.

In weiser Voraussicht habe ich erstmals bei einer Vortour einen unserer Docs mitgenommen, der auch prompt zu tun bekommt: Ein Fotograf wird höhenkrank. Gunnar muss mit ihm zurück in die argentinischen Niederungen.

Aber letztlich haben auch wir keine Chance, bei der Vortour den Krater voll zu erkunden. So verlassen wir diesen seltsamen Ort und beauftragen Gerry und seinen Schwager, die Strecke zu Fuß abzulaufen und für uns zu kartografieren, bis wir mit den Teams zur Haupttour wiederkommen.

While still in Germany, we had managed to discover whose land we would have to drive over if we wanted to explore the Galán crater – which as it turned out, had clearly not been driven by anyone thus far. The land belonged to a Frenchman living in Paris. A short flight later, we had our permit.

It was time to test the route ourselves. The pre-scout vehicles were shipped to Buenos Aires, and then we headed in convoy to Salta. A mere 1,553 miles. The tour route had finally been approved. We planned to head from Salta to Calama in the Atacama desert, via San Pedro over the Socompa Pass, and then back to Salta. A round trip of around 1,000 miles, which was perfect for the new Experience Tour. All we had to do now was to add the crater to the route.

Craters are fascinating in and of themselves – this one even more so. From entrance to exit, it was approximately 19 miles, and all we had to go on was the entrance point, which we had found online. The actual route through and the exit remained unknown quantities. We travelled across the steppe-like farmland belonging to the Frenchman until the way narrowed down to a trail barely wide enough to accommodate a donkey and cart. It was past midday before we arrived at the entrance. And at an altitude ranging between 13,000 and 16,000 feet, man and machine alike were constantly gasping for air. The only way we could make progress at all was by tricking the vehicles' electronic sensors. Perhaps we were suffering from altitude sickness ourselves; we covered the altitude sensors in the Discovery's engine management system with resin, thus creating the impression (as far as the engine was concerned) that we were at an altitude of 4,000 feet. The cars produced more smoke as a result, but with performance still down, we decided to free the engines of this unnecessary gag.

Prudently, and for the first time on a pre-scout, I had chosen to bring one of our doctors along. He was needed almost immediately. A photographer started suffering from altitude sickness, and Gunnar had to accompany him back down to the Argentinean lowlands.

At the end of the day, we were also unable to completely recce the crater. As we left this unusual place I asked Gerry and his brother-in-law to complete the section on foot and map the entire stretch before we returned with the teams.

Nur wer genau hinsieht, erkennt ein kleines Land-Rover-Logo auf dem Wegweiser. Waren Gleichgesinnte schon vor uns hier? Oder ist es ein Hinweis, dass man ohne Land Rover hier nicht weiterkommt? Die folgenden Pisten und Offroad-Abschnitte sind jedenfalls eine Freude für jeden Entwicklungsingenieur auf Testfahrt.

If you look closely, you can see the tiny Land Rover logo on the sign. Were friends here before us? Or was it an indication that, without Land Rover, the road ends here? The following tracks and trails are nevertheless a joy for every vehicle-development engineer on shakedown.

DIE FINSTERNIS

THE DARKNESS

Wir sind in Südamerika zur Haupttour bereit. Gerry und sein Schwager haben ihn natürlich nicht geschafft, den mühsamen Marsch durch erkaltete Lava und brennende Sonne. Aber Hand aufs Herz: So eine 30-Kilometer-Wanderung ist selbst für einen Österreicher mit großer Klappe nicht so einfach zu erledigen. So versuchen wir erstmals seit Beginn der Land-Rover-Experience-Haupttouren, einen Weg zu finden, den wir vorher nicht bereits ausprobiert haben.

Wir wollen unbedingt durch den Krater – und die Teams wollen es auch. Obwohl wir hinter unserem Zeitplan hängen und den Krater auch umfahren könnten, wagen wir das Abenteuer. Es ist bereits 17 Uhr, als wir am Eingang ankommen. Der Plan: 30 Kilometer fahren, dann gegen Mitternacht Campsite aufbauen. Eigentlich ein wunderbares Vorhaben.

Doch gleich am Eingang zeigt uns der Boden, dass er nicht gewillt ist, sich uns anzupassen. Wir müssen uns nach ihm richten. Wir tasten uns am Rand eines Salzsees entlang – auf Google Earth war nicht zu erkennen, wie weich der Untergrund ist. Inzwischen läuft jeder Beifahrer vor dem Auto seines Piloten, um den Boden zu testen, und es wird immer dunkler. Und dunkler. Bis es stockdunkel ist. Also schwarz. Tiefschwarz.

Die erkalteten Lavamassen fressen jedes Restlicht, sodass einige Teams nun vollends die Orientierung verlieren. Und auch wir Reiseprofis müssen uns mehr auf unsere Erfahrung als auf unsere Augen verlassen. Wir erahnen Felsen und Steine am Kraterrand im fahlen Licht der Scheinwerfer mehr, als dass wir sie wirklich wahrnehmen.

Die „Fußgänger" können ihren Weg nur noch mithilfe von Stirnlampen erraten, trotzdem verlaufen sich einige. Ich muss sie zurückholen und beschließe, dass nur noch die Verantwortlichen wie Hans und ich mit unseren Autos den Weg suchen, die Teams dann nur noch vorsichtig folgen. Es ist einfach zu gefährlich für die ungeübten Teilnehmer.

Aber auch auf diese Weise kommen wir kaum voran. Immer wieder bleibt ein Auto stecken, erkennt ein Scout zu spät eine Sackgasse, muss irgendwer um einen viel zu großen Felsbrocken herumrangieren. Die Zeit vergeht, und als ich endlich eine kleine Ebene entdecke, auf die alle zehn Autos samt Zelten passen, ist es 4 Uhr morgens. Die Aufmerksamkeit ist nun völlig verbraucht, die Kraft verschwunden, die Laune durchwachsen. Ich beschließe, dass wir hier bleiben. Es ist verdammt kalt, deswegen werden die Bodenzelte extrem schnell aufgebaut. Koch Stefan kreiert ein Gebräu, dass uns trotz der Strapazen glücklich macht: Kaffee mit Chilipulver.

Am nächsten Morgen um halb sieben wache ich auf und bin putzmunter, als ich nach draußen blicke. Es ist schlicht nicht ersichtlich, wie wir hierher gekommen sind. Alles, was ich rundherum sehe, ist eigentlich unfahrbar: senkrechte Wände um uns herum oder große Felsbrocken, die wir niemals hätten bewegen können. Ich weiß bis heute nicht, wie wir es in der niemals wieder so empfundenen Dunkelheit geschafft haben, das kleine Plateau zu erreichen. Aber manchmal ist das auch nicht wichtig. Wichtig ist, es überhaupt zu schaffen. Und dafür sind wir hergekommen.

Letztlich verhilft uns die Argentinien/Chile-Tour zu unserem kompletten Durchbruch in der Abenteuer-Branche. Wir haben bewiesen, dass wir mit Land Rover überall hinkommen. Deswegen schaut die Company über den Tellerrand hinaus und entschließt sich, ein Presse-Event mit mehr als 120 Journalisten aus aller Welt mit den Autos hier in Südamerika zu veranstalten – das überaus erfolgreich absolviert wird.

We were ready to start the main event in South America. Naturally, Gerry and his brother-in-law hadn't managed the physically debilitating march across the solidified lava field under the burning sun. But if we're being completely honest here, the 19-mile walk was a long way, even for an Austrian with a big mouth. So for the first time ever on a Land Rover Experience Tour, we would be attempting a route that we hadn't previously tested.

For us, it was essential that we drive the crater, and the teams felt the same way. Although we were behind schedule and could have circumvented the crater altogether, we decided to take the plunge. It was already 5 in the afternoon when we arrived at the entrance. The plan was to drive the 19 or so miles and set up camp around midnight. Actually, it was a wonderful plan.

From the outset, though, the ground wasn't willing to go along with our plan, and we had to bow to its demands. We explored the edge of a salt lake – on Google Earth we hadn't been able to ascertain how soft the ground was. Meanwhile all the co-drivers had taken to walking in front of their vehicles to test the ground. It was getting darker by the minute, and very soon it was absolutely pitch black.

The solidified lava formations literally swallowed whatever light there was, and as a result, some of the teams could no longer recognise east from west or north from south. We, the travel professionals, had to rely more on our experience than on our eyes. Rock faces and stones on the edge of the crater, which can just be made out at long range using the headlights, are more figments of our imagination than real geographical features.

The "pedestrians" were now almost completely reliant on their own personal headlamps – yet some managed to lose their way. I had to go out and get them while at the same time deciding that, as Hans and I were in charge, it was our task to lead the way, leaving the teams to follow us. For the participants, who were unused to such situations, it had become simply too dangerous.

This method didn't improve our speed over the ground, however. Again and again, vehicles bogged down, and we entered one dead-end after the next before recognising our mistake and having to backtrack, or we had to manoeuvre around a large rock. Hours passed, and by the time I had discovered a flat area large enough for us to park up the vehicles and pitch our tents, it was 4 am. People's powers of concentration were gone by now, and the same could be said for their stamina – the mood was so-so at best. I decided that we would pitch camp here. It was absolutely freezing, and for that reason we put the tents up as quickly as possible. Stefan made up a drink that perked us up a bit: coffee with chilli powder.

I awoke at 6:30 that morning and was gobsmacked when I looked out of the tent. It was impossible to see how we had got here. The terrain appeared virtually impassable in every direction, as far as the eye could see. Vertical rock faces and huge boulders, which we would never have been able to move, were scattered across the landscape. To this day, I have no idea how we managed to find the plateau in the darkness. Sometimes the "how" isn't important – what is important is that you achieved it in the first place. And that was why we were here.

In the final analysis, the Argentina/Chile Tour helped to establish us as a significant player in the adventure market. We had successfully shown that we could literally go anywhere with Land Rover. Land Rover also demonstrated that it could think "out-of-the-box" and chose to run a media event for 120 international journalists with the vehicles in South America – a roaring success.

DOMINIK DOERR

geb. 25.11.1966 // Facharzt für Innere Medizin, Sport- und Notfallmedizin,
Notarzt in der Luftrettung, Internist, Verbandsarzt des Bundesverbandes deutscher Gewichtheber

born 25 November 1966 // specialist in internal medicine, sports and emergency medicine,
helicopter rescue doctor and physician for the German Weightlifting Federation

Du bist der zweite Doc der Land Rover Experience Tour. Wie bist du dazu gekommen?

Dominik: 2006 habe ich die G4 Challenge mitgemacht, da habe ich Hans kennengelernt. Gleich darauf war ich bei den Touren 2007 in Argentinien, 2008 in Malaysia, 2011 in Bolivien und bei der Jubiläumstour auf den Spuren der Seidenstraße dabei.

Wobei wurde dein Fachwissen benötigt?

Dominik: Eingreifen musste ich schon bei der G4: ein Polytrauma, ein Höhenlungenödem sowie einige leichtere Fälle von Höhenkrankheit; in Argentinien/Chile wie auch in Bolivien gab es ebenfalls leichtere Fälle von Höhenkrankheiten und Wundversorgungen, in Malaysia hauptsächlich Wundversorgungen und die Versorgung von Blutegelattacken.

Immer wieder diese Höhenkrankheit. Ist dagegen denn gar kein Kraut gewachsen?

Dominik: Nein. Grundsätzlich besteht schon ab etwa 3 000 Meter – bei manchen Menschen schon ab 2 500 Meter – ein Risiko, höhenkrank zu werden. Es gibt keine wirklich sinnvolle Vorbeugung und auch keine Faktoren, mit denen man eine Vorhersage treffen könnte, wer höhenkrank wird und wer nicht. Auch körperliche Fitness hat keinen Einfluss darauf. Allerdings kann sie dafür sorgen, dass man mit guter Konstitution in der Höhe leistungsfähiger ist.

Wie testest du auf den Touren, ob es den Mitfahrern gut geht oder nicht?

Dominik: Mit dem Pulsoximeter kann ich die Sauerstoffkonzentration im Blut abschätzen – aber nicht wirklich messen, da dies eine Genauigkeit impliziert, die unter Extrembedingungen nicht gewährleistet ist. Sie gibt aber Hinweise, ob sich eine Hypoxie, also ein Sauerstoffmangel, anbahnt oder nicht.

Welches Erlebnis ist dir besonders im Gedächtnis hängen geblieben?

Dominik: Beeindruckende Momente gab es reichlich. Als ganz besonders bleibt mir unsere Übernachtung auf dem Socompa-Pass an der chilenisch-argentinischen Grenze in Erinnerung, als wir aufgrund einer sturen Zoll-Bürokratin in der Distrikthauptstadt Salta nicht gleich nach Argentinien einreisen konnten und „gezwungenermaßen" ein schönes Fest mit den Zöllnern beider (!) Seiten veranstaltet haben – und es schließlich zum Handschlag zwischen den beiden jeweiligen Kommandanten kam, was nach dem Falklandkrieg (die Chilenen haben die SAS, die Spezialeinheit der Engländer, unterstützt) auch heute noch nicht selbstverständlich ist.

You are the second doctor to take part in the Land Rover Experience Tour. How did that come about?

Dominik: In 2006 I took part in the G4 Challenge, where I met Hans. Pretty much straight after I took part in the Argentina Tour in 2007, in Malaysia in 2008, Bolivia in 2011 and the anniversary tour along the Silk Road.

On which tours were you required to go to work?

Dominik: I needed to intervene on the G4 Challenge: polytrauma, a pulmonary oedema, as well as mild cases of altitude sickness; in Argentina/Chile as well as Bolivia we also had some mild altitude sickness and wounds that needed to be treated; in Malaysia it was largely wounds and treatment of leech bites.

I keep hearing altitude sickness. Is there nothing that you can do?

Dominik: No. The risk of contracting altitude sickness is ever-present from about 9,800 feet upwards, for some people even from 8,000 feet. There is no really sensible prophylaxis and no factors by which one can predict who is likely to suffer and who isn't. Physical fitness has no real influence, either. Having a good constitution does mean that one is more physically able at altitude, however.

On tour, how do you test the participants' condition?

Dominik: The pulse oximeter can estimate the levels of oxygen in the blood. It is not so precise as to be able to measure specific levels, as this is not possible in extreme conditions. However, it gives me an indication of whether or not there is a danger of hypoxia or oxygen depravation.

Is there any particular incident that has really stuck in your memory?

Dominik: There have been many impressive moments, but one incident really stands out, and that was our enforced overnight stay on the Socompa Pass on the Argentinean-Chilean border as the result of a particularly bureaucratic civil servant in the regional capital of Salta. Given the fact that in the Falklands War the Chileans had supported the British Special Air Service against the Argentineans, the party we had with the customs officers from both (!) sides of the border, and the handshake between the two commanding officers, was something you couldn't take for granted – even in 2007, many years after the war.

MALAYSIA

MALAYSIA
2008
7 FREELANDER, 4 DEFENDER,
1 AMBULANCE DISCOVERY
STRECKE / DISTANCE: 1200 KM / 750 MILES

Erholungsreise? Noch glauben die Teilnehmer der achten Land Rover Experience Tour daran. Sie werden in einem luxuriösen Hotel verwöhnt, dürfen im Wasser planschen und die Seele baumeln lassen. Der Blick in den Dschungel verrät noch nicht, dass dies eine der anstrengendsten Touren wird – denn der Regen wird kommen …

The vacation of a lifetime – or so participants in the eighth Land Rover Experience Tour thought at first. Spoilt in a luxury hotel, bathing in the pool, forgetting about your worries. The jungle would turn out to be one of the most strenuous tours thus far – as rain was on its way…

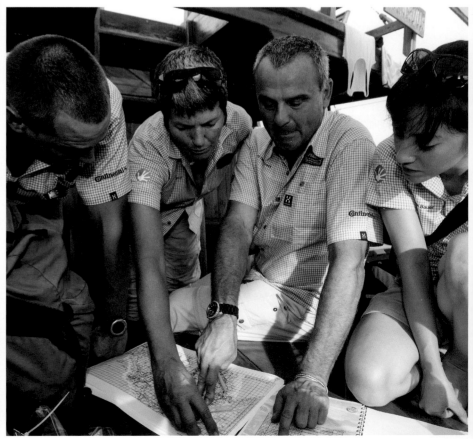

DIE FEHLEINSCHÄTZUNG
THE MISJUDGEMENT

Australien? China? Malaysia? Wie üblich zerbrechen wir uns die Köpfe, wie wir die große vorherige Experience Tour wieder einmal toppen können. Drei Destinationen schlagen wir Land Rover vor, unser Favorit ist eindeutig Malaysia. Ziel: der Dschungel. Den kennen wir bereits aus Mittelamerika, der verspricht Abenteuer bis in jeden Bach und jede Wurzel. Wie Recht wir damit behalten sollen, stellt sich allerdings erst später heraus.

Natürlich wird Malaysia gewählt. Unsere ersten Befürchtungen, organisatorische Probleme mit den Autos zu bekommen, eventuelle Sprachschwierigkeiten, asiatisches Chaos oder zu verschiedene Kulturkreise, erweisen sich als Luftblase. Die Menschen sind extrem freundlich, hilfsbereit, und die lange englische Herrschaft über das Land hilft bei der Verständigung enorm. Noch nie war es so einfach, die benötigten Autos einzuführen inklusive des voll ausgerüsteten Ambulanz-Discovery.

Unsere erste Reise nach Malaysia zur Guide-Suche endet schon bei der ersten Agentur, die wir anpeilen: Hier finden wir engagierte junge Offroad-Fans. Besonders einer sticht heraus: Shah, ein Malaie, der dort mit kurzer Hose und gelben Kniestrümpfen parat steht wie ein junger Offizier einer Fantasiearmee. Noch nie vorher konnten wir uns so schnell – und nach so herrlichem Essen, besten Hotels und perfekter Landeseinführung – wieder in Deutschland unseren Orga-Aufgaben widmen.

Die Reisestrecke ist schnell gefunden: von der Insel Langkawi vor der Nordwestküste Malaysias etwa 1 200 Kilometer durchs Land auf die andere Seite zur Ostküste ins Strandhotel. Dazwischen: Dschungel, was sonst. Und nichts anderes. Dass wir wohl auch mal den einen oder anderen umgekippten Baum zerteilen werden oder auch eine Brücke bauen müssen, ist mir so klar wie nichts. Deswegen gibt es in den Qualifikationscamps bereits eine komplette Ausbildung an Stihl-Kettensägen, denn auch im Urwald kann man nicht einfach drauflos zerkleinern. Das will gelernt sein, schon alleine damit nicht irgendwem rein zufällig so ein Urwaldriese auf seinen Abenteurerkopf fällt.

Für die Qualifikationscamps melden sich nun rund 20000 abenteuerhungrige Menschen – eine tolle Bestätigung, dass wir auf dem richtigen Weg sind. Wenn die späteren Sieger allerdings gewusst hätten, was auf sie zukommt, hätten die meisten wohl dankbar abgewunken.

Where to next? Australia? China? Or Malaysia? We started scratching our heads and wondering how we could top the previous year's amazing Experience Tour. We suggested three possible destinations, and our clear favourite was Malaysia. Objective: jungle. We knew the jungle from the Central American tour, where adventure could be found pouring from every stream and hiding behind every root. We would later discover just how right we had been.

Of course it had to be Malaysia. Any initial fears – regarding vehicle shipping, possible language difficulties, Asian chaos or simply cultural diversity – turned out to be groundless. The local population was extremely helpful, and the fact that it was a former British colony helped communication enormously. Importing the vehicles, including the Discovery ambulance with all its medical supplies on board, had never been so simple. Our first trip to Malaysia to search for a guide came up trumps with the first agency we approached. We encountered highly motivated, young off-road fans, and one in particular immediately caught our attention: Shah was a Malay wearing shorts and yellow socks, and to be honest, he looked like an extra from a Beatles movie. In next to no time, having enjoyed fantastic food, amazing hotels and a perfect introduction to the country, we were back in Germany getting on with organising the main event.

We were able to put the route together in rapid time: starting from the island of Langkawi off the north coast of Malaysia and then heading some 750 miles across the country towards the east coast finishing in a hotel on the beach. And in between: nothing but jungle. Removing trees that blocked our route and building the odd bridge or two were on the agenda – and ultimately what the Experience was all about. For the selection camps, we had prudently planned a complete training session on handling Stihl chainsaws, as we wouldn't be able to hack everything into matchwood in the rain forest. We needed a proper training course to ensure that the participants wouldn't start felling trees onto one another.

That we had 20,000 would-be adventurers apply for the selection camps was a fantastic confirmation that we had made the right decision. That said, if the lucky six winners had known what awaited them in the rainforest, most of them might have reconsidered coming at all.

Auf Regen folgt Schlamm: Schon kurz nach dem Start wird klar, dass der Konvoi stellenweise höchstens im Schritttempo vorankommt und immer beisammenbleiben muss, um sich gegenseitig zu helfen – sowohl mit Muskelkraft als auch mit Winden. Kein Wunder, dass am Abend alle Mitreisenden an Ort und Stelle umfallen und schlafen.

Rain is followed by mud. Relatively soon after the start, it was clear that much of the route could only be driven at walking pace and that vehicles would have to stick together in order to be able to help each other with muscle power and winches. It wasn't surprising, then, that in the evening everybody stayed put and slept where they were.

DER BAUM
THE TREE

Wir lernen schnell. Zum Beispiel, dass eine Kettensäge, mit der man einen deutschen Durchschnittsgarten nach allen Regeln der Kunst in sämtliche Kleinteile zerlegen kann, im Dschungel nur ein stumpfer Zahnstocher ist. Natürlich treffen wir bereits auf der Vortour schnell auf einen umgekippten Baum, der den Weg – meistens alte Holzfällerpisten – komplett blockiert. Mit unserer motorisierten Kindersäge schaffen wir gerade mal einen Schnitt von 20 Zentimeter Tiefe in das Hartholz des etwa 120 Zentimeter dicken Stammes, bevor sich die Kette erstmals mit hässlichem Geräusch verabschiedet. Zunächst legen wir sie akribisch wieder in ihre Führung, aber immer öfter springt sie heraus und wird stumpf. Mit Nagelfeilen schleifen wir die Kette nach, und drei Stunden später arbeiten wir immer noch an dem hartnäckigen Stück Dschungelholz mit der Säge – und inzwischen auch mit den Winden der Autos.

Für uns ist klar: Die Land Rover Experience Tour wird mit solchen Aufgaben fertig und wächst daran. Egal was kommt, wir bleiben auf dem Weg. Und lösen solche Probleme nicht so wie zum Beispiel die Rainforest Challenge: Die bricht durchs Gehölz ohne Rücksicht auf Verluste – sei es bei sich oder in der Natur. Die lassen sogar Autos im Dschungel zurück, wenn es gar nicht anders geht. So etwas kommt für uns nicht in Frage. Was mit auf die Tour kommt, nehmen wir auch wieder mit nach Hause.

Doch die Frage stellt sich auf der Vortour nicht. Ein bisschen Matsch, ein bisschen Schlamm, mal eine weggefaulte Brücke – perfekt für die Experience Tour. Dazu Kultur, zum Beispiel ein Besuch in den Cameron Highlands nahe der Hauptstadt Kuala Lumpur, wo es neben wunderbarem Tee und leckeren Erdbeeren vor allem die größte Dichte an alten Land Rover der Serien II bis III gibt. Der Grund: Viele Solihuller ließen die Briten einfach dort zurück, als Malaysia 1963 aus dem Commonwealth entlassen wurde; immer mehr kamen im Laufe der Zeit hinzu, weil sie sich als zuverlässig erwiesen. Da die nun teils schrottreifen Lastenträger hier weder Steuern bezahlen müssen noch einer technischen Überwachung unterliegen, so lange sie ein großes „CH" auf den Seiten tragen und das fest definierte Gebiet der Cameron Highlands nicht verlassen, dienen die meisten von ihnen bis heute als unverzichtbare Transportmittel – wenn sie auch inzwischen mit japanischen Getrieben, koreanischen Motoren und selbstgemachten Ersatzteilen gespickt sind. Nach Schätzungen fahren hier in einem Gebiet von rund 700 Quadratkilometern etwa 7 000 Land Rover.

We learnt quickly. For example, that a chainsaw designed to chop the average German garden into bits is nothing more than a blunt toothpick in the jungle. On the pre-scout recce we encountered more than one tree blocking the logging routes. Our toy chainsaws could barely cut 8 inches into the four-foot-wide hardwood trunk before the chain stopped with a disturbing gurgling noise. We meticulously re-positioned the chain in its guide, but to no avail, as it repeatedly jumped out of the guide before rapidly going blunt. We sharpened the chain teeth with nail files, but three hours later we were still at work on this stubborn piece of timber, having also reverted to using the winches on the vehicles to remove it.

For us, it was almost a matter of principle. The Land Rover Experience Tour has to deal with situations like these – they are what make the tour so special. Regardless of what is in the way, we stick to the prescribed route, in contrast to an event such as the Rainforest Challenge, which has no scruples when it comes to tearing through the undergrowth, no matter the cost to man, material or the environment. Vehicles that can't be recovered are simply left behind in the jungle. For us, this is simply out of the question. What comes on the tour goes home with the tour.

The pre-scout recce was not dogged by such issues, though. There was a bit of dirt, a bit of mud and the odd rotten bridge to repair – all of which would be perfect for the Experience Tour. On top of that, we had a true cultural highlight in the Cameron Highlands region near the capital city of Kuala Lumpur. Aside from fabulous tea blends and delicious strawberries, the region is also famous for its large population of historic Series II and III Land Rovers. When Malaysia officially left the Commonwealth in 1963, the British left many of their Land Rovers behind. Many more joined the original vehicles over the years, as they were simple to maintain. Today, the Land Rovers of the Cameron Highlands are immediately recognisable, thanks to a large "CH" painted on the side that exempts them from tax and any form of vehicle inspection but also restricts their operation to the Cameron Highlands. To all appearances now on their last legs, the workhorses are very popular and have been kept on the road with all manner of Japanese gearboxes, Korean engines and a host of other DIY parts. It is estimated that there are over 7,000 Land Rovers on the job in the 270-square-mile region.

Keine Pause im Kampf ums Fortkommen: Die Tour durch den malaysischen Dschungel wird zur echten Feuerprobe für Körper und Geist. Noch nie war Teamfähigkeit so wichtig wie hier.

No rest for the wicked keen to make progress. The tour through the Malaysian jungle proved a true ordeal for body and spirit. Never before had team spirit been so important.

DIE SCHALTER

THE SWITCHES

Als die Haupttour startet, schauen sich die Gewinner – wie meistens bestehend aus drei Frauen und drei Männern – erst mal irritiert um. Wir bringen sie auf die Insel Langkawi, wo es keine Autos zu genießen gibt, sondern nur hellblaue Lagunen, Sonne sowie ein Top-Hotel. Und als wir schließlich mit einem Motorsegler nach einer vierstündigen Bootstour aufs Festland übersetzen, beschweren sie sich bereits scherzhaft über diese „Urlaubsreise".

Am Festland finden sie dann ihre Freelander vor: völlig serienmäßig ausgestattet bis auf etwas grobstolligere Reifen von der Continental-Marke Uniroyal, einen extra montierten Unterfahrschutz sowie Dachgepäckträger mit Ersatzrädern. Bereits in Jordanien hatte sich gezeigt, welchen Vorteil manchmal kleinere und leichtere Geländewagen haben, und so bin ich guter Dinge, was die Leistungsfähigkeit der Freelander angeht. Die für schweres Gelände nicht optimale Bodenfreiheit macht mir etwas Sorgen. Aber die Vortour haben die Wagen ja auch problemlos geschafft – was soll schon werden?

Insgesamt fährt ein Dutzend Land Rover mit, die ich in drei Gruppen einteile. Die drei Gewinnerteams sollen jeweils führen, um ihrer Aufgabe – diesmal ausschließlich Navigieren – gerecht zu werden.

Ich fahre ganz hinten in der Ambulanz nach dem letzten Dreierpack, neben mir Doc Dominik. Vor mir lenkt Journalistin Melanie den Führungs-Freelander unserer kleinen Einheit, und sie meldet sich über Funk: „Ich wollte gerade mein iPhone einstöpseln, da geht das Navi aus." Wir halten kurz an, ich fummele etwas an den Schaltern, und schon funktioniert alles wieder. Melanie ist begeistert.

Wir sind noch keine 3 Kilometer weitergefahren, da meldet sich Melanie wiederum: „Ich glaube, mein linkes Vorderlicht geht nicht." Ich gebe zu, mir ist etwas langweilig, und im tiefsten Inneren bin ich immer mal wieder ein kleiner Junge, also antworte ich: „Du hast wahrscheinlich den CO_2-Schalter angeknipst, denn die Autos sind ja Prototypen."

Stille. Eine merkwürdige Stille. Niemand nutzt den Funk. Zeit für mich, grinsend nachzusetzen: „Die Freelander haben vier CO_2-Schalter. Das bedeutet, man kann die vier Lichtquellen an den Fahrzeugecken einzeln ausschalten. Aber nie die beiden hinteren oder die beiden vorderen Leuchteinheiten gleichzeitig. Aus Sicherheitsgründen. Mit dem System wird die Generatorleistung reduziert und man senkt automatisch den CO_2-Ausstoß."

Von vorn kommt nur ein trockenes „Okay" durch den Äther, und der Doc und ich haben Mühe, uns vor Lachen im Sitz zu halten. Das wird nicht besser, als nach zwei Minuten Melanies Beifahrer – logischerweise ebenfalls ein Journalist – sich auf unserem Kanal meldet: „Kannst Du das noch einmal wiederholen?"

Ich bin ja im Grunde ein freundlicher Mensch, deshalb erkläre ich die ganze Chose noch einmal, gespickt mit ein paar hanebüchenen technischen Raffinessen. Dann frage ich Melanie: „Sag mal, hast du vielleicht vor dem Start schon auf einen der CO_2-Schalter gedrückt? Dann geht nämlich das Navi aus. Das ist technisch noch nicht so ausgereift." Das weckt inzwischen einen Autojournalisten in Auto Nummer zwei unserer Dreier-Kolonne: „Echt?" Nachdem ich nicht mehr ganz so viel prusten muss, kläre ich die Geschichte auf, ehe der Redakteur die Geschichte der „neuen CO_2-Schalter von Land Rover" online stellt.

Als wir als letzter im Mini-Konvoi abends in der fast romantischen Dschungel-Campsite mit Lagerfeuer und ohne Zeitdruck ankommen, haben wir beschlossen, das Schalter-Spiel noch etwas fortzuführen. Als Land-Rover-Pressechef Paul auf mich zukommt, nehme ich ihn sichtlich erregt beim Kragen, schleppe ihn in eine dunkle Ecke und frage ihn, warum er mich über die CO_2-Schalter nicht aufgeklärt hat. „Welche CO_2-Schalter?", fragt er verdutzt zurück. „Ich dachte, man könne aus Sicherheitsgründen nur zwei Quellen auf einmal abschalten", knurre ich ihn an und kippe die Story ins Absurde, „aber es geht auch einzeln!" „Sag bloß kein Wort", antwortet Paul nach Luft schnappend, „das darf nicht rauskommen!" Meine Gruppe, die das Zwiegespräch planmäßig mitbekommt, macht sich vor Lachen inzwischen fast in die kurzen Hosen.

Jetzt bin ich in meinem Element. Und erhöhe den Druck: „Der Auto-Journalist hat das bereits mitbekommen, ich habe ihn schon telefonieren sehen." Paul ist völlig aufgelöst und informiert Christian Uhrig, unseren Marketingchef. Der antwortet: „Ich habe bereits davon gehört …"

Bevor ich meinen Job verliere, löse ich das Rätsel dann schnell für alle auf. Ein Highlight will ich allerdings noch draufsetzen, und zwar mit einem Fernsehinterview – just for fun und für mein persönliches Video-Album. So bitte ich die mitreisenden Jungs von „Abenteuer Auto", mit mir ein gefaktes Gespräch zu diesem Thema zu führen. So stelle ich einen Freelander vor eine Palmölfabrik, die alle 30 Sekunden eine grauenhaft schwarze Wolke aus einem Ofenrohr ausstößt, setze mich ins Auto und fabuliere über die sagenhaften CO_2-Schalter, unter anderem mit einer Close-up-Aufnahme der ersten vier Radiostationstasten. Und immer, wenn der Interviewer etwas über Zukunft und Innovation fragt, stänkert hinter dem Freelander eine schwarze Wolke hervor. Es fällt mir wirklich schwer, halbwegs ernst dabei zu bleiben.

Das Lachen gefriert mir allerdings, als ich nach der Tour erfahre, dass die Spaßvögel von „Abenteuer Auto" vergessen haben, das Pseudo-Interview herauszuschneiden, bevor sie das ganze Material ihrer Redaktion überließen. Ich fahre persönlich und ein bisschen zu schnell zu deren Hauptsitz nach München, um das Material noch rechtzeitig zu sichern.

As we kicked off the main event, the six winners, as always three men and three women, were initially somewhat confused. We had brought them to the fabulous island of Langkawi, where there are no cars at all, just beautiful blue lagoons. And then we put them in a luxury hotel. Finally we jumped aboard a motor yacht for a four-hour voyage to the mainland. No wonder, then, that jokes about luxury holidays started coming thick and fast.

Once on the mainland, they encountered their Freelanders. Other than specialist Continental rough-terrain, off-road tyres, additional underbody protection plates as well as roof racks and spare tyres the vehicles were all standard, as they had come from the factory. We had already seen the benefits of smaller, lighter four-wheel-drive vehicles on the Jordan Tour, so I was not at all worried that the Freelanders would not be up the job. Lack of ground clearance was an issue I thought might cause us some heartache in this terrain. That said, they had mastered the pre-scout recce without a whimper.

We had twelve Land Rovers in all, which I divided into three groups. The three teams of participants were assigned the task of leading each group – and, of course, navigating their way through the jungle.

I was driving the ambulance with Dominic the doctor on board and took up my position at the end of the last team of vehicles. In front of me, the journalist Melanie, who was driving the lead Freelander in our group, radioed, "I just connected my iPhone, and the GPS screen went dead." We stopped, and I played around with the switches and got everything working again. Melanie was impressed.

2 miles down the track, Melanie was on the radio again: "I think my left front light isn't working." OK, I was bored, and deep inside I am still a little boy, so I answered, "You probably hit the CO_2 switch by mistake as the cars are prototypes."

Silence. A very strange silence. Nobody was using the radio. Time for me to go one step further while grinning from ear to ear, "The Freelander is equipped with four CO_2 switches you can use to switch off the lights on all four corners of the vehicle individually, but never both lights at the front or both lights at the rear simultaneously for safety reasons. The system is designed to reduce demand on the alternator, thereby reducing the vehicle's CO_2 emissions."

From up ahead we heard a dry "Okay" over the airwaves, and the Doc and I struggled to prevent ourselves from breaking out in fits of giggles. After two minutes things got more complicated when Melanie's co-driver, who was also a journalist, spoke up, asking, "Can you repeat that, please?"

I am a nice guy, so I explained the whole thing once again, though this time with a topping of technical mumbo-jumbo for good measure. Then I asked Melanie, "Did you press one of the CO_2 switches before we set off today? That might explain why the GPS screen went dead – the system still has a few bugs." By now, one of the car journalists in our group had woken up to the conversation and spoke up on the radio: "Really?" After I stopped laughing, I came clean over the tale before the journalist put the story about "Land Rover's CO_2 switch" online.

That evening, as our mini-convoy rolled up in relaxed fashion in front of the almost romantic jungle campsite complete with campfire, we decided to give the switch story an extra airing. As Land Rover PR manager Paul walked over to me, I grabbed him by the arm and took him over to a corner of the campsite and asked him why he hadn't told me about the CO_2 switch. "What CO_2 switch?" he asked, bewildered. "I thought you could only switch two lights off simultaneously for safety reasons," I whispered, now adding an even more absurd twist into the tale, "They can be switched off individually." Paul, who was still completely bewildered, just said, "That's enough – none of this must ever get out!" My group, which was listening to the conversation on the sly as planned, struggled to keep quiet.

Of course now I was on a high, so I turned up the pressure a little: "The journalist has already found out, and I could see that he was on the phone. Paul was now more than just a little confused and informed our head of marketing, Christian Uhrig, who commented, "I've heard about this, too…"

Before someone fired me, I once again came clean with the truth. But there was still a final chapter to the tale, one involving a TV interview – just for fun, for my own personal video album. I asked the guys from the German TV programme "Abenteuer Auto" to do a fake interview on the topic. I parked a Freelander in front of a factory producing palm oil and waxed lyrical about the amazing CO_2 switches with a close-up of the four radio-station buttons. Every time the interviewer asked about the future and innovation, a cloud of black smoke billowed out behind the Freelander. It was very difficult to keep a straight face.

I soon stopped laughing, though, when I heard that the TV jokers had forgotten to remove the fake interview before handing their material over to the studio. I personally drove to their head office in Munich, and at risk of losing my driving licence, to make sure that the material wasn't broadcast.

Die Strapazen lassen sich leichter ertragen, wenn der Magen gut versorgt wird – natürlich mit leckerem Essen aus der einheimischen Küche.

Hard work is easier to cope with on a full stomach – naturally thanks to the culinary delights of local cuisine.

DER SCHLAMM
THE MUD

Der Abend am Lagerfeuer wird für ein paar Tage der letzte sein, an dem wir so richtig herzhaft lachen können. Denn es fängt an zu regnen. Und wenn es im malaysischen Urwald regnet, dann bedeutet das eimerweise Wasser pro Quadratmeter Boden, was im Dschungel Schlamm bis zu den Kniekehlen und auch höher nach sich zieht.

Ich habe die Kombination von Regen und Boden tatsächlich unterschätzt. Erste Maßnahme gegen die Naturgewalten: Der Konvoi muss zusammenbleiben, damit sich die Fahrzeuge und Mannschaften gegenseitig helfen können. Daraus folgt, dass wir statt dem von uns anvisierten Schnitt von 30 Kilometern pro Stunde etwa 3 schaffen. Immer wieder bleiben die Freelander hängen. Aber der Ambulanz-Discovery und die Defender ebenso – der Schlamm ist verdammt tief.

Zu tief zum schnellen Vorankommen, aber nicht zu tief für die Land Rover Experience Tour. Zeitweise bauen wir Steine unter die Sandbleche, damit wir eine „Pfütze" passieren können, an anderen Stellen nutzen wir das komplette Equipment an Winden, wieder woanders müssen nicht nur die Teilnehmer und das Orga-Team in den Schlamm tauchen und schieben, sondern auch die begleitenden Journalisten. An mehreren Stellen müssen wir mit Muskel- und Motorkraft einen Freelander mit Winde durch die Schwachstelle bugsieren und ihn dann umdrehen, damit er über seine Winde samt Umlenkrollen die anderen Autos nachholen kann. Es ist knallhart, es ist teuflisch anstrengend, es ist übermäßig ermüdend, aber es funktioniert.

Der Brückenbau, der immer mal wieder notwendig wird, ist dagegen kein Problem – unsere auf der Haupttour mitgeführte Säge (diesmal im XXXL-Format) erweist sich als dschungeltauglich. Unsere Erfahrung damit ist inzwischen groß, die Arbeitsabläufe sind klar gegliedert, der Spruch der Reise lautet: „Mut zur Brücke".

Wir campen nachts direkt auf der Straße, auf dem Waldboden, in den Autos, auf den Autos, oder was sich auch immer anbietet – falls man nicht sowieso einfach am Ort der letzten Bergetätigkeit in tiefen, unruhigen Schlaf fällt. Mehr als vier bis fünf Stunden pro Nacht sind nicht drin, und bei einigen Mitfahrern schwinden Kräfte und Laune erstaunlich parallel. Alina, unsere einheimische Köchin, schafft es zwar jeden Abend, ein unendlich leckeres Mahl zu kredenzen, aber nahezu 100 Prozent Luftfeuchtigkeit, 40 Grad Hitze und immer wieder dieser Schlamm machen uns schwer zu schaffen. Nur selten gibt es Abwechslung in Form einer offiziell genehmigten Querung der einen oder anderen Autobahn, wofür wir die Leitplanken ab- und natürlich auch wieder anmontieren müssen.

Und dann sind da ja noch die Viecher. Nicht die großen jagen uns Angst ein, sondern die kleinen: Schlangen, Spinnen, Raupen und der ganze Mikrokosmos der fliegenden, krabbelnden, stechenden, saugenden oder einfach nervenden Insekten. Tiere, die wir in unserem Leben noch nie gesehen haben. Zum Beispiel fette Wespen, die nachts angezogen werden durch das hell erleuchtete Laptop, das als Navigationshilfe fungiert, und durch einen kleinen Spalt ins Auto geflogen kommen. Oder kleine malaysische Blutegel. Die docken gerne – aufgrund ihres körpereigenen Betäubungsmittels unfühlbar – an den menschlichen Körper an, saugen sich voller Blut und verabschieden sich selbstständig. Am Tatort hinterlassen sie ein Blutverdünnungsmittel, wodurch sofort die Blutung beim Wirt einsetzt und alle eventuellen Schadstoffe ausgewaschen werden. Und weil das so ist, sollte man sie gewähren lassen, bis sie satt sind – das ist der beste Weg, einer Infektion aus dem Wege zu gehen. Nicht schön, aber sinnvoll. Der Dschungel hat eben seine eigenen Gesetze.

Gesetze hin, Gesetze her – kurz darauf kaufe ich für ein insektenfreies Auto in einem malaysischen Tante-Emma-Laden irgendein hochgiftiges Zeug, sprühe es in mein Domizil, schließe es für eine Stunde luftdicht ab und warte. Ich muss gestehen, klammheimlich freue ich mich auf das Gemetzel im Inneren. Ob ich dabei irgendeine seltene Insektenart auslösche, ist mir letztlich nicht nachzuweisen – gesichert ist dagegen die Erkenntnis, dass später zu Hause die sonst nicht gerade zimperlichen Fahrzeugaufbereiter mit Pinzetten massenhaft fremdartige und vielbeinige Geschöpfe aus den verwegensten Ecken des Autos ziehen werden.

Richtig schlimm aber sind die Hautrötungen, einhergehend mit Juckreiz und Pusteln, die plötzlich die halbe Mannschaft befallen. Da ist selbst der Doc ratlos, denn es gibt keine Regelmäßigkeiten, aus denen sich die Ursache herauslesen lässt. Auch hier erweist sich Köchin Alina als rettender Engel: Sie tippt auf Raupen. Und sie hat Recht. Viele Mitreisende sind mit Raupen in Berührung gekommen, die mit feinen, aber giftigen Härchen ausgestattet sind. Durch Kratzen verteilen die Betroffenen die tierische Essenz auf weitere Hautbereiche. Da hilft nur: Ausbaden. Was sich aber nicht überall anbietet. Ich persönlich bade grundsätzlich in keinem Bach, bei dem ich den Grund nicht sehe.

Wer weiß, was da noch so alles drin ist …

That evening around the campfire marked the last time for the next few days that people were really able to have a laugh. A day later, it started to rain. When it rains in the Malaysian jungle it comes down in buckets – meaning mud up to your knees and higher.

I underestimated the effect the rain would have on the ground. Our first countermeasure was to keep the convoy together so that everybody could help one another. As a result, rather than our average of 19 miles per hour, we managed a mere 2. The Freelanders were getting stuck on a regular basis but even the Defender and the Discovery ambulance were having problems. The mud was pretty deep.

OK – it was too deep for us travel quickly, but it wasn't too deep to stop the Land Rover Experience Tour. At times we needed to place stones underneath our sand channels in order to be able to cross the odd "puddle". There were times when the full complement of winching equipment had to be unpacked to enable if we wanted to move at all. On other occasions the whole team – meaning the participants, organisers and all the journalists – were out of the vehicles and in the mud, pushing and heaving for all their worth. At numerous locations the mix of muscle and motor was the only way to get a Freelander through a particularly difficult part, only then to turn the vehicle around to use its own winch and return pulleys to haul the following vehicles through the mire. It was really tough, physically strenuous, and just downright exhausting. But it worked.

Building bridges, however, posed no problems at all. This time we had a full-size chain saw, which was more than "jungle-approved". We had acquired a lot of experience in the team, work processes were clearly defined and the motto of the trip became "Bridge the gap with courage".

At night we slept on the track, on the forest floor, in the cars, on the cars, or wherever we could find a comfortable spot after the most recent winching session. Four or five hours of unruly, fitful sleep were the maximum. As a result, for some of the team, stamina and mood began to deteriorate almost concurrently. Our local chef, Alina, managed to work culinary miracles every night, but the 100 percent humidity, the 40-degree heat (104 degrees Fahrenheit) and the incessant mud started to eat away at our strength. Every once in a while, there was the welcome relief of a brief stretch of motorway between jungle sections, for which we had to first dismantle and then re-assemble the Armco safety barrier…

Did I mention the insects? We weren't worried about the big stuff, but the little creatures caused us sleepless nights: snakes, spiders, caterpillars and the entire community of crawling, biting, sucking or just plain nerve-wracking insects. These included things I had never seen before, such as the huge wasps that managed to fly into the car attracted by our navigation laptop's display. Or the small Malaysian leeches, which, once attached to the human body, can't be felt thanks to the anaesthetic they inject into you. They suck out as much blood as they can before going on their way, leaving a blood thinner in the bite and thus allowing whatever pollutants or other harmful substances in the body to be washed out – which is a good thing, because it is the most effective way of getting rid of infection. The jungle has its own set of rules.

Rules or not, I wanted an insect-free car and bought the bug equivalent of nerve gas at some Malaysian kiosk, sprayed the car full, closed it for an hour and waited. Of course on the quiet I was looking forward to the insect carnage to come. Whether or not I was responsible for the annihilation of a rare breed of insect is probably difficult to prove now – however, when the vehicles returned to Germany the valets took to using pincers to remove the vast range of exotic bugs and caterpillars that had died a horrible death in the inner confines of the car.

A much bigger problem were the itchy red marks and pustules that seemed to attack the team over night. Even our Doc didn't know where they came from, as there was no uniformity from which one could determine the source. Alina the cook suggested that caterpillars might be the miscreants. And she was right. Many in the team had come into contact with the caterpillars whose fine hairs were full of poisonous fluid. All the host had to do was scratch, thus spreading the fluid to other parts of the body. The only way to treat the problem was to bathe. Baths were at a premium in the jungle, and I have learned never to go bathing where I can't see the ground. You never know whom you might be sharing your bath with.

STEFAN AUER

geb. 13.2.1966
gelernter Koch, Berufskraftfahrer,
Sprengmeister, Sicherheitsfachkraft
und seit 2004 flexibelstes LET-Teammitglied

born 13 February 1966
trained chef, truck driver, explosives expert, security specialist
and since 2004 the most versatile man in the LET team

Trägt man als Österreicher das Offroad-Gen von Geburt an in sich?

Stefan: So ungefähr. Schon früh habe ich Spaß an Offroadern gehabt, besonders in dem damaligen Skigebiet Silvretta Nova. Da musste ich mit Allrad-Lastern hoch auf die Berge, zur Pistenrettung, zum Lawinensprengen, zum Liftbau. Irgendwann war ich dann stellvertretender Pistenchef und fuhr privat einen Puch G. 1997 hab ich an der Camel Trophy teilgenommen, es ging in die Mongolei. Prompt gewann ich mit einem Kollegen die Trophy, und von da an war ich bei den weiteren Camel-Touren als Mitverantwortlicher dabei. Dann lernte ich Dag kennen, und inzwischen fahre ich jede Tour mit.

Als was?

Stefan: Als alles. Dag kann mich für fast jede Aufgabe einsetzen. Er kann mich alleine kilometerweit vorneweg schicken, er kann mich als Lumpensammler weit hinten einsetzen, und er weiß, alles funktioniert in seinem Sinne. Zur Not schraube ich auch an den Autos herum, bis sie wieder funktionieren. Ich arbeite nebenbei als Motorradmechaniker, halte eine komplette Fahrzeugflotte in Schuss und habe meinen original Camel-Discovery von 1997 gekauft, um ihn zu restaurieren.

Gibt es etwas, was dich wirklich mal umhaut?

Stefan: Nicht viel. Mein Albtraum ist eigentlich nur Schlafmangel. Wenn ich mal zwei Nächte hintereinander nur etwa zwei bis drei Stunden Schlaf bekomme, werde ich etwas grantig …

Was hat dich auf den diversen Touren besonders beeindruckt?

Stefan: Neben ein paar wirklich herausfordernden Streckenabschnitten wie der matschglatten steilen Piste in Malaysia oder der Strecke durch den Krater in Argentinien bei pechschwarzer Nacht war es ein Ausflug mit der malaysischen Köchin Alina auf einen Markt der Einheimischen in Kuala Lumpur. Als gelernter Koch war ich fasziniert von dem großen Angebot und besonders von den noch völlig unausgenommenen Tieren, die da bei 100 Prozent Luftfeuchtigkeit und 45 Grad herumlagen.

Hast du ein Rezept, in solchen Situationen auf alle Fälle gesund zu bleiben?

Stefan: Klar! Am besten morgens einen Schluck selbst gebrannten Enzianschnaps. Wenn das nicht geht: Cognac oder Wodka tun's auch. Selbst abends.

Is it fair to say that Austrians are born with an off-road gene?

Stefan: Pretty much. I was into off-roading from an early age, particularly in the Silvretta Nova skiing region. I had to take four-wheel-drive trucks into the mountains as part of the mountain rescue team as well as to support avalanche blasting and ski lift construction. I became head of the ski piste team. Privately I ran a Puch G. In 1997 I took part in the Camel Trophy, which was in Mongolia that year, and won the event with a colleague. From then on I was part of the organisation team for all subsequent Camel Trophy events. I got to know Dag and have accompanied every tour ever since.

Doing what?

Stefan: Everything. Dag can put me on almost every task. He can send me miles up front on my own, I can play tail-end-charlie at the back, and he knows he can rely on me. If necessary, I know a thing or two about the vehicles and can get them going again. I also work as a motorcycle mechanic, keep a complete vehicle fleet on the road and bought my original Camel Trophy Discovery from 1997 with the intention of restoring it.

Is there anything that really gets you down?

Stefan: Not much. My personal nightmare is lack of sleep. A couple of nights in succession where I only get two or three hours make me a little grumpy...

What has impressed you most on all the tours?

Stefan: Alongside a couple of really challenging sections such as the slippery slope in Malaysia or the crater drive in the dead of night in Argentina, I think what impressed me most was a trip to the local food market in Kuala Lumpur with our Malaysian cook Alina. As a trained cook, I was fascinated by what was on offer, and by the uneviscerated animals which were everywhere in the 100-percent humidity and 45-degree (113 degrees Fahrenheit) heat.

What is the secret to staying healthy in those circumstances?

Stefan: Simple! Every morning I have a drink of homemade gentian schnapps. If that isn't available, then cognac or vodka works, too. Even at night.

DER HANG
THE SLOPE

Mit breitem Grinsen quittieren wir das Ende der fast übermenschlichen Dschungeldurchquerung – nicht ahnend, dass Malaysia noch eine Sonderprüfung für uns bereithält. Vom Höhenzug, auf dem wir uns die Matschschlacht lieferten, führt ein schmaler Feldweg runter auf Meeresebene, wo sich unser Endpunkt befindet. Dazwischen liegt ein Gefälle von bis zu 30 Prozent. Zwischen Bäumen und Büschen schlängelt sich der Weg etwa 3 Kilometer ins Tal, mit einem Plateau zum Ausruhen in der Mitte. Schlimm ist allerdings nicht die steile Abfahrt, sondern dass der Weg ebenso nass ist wie der Dschungel vorher und damit spiegelglatt.

Hans probiert es – wie dankenswerterweise so oft – als Erster. Mit seiner Erfahrung am Steuer von Geländewagen schafft er es, seinen Defender mit teils blockierenden Rädern schadlos aufs Plateau zu setzen. Einer Teilnehmerin gelingt es auch noch, unter Einsatz ihres Lebens einen Freelander dort abzustellen, dann brechen wir die Aktion ab: zu gefährlich. Wenn ich nur an die Vier-Tonnen-Ambulanz denke …

Aber runter müssen wir, es gibt keinen anderen Weg. Also was tun? Ich weise an, alle Kunststoffseile von den Winden zu lösen, die daran angebrachten Haken bis auf einen abzuschneiden und die Enden zusammenzuknoten. Das so entstandene lange Seil schlagen wir zweimal um einen dicken Baumstamm als Umlenkung, haken es beim ersten Versuchsfahrzeug ein und lassen es mit Muskelkraft und im ersten Gang herunter. Es funktioniert – aber es dauert lange. Zu lange.

Da hat unser Guide Atec eine Idee. Er setzt sich in einen Freelander, fährt langsam auf die steile Stelle zu, lässt sich abkippen, knallt brutal den Rückwärtsgang rein und bremst den Wagen durch volle Pulle Gas ab, bis er ganz unten ist. Die Aktion „Rückwärtsgangbremse" ist ungewöhnlich, sinnvoll aber auch tückenreich, wir können sie also nicht den Teams überlassen. Die Instruktoren bringen auf diese Weise alle Autos ins Tal.

Wundert es jemanden, dass ich auf dieser Tour rund zehn Kilo abnehme? Und bis auf eine Garnitur als Andenken meine völlig verschlammten Klamotten noch vor Ort pulverisiere? Und wir keinen einzigen Offroad-Touristen für eine folgende Experience-Reise in dieses wunderschöne Land finden?

The first jungle crossing, which had demanded almost superhuman qualities of each and every one of us, came to an end, and, not surprisingly, we were full of beans – little did we know that Malaysia had held a little test in store for us. From the range of hills where we had fought in the mud, there was a very narrow track that took us back down to sea level and the end of the tour. With a 30-degree incline. Between trees and bushes, the two-mile track with a plateau in the middle led all the way down into the valley. The problem, however, wasn't the incline; it was that the track was as wet as the jungle had been, and as slippery as the world-famous Cresta bob run.

Generously as ever, Hans volunteered to go first. Only thanks to his immense experience with four-wheel-drive vehicles and despite occasionally locking up all four wheels on the way, he managed to reach the plateau unscathed. One of the participants also managed to get her Freelander to the plateau, too, though she risked her life doing it. We decided enough was enough. It was simply too dangerous. The thought of taking the four-ton ambulance down there was terrifying…

It was the only route down, though, so we had no choice. What could we do? I advised the teams to remove the kinetic ropes from the vehicle winches, to remove all the attached hooks but one, and then to knot them all together. We belayed the rope twice around a large tree and attached the other end with the hook to the first vehicle, which went down the track in first gear supported by our muscle on the other end of the rope. It worked, but it took too long.

Atec, our guide, then had an idea. He climbed into a Freelander, drove to the top of the slope, crawled over the apex, slammed it into reverse and drove forwards down the hill in reverse using engine braking to control the vehicle until he reached the bottom. "Reverse gear braking" was unusual, made sense, but was very risky, so we decided to let the instructors bring the vehicles down the hill.

Would it surprise anybody that I lost ten kilos on this trip, and that – apart from a single shirt I kept as a souvenir – all the rest of my work clothes, which had been completely ruined by the permanent mud bath, were incinerated in Malaysia? Not one paying customer was prepared to book the Experience Tour in this beautiful country. I wonder why.

BOLIVIA
2011
12 DEFENDER,
1 AMBULANCE DISCOVERY
STRECKE / DISTANCE: 1650 KM / 1,030 MILES

BOLIVIEN

BOLIVIA
2011
12 DEFENDER,
1 AMBULANCE DISCOVERY
STRECKE / DISTANCE: 1650 KM / 1,030 MILES

DER DEFENDER
THE DEFENDER

War Malaysia zu hart? Zumindest sind einige der Teilnehmer an die Grenzen ihrer Kräfte gekommen. Vielleicht ist Südamerika berechenbarer? Klar, Australien ist wieder in der Lostrommel, und zur Abwechslung mal Äthiopien. Aber es wird Bolivien. Ich glaube, das Land ist etwas sanfter als Malaysia, aber mit genug Abenteuerpotenzial ausgestattet.

Sofort kommt die Frage: Ist das Land sicher genug? Südamerikanische Mafia, hohe Kriminalität und ein kaum berechenbarer Präsident – ich beschließe, Bolivien ist sicher. Und die Team-Fahrzeuge sollen Defender sein, weil das Modell nun einen neuen Motor unter der Haube hat. Es wird Zeit, Land Rovers Urvieh mal wieder auf große Tour zu schicken.

Den richtigen Guide zieht Hans aus dem Ärmel: Ciro, Sohn eines bolivianischen Minenbesitzers, gebürtiger Bolivianer mit nordamerikanischem Pass. Den hat Hans im Urlaub kennengelernt. Da wir dringend einen Defender für Fotos in Bolivien brauchen, um ein bisschen für die Tour zu werben, wird Ciro als Erstes beauftragt, einen zu mieten. Wir wollen unterdessen unsere eigene Defender-Flotte aus Deutschland zum Seehafen im chilenischen Arica entsenden, um sie dann auf dem Landweg nach Bolivien temporär einzuführen – Bolivien selbst besitzt keinen Zugang zum Meer. Alles tolle Ideen. Bis auf die Tatsache, dass Ciro weder einen Wagen zum Mieten noch einen zum Leihen findet. Ich disponiere kurzfristig um: Er soll einen gebrauchten Landy kaufen.

Was Malaysia too tough? Some of the participants were well and truly at the end of their tether by the end of the tour. Perhaps the risks in South America were easier to calculate? Australia was back on the agenda, and there was even talk about going to Ethiopia. However, Bolivia got the vote. I thought the country would be easier going than Malaysia while still being able to offer enough adventure.

The first questions came soon enough: was the country sufficiently safe? South American mafia, a high crime rate and an unpredictable president – I decided Bolivia was safe. The teams would get Defenders, as it had just received a new engine. It was time to send Land Rover's original back on tour.

Once again, Hans had another ace up his sleeve – this time it was the perfect guide. Ciro was the son of a Bolivian mine owner – a native Bolivian, but with a US passport. Hans had met him on holiday. As we urgently needed a Defender for a photo shoot in Bolivia to do the usual pre-tour publicity, it was Ciro's first assignment to rent one. Meanwhile, we had also decided to ship our own Defender fleet from Germany to the deep-sea port of Arica in Chile, from whence we would import the vehicles overland into Bolivia on temporary papers, as Bolivia has no coastline. All very good ideas, except that Ciro wasn't able to rent or even borrow a Land Rover. We changed plans and told him to buy a used Defender.

Nach erschreckend langer Suche findet Ciro in der Hauptstadt Santa Cruz tatsächlich ein leidlich brauchbares Exemplar und begibt sich auf den Weg nach Cochabamba, zum Startort der neuen Tour sowie Hans' und meinem momentanen Aufenthaltsort. Doch Ciro kommt samt Auto schließlich auf einem Anhänger an. Die „Karre" ist schon auf diesem kurzen Weg verreckt. Freundlicher ausgedrückt: Der TDI-Motor des sehr gebrauchten Solihullers hat bereits auf dieser Fahrt Aussetzer. Ich teste sofort den alten Wagen. Er springt an und läuft leidlich rund, aber es wird auch deutlich: Es fehlt Leistung. Keine gute Voraussetzung für Foto-Fahrten in der am höchsten gelegenen Großstadt der Welt, La Paz (auf 4 000 Metern). Dort denkt man ja schon, wenn man aus dem Flugzeug steigt, man hätte auf nüchternen Magen und auf ex drei große Gläser Champagner getrunken. Der magere Sauerstoffgehalt der Luft euphorisiert einen tagsüber ein bisschen, und nachts kann man nicht schlafen.

Aber wer kann hier in Cochabamba mal eben einen Defender-Motor reparieren? Land Rover leider nicht – ist hier nicht offiziell vertreten. Freie Autowerkstätten? Die winken ab: Japanische Massenware kriegen sie hin, aber so eine englische Wertarbeit dann doch nicht. Der VW-Händler? Zuckt freundlich mit den Achseln. Vielleicht die Lkw-Schrauber um die Ecke? Tatsächlich. Deren Antwort: „Kein Problem."

Völlig unkompliziert checken sie sofort den Kompressionsdruck, stellen fest, dass er nicht vorhanden ist, und beginnen, den Motor zu zerlegen. Über neue Kolben, Kolbenringe und so weiter sollen wir uns keine Gedanken machen, teilen sie uns mit. Ebenso seien die Kosten völlig überschaubar. Sagen sie mit dem Augenaufschlag eines anhänglichen Cockerspaniels.

Mit mulmigem Gefühl, aber in der Gewissheit, wenig Zeit, keine Wahl und den Zwang zum Vertrauen zu haben und deshalb auf die Truckerversprechen angewiesen zu sein, verziehen wir uns in ein Hotel. Um abends gegen 20 Uhr wieder in der Werkstatt aufzutauchen. Vertrauen ist gut, Kontrolle ist besser, deutsche Gründlichkeit ist am allerbesten.

Mir stockt der Atem: Der Motor liegt in gefühlten 1 000 Einzelteilen auf dem Boden – ohne dass der Block ausgebaut worden ist. Ein bolivianischer Feinmotoriker steht breitbeinig auf den Vorderkotflügeln und hont mit einer Bohrmaschine die Brennräume. Ein zweiter sinniert darüber, wo man übergroße Kolben herbekommen kann. Und ein dritter kümmert sich um die Ventile, die Ventilsitze und die Kurbelwelle – was das genau bedeutet, ist nicht so richtig ersichtlich. Mit noch gemischteren Gefühlen als zuvor verziehen wir uns für eine unruhige Nacht wieder ins Hotel.

Morgens Punkt 8 Uhr stehen wir wieder bei den Truckerschraubern auf der Matte: Der Wagen ist fertig. Der Motor läuft. Sauber und rund. Wir werden gebeten, zwei Stunden durch die Stadt zu cruisen, um den Motor einzufahren, und dann für einen Ölwechsel wiederzukommen. Der Preis für diese perfekte Arbeit: umgerechnet 500 Euro.

Ich würde jederzeit wieder eines meiner vielen Tourenfahrzeuge bei den „Steh-Honern" in Cochabamba reparieren lassen!

After a painfully long search, Ciro found a reasonably usable vehicle in the capital, Santa Cruz, and immediately headed to Cochabamba, which was both where we would be starting the new tour and where Hans and I were staying. Ciro turned up, however, with the Defender on the back of a flatbed truck. The Landy had already conked out on the short trip from the capital. The truth was that the TDI engine of the rather long-in-the-tooth Solihull legend had suffered a number of misfires. I tested the vehicle immediately. It started and ran reasonably enough on tickover, but it was obvious that it was down on performance, which did not bode well for a photo shoot in the highest capital city on the planet, La Paz (13,000 feet). When you arrive in La Paz and walk off the plane, it feels as if you've just knocked back a bottle of champagne on an empty stomach. The thin oxygen produces a permanent sense of euphoria during the daytime, and at night you can't sleep.

We needed to find someone in Cochabamba who could repair the Defender's TDI engine. Land Rover was out of the question – there was no official dealership here. Independent workshops ran a mile. Japanese products, yes – an exotic Brit? No way. The VW dealer? He just smiled and shrugged his shoulders. What about the truck repair place round the corner? Their answer was a remarkable "No problem".

With out any ado, they checked the compression (there wasn't any) and then started to take the engine apart. We wouldn't have to worry about pistons, rings and such, and the costs wouldn't be exorbitant, either – and all this with the grateful look of a loyal cocker spaniel who has just been given a bone…

With a sense of unease but also the realisation that we had neither the time nor a choice and therefore had to trust the truck repairman, we found a hotel only to return to the workshop at 8 o'clock that night. Better safe than sorry and all that, and the meticulousness of the Germans is the best guarantee of all.

I had to fight for breath. It looked as if the motor had been reduced to a sea of 1,000 parts on the floor, not counting the block, which was still in the engine bay. A Bolivian "specialist" straddled the front wings using a drill to grind down the combustion chambers. Another technician was considering where to get hold of larger pistons, while a third was working on the valves, the valve seats and the crankshaft. What it actually all meant was not exactly clear. With more mixed feelings, we trudged back to the hotel with the prospect of an unruly night ahead of us.

The following morning at 8 o'clock on the dot we were back at the workshop. The vehicle was ready. The engine was running and sounded smooth. We were asked to spend two hours running it in around town, and then to come back to change the oil. The cost of perfection? € 500.

I would repair any of my expedition vehicles at the "straddling grinders" in Cochabamba.

Das südamerikanische Land bietet alles, was das Offroader-Herz begehrt: enge Schotterpisten, einsame Wege bis in die Wolken und natürlich Wasserdurchfahrten.

This South American country has everything an off-roader has ever dreamed of: narrow gravel roads, lonely trails into the clouds and river crossings.

DAS GESETZ
THE LAW

Die erste Fahrt durch Bolivien mit dem Foto-Defender überzeugt mich bereits, das richtige Land gewählt zu haben. Dennoch kommen mir die Haupt- und Nebenstraßen noch ein wenig soft vor. Doch wir werden schon die richtigen Pisten finden.

Allerdings brauchen wir dringend unsere Autos – und die stecken mal wieder fest. Und zwar in Arica. Was wir beim Verschiffen nicht bedacht haben: Es gibt ein bolivianisches Gesetz, das es nur Dieselfahrzeugen mit Motoren mit mehr als 4 Liter Hubraum erlaubt, ins Land einzureisen. Der wunderbare Defender-Motor glänzt in Deutschland aber mit einem sparsamen 2,4-Liter-Diesel – was die bolivianischen Zöllner in keinster Weise erweicht.

Hätten wir von dem uns völlig sinnlos erscheinenden Gesetz vorher erfahren, hätten wir schon bei der Verschiffung in Deutschland die Wagenpapiere (illegal, aber zeitsparend) auf 4 Liter Hubraum umgeschrieben. So ähnlich hatte es übrigens auch der Erstbesitzer des Defender gemacht, dessen Wagen wir in Bolivien gekauft haben: Die Bastelbude besitzt angeblich 4,1 Liter Hubraum.

Klar, hier passt man einfach die Papiere an die Gesetze an. Die Vorschrift soll übrigens vermeiden, dass sich viele Menschen Autos mit kleinen Dieselhubräumen kaufen – in der Hoffnung, dass sich große sowieso niemand leisten kann. So sehr ich auch dieses Gesetz drehe und wende, ich finde keine Lücke. Damit stecken nun alle Autos fest – auch die Ambulanz, die immerhin mit 3 Litern Hubraum ausgestattet ist.

Es bleibt mir nichts anderes übrig, als mir geduldig, aber nachdrücklich den Weg zum Volkspräsidenten Evo Morales freizuquatschen. Der hat einst unser Tour-Vorhaben genehmigt und sich davor sogar für die Durchführung einer Dakar-Rallye in seinem Land starkgemacht. Ciro schafft es tatsächlich bis in die oberste Etage der Regierungsebene. Als der Präsident von unserem Debakel erfährt, erlässt er sofort eine „Lex Land Rover": „Ley 830" besagt, dass Land Rover ein Jahr lang Fahrzeuge einführen darf, die nicht an einen bestimmten Fahrer gebunden sind und die weniger als 4 Liter Hubraum aufweisen dürfen.

Our first journey with the photo-shoot Defender across Bolivia convinced me that we had made the right decision to come here. While the main and secondary roads seemed a little soft for our purposes, I was convinced we would ultimately find the right routes.

We urgently needed our own vehicles – and of course, once again, they were stuck in customs in the port of Arica. When we drew up the shipping papers, we had overlooked one important point. Under Bolivian law, only diesel-engine vehicles with a capacity of more than 4 litres may be imported into the country. The extremely efficient Defender engine performs brilliantly in Germany and elsewhere in the world with a capacity of just 2.4 litres; still, the Bolivian customs officials would not yield.

Had we known about the law beforehand – a law, by the way, that appeared to make no sense whatsoever – we could have modified the vehicle documentation accordingly, thus giving the Defenders 4-litre engines. This is illegal, but it saves time. It was also how the Defender we were already running in Bolivia had been purchased by its first owner to begin with. According to its paperwork, it had a 4.1-litre engine. In Bolivia, people adjust the paperwork to fit the law. The legislation is designed to prevent people from buying cars with small diesel engines in hopes that nobody can afford to buy larger diesel engines. The more I looked at this law, the less I saw any way of getting around it. And it meant that all our vehicles were stuck – including the ambulance, which at least had 3 litres under the bonnet.

My only chance was to remain patient and approach President Evo Morales directly. He had originally given us his approval to run the tour in Bolivia in the first place and had personally supported the Dakar rally raid in his country. Ciro managed to reach the top level of government, and when the President heard of our problem, he enacted a "Lex Land Rover" – "Ley 830" – that provided for the import of our vehicles for one year, vehicles that were not legally linked to any one specific driver and that could be under 4 litres in capacity.

DIE BLOCKADE
THE BLOCKING

Natürlich finden wir auf der Vortour die abenteuerlichsten Routen. Persönlich enttäuscht bin ich allerdings vom „Camino de la Muerte", der „Todesstraße", einst die angeblich gefährlichste Straße der Welt. Weil es inzwischen eine Umgehungsstraße gibt, sind das Gefährlichste auf dieser Piste heute Fahrradfahrer, die die Straße als sportliche Abfahrt sehen sowie von Cocablättern vollgedröhnte Einheimische auf dem Motorrad, die weiß der Himmel wohin unterwegs sind.

Eine Herausforderung ist die Straße zumindest nicht für uns. Bis auf den Schreckmoment, als einer der oben beschriebenen Bolivianer mit seinem Zweirad hinten auf meinen Defender auffährt und ich ihn schon im unendlichen Abgrund wähne. Als ich ihn dort nicht erblicke, schaue ich hinters Auto. Da liegt er unter seinem Motorrad, grinst, platziert einen dicken Packen Cocablattmatsch zurück in die rechte Wange, faselt etwas von „Sorry, Sorry", schwingt sich wieder auf sein Gefährt und wankt weiter den Berg hinunter. Nein, die Zeiten, in denen sich begegnende Autos so gegenseitig wie regelmäßig in den Abgrund schubsten, sind definitiv vorbei.

Aber wir finden trotz der ungenauen russischen Generalstabskarten und dank der Mithilfe diverser grünzahniger Cocabauern, die wir über etliche Andenkilometer als Kurzzeit-Lokalguides mitnehmen, doch noch perfekte Experience-Wege – oft Minentracks. Die sind nicht nur extrem schmal und bestehen aus Schotter, sondern ihre Spitzkehren sind teilweise auch noch so eng, dass wir mit den Defendern rangieren müssen. Und das ist kein Spaß. Links begrenzt eine mindestens 1 000 Meter hohe Felswand den Spielraum, rechts ein gut 1 000 Meter tiefer Abgrund. Wie gesagt: Der Camino de la Muerte ist dagegen eine Touristenattraktion für Pauschalreisende. Ich muss aber gestehen, ich baue die Straße trotzdem in die Haupttour ein. Allein schon wegen ihres Namens.

Während wir solche fahrerischen Herausforderungen selbst im Griff haben, sind wir gegen eine typisch bolivianische Protestart nahezu machtlos: Blockaden. Die hat Evo Morales einst erfunden, als er noch nicht Staatsoberhaupt war. Und die wenden nun unzufriedene Dorfbewohner gegen ihn selbst an. Das Prinzip ist einfach: Da es nicht so viele Straßen gibt, blockiert man bei allgemeiner politischer Unzufriedenheit die wichtigen (und manchmal auch die unwichtigen) Zufahrts-, Durchfahrts-, Haupt- und Nebenstraßen durch Steine, Felsen oder Menschen. Die Folge: Eine ganze Region wird von Nachschub aller Art abgeschnitten. Zum Beispiel Kraftstoff. Oder Nahrungsmittel. Oder Unterhaltungselektronik. Völlig egal – irgendjemand wird sich schon ärgern und bei den Obersten in der Regierungshauptstadt La Paz anklopfen.

Natürlich geraten auch wir auf der Vortour prompt in so eine Blockade. Ein ganzes Dorf ist auf den Beinen, und so ein Konvoi von vier Beulen (ohne Aufschriften, gut ausgerüstet) kann keinen Einheimischen gehören. Also entweder Ausländer oder Regierungsfahrzeuge – genug Gründe, sie aufzuhalten.

Sofort stehen Hunderte von Menschen um uns. Guide Ciro dolmetscht das bolivianische Spanisch: mal wieder allgemeine Unzufriedenheit. Aha. Und als die Blockierer erkennen, dass wir eine Filmkamera im Gepäck haben, wünscht sich der Bürgermeister freundlich, aber nachdrücklich ein Fernsehinterview. So postieren wir die Landys als Lichtgeber um den Platz an der Hauptstraße herum, und Land-Rover-Marketingchef Christian Uhrig diskutiert eine halbe Stunde mit dem aufgeregten Dorfchef. Ciro vermittelt dabei immer diplomatisch. Mit der Zusage, das aufgenommene Gespräch bei einem deutschen Fernsehsender abzugeben, lässt uns die zwar nicht bedrohlich wirkende, aber doch deutlich in der Mehrzahl befindliche Menge ziehen.

Ich muss gestehen, wir finden nicht die Zeit, den Sender zu besuchen.

Of course we were able to find the most challenging routes on the pre-scout recce. I personally was disappointed by the "Camino de la Muerte" or "Road of Death" that was allegedly once the most dangerous road on the planet. As it has since been bypassed, the most dangerous things left on the road are cyclists who view the route as a sporting downhill run and motorbiking locals high on coca leaves who are probably just out for the buzz. The road is certainly no longer a challenge for us. That is, it wasn't until the moment one of the aforementioned locals rammed my Defender from behind with his motorbike. He suddenly disappeared from view, and in my mind's eye I could see him heading to a better place. I jumped out of the Defender and saw him lying on the road underneath his bike, grinning as he pushed another wad of coca leaves into his mouth. He mumbled "sorry, sorry", jumped back on his bike and headed down the mountain. One thing is certain, however: the days when one vehicle would shove another over the edge and into the abyss on a regular basis were well and truly over.

Nevertheless, despite our inaccurate Russian military maps, and thanks to the help of countless green-toothed coca farmers whom we consulted over many miles in the Andes as short-term guides, we were able to find routes (often mining roads) that suited the Experience Tour perfectly. Narrow, gravel roads with switchbacks so tight that taking a Defender through the corner nearly required a three-point turn every time. And it was no joke. To the left, a 3,000-foot wall of rock; to the right, a 3,000-foot drop, with nothing in between. By comparison, the Camino de la Muerte was a walk in the park for tourists. Nevertheless, the famous road featured on the tour simply because of the name.

While we can control the driver-challenge aspect of the tour, we are completely helpless when faced with the common form of Bolivian protest: the roadblock – a method Evo Morales himself invented before he rose to power and that dissatisfied villagers now use against him. The idea is as simple as it is effective. Where roads are few, political dissatisfaction is expressed by blocking the major arterial (and sometimes the less important) routes, access roads and bypasses with stones, boulders and even people. As a result, a whole region can be cut off from all manner of supplies, be it fuel, food or even electronic goods. Somebody is always bothered enough to knock on the door of the head of the government in La Paz.

On the pre-scout recce, we ran into just such a protest. The whole village was on its feet, and it was obvious that our four Defenders – which lacked dents, were covered in logos and were obviously well equipped – didn't belong to locals. I.e., we were either foreigners or the government, and either way, that was reason enough to keep us there.

In an instant, we were surrounded by hundreds of people. Ciro translated from Bolivian Spanish. Once again, the issue was general dissatisfaction with the way the country was being run. And the protesters noticed that we had a camera team on board – now the mayor made it clear in friendly but firm terms that he wanted a TV interview. We positioned the Land Rovers alongside the main road, where they could provide light, and Land Rover's head of marketing Christian Uhrig debated for half an hour with the agitated mayor. Ciro played the perfect diplomatic middleman. Having agreed to pass on the material to a German TV broadcaster, the crowd, which hadn't appeared threatening but nevertheless outnumbered us considerably, allowed us to continue on our way.

As it happens, we never found the time to visit a German broadcaster.

CHRISTIAN UHRIG

geb. 4.6.1960
Leiter Marketing bei Land Rover Deutschland,
Experience-Verantwortlicher und Sparringspartner; im früheren
Leben u. a. Management Supervisor bei Werbeagenturen und
Studium der Forstwissenschaft

born 4 June 1960
Head of Marketing Land Rover Germany, Project Manager
Land Rover Experience and sparring partner; in another life,
management supervisor in an advertising agency and a degree
in forest economics

Bei welchen Touren warst du dabei?

Christian: Ich konnte bisher bei allen zehn Tourdestinationen dabei sein. In Jordanien erst ab Start des Reiseprogramms in 2001, in jenem Jahr habe ich meinen Job bei Land Rover begonnen. Es ist eigentlich unfassbar, dass wir schon zehn so komplett unterschiedliche Abenteuer überall auf der Welt durchführen konnten.

Welche Tour hat dir am besten gefallen?

Christian: Die Frage ist sehr schwierig und eigentlich nicht zu beantworten, denn mir liegt jede Tour sehr am Herzen. Jedes Ziel hatte seinen ganz besonderen Charme und Charakter, der jeweils einmalig war. Der Dschungel in Belize, die Pampa in Argentinien, der Etosha-Nationalpark in Namibia, die Highlands in Schottland oder die Anden in Bolivien. Das nachhaltigste Erlebnis erzeugten aber ganz gewiss die Weiten des tibetischen Hochlands mit der faszinierenden Hauptstadt Lhasa auf dem „Dach der Welt" bei der Pre-Scout-Tour im Jahr 2012. Vor allem die tibetischen Mönche, mit ihrem ganz besonderen Schicksal, waren so freundlich und entspannt, als sei hier der friedlichste Platz auf der Erde. Ein weiteres ganz spezielles, überraschendes Highlight für mich war sicherlich Island, weil es bei einer sehr kurzen Anreise maximales Abenteuer und menschenleere Wildnis abseits der Straßen erlaubte. Man kam sich manchmal schlicht vor wie auf dem Mond, wenn da nicht diese gleißenden Farben, die Gletscher und die rauschenden Gewässer gewesen wären. Wie die Menschen hier auf Trolle als Fabelwesen kamen, ist kein Wunder.

Gibt es dazu ein Ereignis, das dir besonders in Erinnerung ist?

Christian: Ja, wir waren im Jahr 2001 in Island auf einer Pre-Scout-Tour, um eine Campsite zu erkunden. Auf dem Hinweg ging es durch einen schon kräftig fließenden Bach, mit auffälligen Steinmarkierungen im Bachbett zur Orientierung bei der Durchfahrt. Auf dem Rückweg, maximal eineinhalb Stunden später, war der Bach zu einem reißenden Fluss angewachsen. Wir haben es mit Unterstützung eines Trucks geschafft, mehr driftend als fahrend, das rettende Ufer zu erreichen, hinter uns im Schlepptau ein alter Geländewagen, voll besetzt mit einer Familie. Unser Auto war trocken, weil wir die Türen mit Isolierband abgeklebt hatten. Der Jeep sah allerdings mehr aus wie ein Aquarium als ein Auto. Das Wasser stand innen bis zur Höhe der Scheiben und floss jetzt hinaus. Beim Öffnen der Tür ergoss sich nicht nur Wasser und Schlamm auf den Boden, sondern auch Papiere, Kleider und Proviant. Das Gesicht des Fahrers vergesse ich nie.

Wann hattest du zum ersten Mal Kontakt mit Land Rover?

Christian: In den Jahren 1995–1998, während meiner Zeit bei Lintas, einer internationalen Werbeagentur, war ich als Etat-Direktor für Rover verantwortlich und 1997 mit dem Freelander-Launch befasst. Wir hatten in Spanien erstmals die Gelegenheit, ins Gelände zu fahren und später auch über die Treppen an den Strand. Dabei habe ich Dag kennengelernt, der schon damals ein Offroad-Experte war.

Du bist mehr bei den Pre-Scout-Touren als bei den Haupttouren dabei – mit Absicht?

Christian: Für mich persönlich haben die Pre-Scout-Touren den größten Reiz, weil hier die Mischung aus Unerwartetem und Planungsstress, Entscheidungsfindung, Mensch und Natur so unmittelbar zusammentreffen, dass mir das, was gerade passiert, oft unwirklich vorkommt. Ich lehne beispielsweise nach gefühlten zehn Stunden Fahrt an der Motorhaube, bin im Dschungel über die Karten gebeugt, „in the middle of nowhere", und diskutiere über ein Thema, das banal klingt, aber essentiell sein kann. Beispiel: „Wie weit kommen wir heute noch, bis es komplett dunkel wird?" Und plötzlich läuft irgendein langbeiniges Insekt über mein Bein und ich denke: „Bleib jetzt ganz ruhig ..."

Which tours have you been able to accompany?

Christian: I have been on all ten. I started working for Land Rover in 2001, so I was only in Jordan for the start of the customer programme. I can hardly believe that we have managed to put together ten so completely diverse adventure trips all over the world.

Which tour was your favourite?

Christian: That's a very difficult question and almost impossible to answer, as I put my heart and soul into every tour. Each one had its own underlying charm and character, and each was unique. The jungle in Belize, the Argentinean Pampas, Etosha National Park in Namibia, the Highlands in Scotland or the Andes in Bolivia. I think the most lasting impressions were generated by the expanse of the Tibetan Highlands, with its fascinating capital Lhasa "on the roof of the world" during the pre-scout in 2012. The Tibetan monks, considering their own particular situation, were so friendly and relaxed as if they hadn't an enemy in the world.
A special and surprising highlight for me was without a doubt Iceland, as despite the relatively short flight it provided the maximum dose of adventure. Once you had left the road, there was a wilderness totally bereft of mankind. Had it not been for the glistening colours, the glaciers and the wild streams, one could have been on the moon. It's not surprising that people here invented trolls.

Did anything happen that you can remember particularly well?

Christian: Oh yes. In 2001 we were in Iceland on a pre-scout recce looking for a campsite. On the way towards the camp, we had crossed a stream that was in full flow where rocks in the water had been marked to help with orientation as one crossed over. On the way back, less than an hour and a half later the stream had become a raging torrent. Using a truck to help us we managed to drive (though drift would be more accurate) across with an older four-wheel drive complete with family in tow behind us. Our vehicle remained dry inside, as we had taped the doors with electrical tape. The Jeep, however, was more of an aquarium than a car. The water inside the vehicle was as high as the windows and just poured out when we opened the doors. It wasn't just mud and water that poured out either, but paper, clothes and food. I will never forget the driver's face.

When did you first come into contact with Land Rover?

Christian: Between 1995 and 1998, while I was working for an international advertising agency called Lintas, I was account director for Rover and was busy with the launch of the Freelander. In Spain we had the opportunity to drive off-road for the first time and via steps down onto the beach. This was where I met Dag, who was already an expert in all things off-road.

You spend more time on the pre-scouts than on the main event – is that intentional?

Christian: I find the pre-scout tours more interesting because their mix of unexpected events, planning stress and decision-making is often so at odds with the environment through which we are travelling. For example, I am in the middle of the jungle, in the middle of nowhere, leaning over the bonnet with maps spread everywhere, having just spent what seems like ten hours behind the wheel and we could be talking about something which sounds banal, but which is in fact crucial to the success of the tour. For example, "How much further can we get before it gets completely dark?" And as I talk, I can feel something with long legs walking up my leg and I'm thinking, "Stay very calm..."

Die Tour lebt nicht nur von unglaublichen Landschaften, sondern auch von Begegnungen der menschlichen Art. Seien es nun andere motorisierte Gruppen, Bauern beim Pflanzen von Coca-sträuchern oder einheimische Kinder – die Neugier, was der andere so macht, ist stets auf beiden Seiten groß.

The tour lives from more than just unbelievable landscapes. It thrives on the people you meet on the way, whether they are other globetrotters, farmers planting their coca crops or local children – the desire to discover how the other person lives is overwhelming for both.

DER KRAFTSTOFF
THE FUEL

Eine Folge von solchen Blockaden ist natürlich auch Kraftstoffmangel. Für uns als Autofahrer durchaus ein Kriterium, das wir in die Planungen einbeziehen müssen. Dazu sollte man wissen: Diesel ist in Bolivien ein durchaus gängiger Kraftstoff. Aber wer den Diesel-Nachschub stoppt, legt Lastwagen lahm. Und alle anderen Dieselfahrzeuge auch. Es sei denn, sie sind Teil der Land Rover Experience Tour.

Aber es gehört schon ein gewisses Geschick dazu, an das bei Blockaden so kostbare Nass zu gelangen. Ciro verrät uns, dass es sich viele Bolivianer zum Volkssport gemacht haben, Kraftstoff in alten Olivenölfässern, in Essigkanistern oder irgendwelchen anderen Behältern zu bunkern. Wir müssen diese Menschen nur finden – und ihnen genug für ihren Schatz bieten. Dann greifen sie zu Schläuchen, schaffen durch die altbekannte Methode des Ansaugens Unterdruck, spucken den ersten Schluck aus und füllen die Tanks.

Der findige Mitarbeiter einer Baufahrzeugfirma kommt auf eine besonders lukrative Idee, uns das Selbstzündungsgebräu zu verschaffen: Er knackt den halbvollen Dieseltank des Caterpillar-Frontladers seines Chefs und füttert mit dem Stoff unsere Defender. Dafür müssen wir ihm versprechen (außer einer gewissen Summe, die sofort in bar zu entrichten ist), ihm für seinen persönlichen Defender auf der Haupttour Ersatzteile mitzubringen. Was ich natürlich auch tue. Ich bleibe nirgendwo lange, aber auch niemandem etwas schuldig.

Apropos mitbringen: Aufgrund dieser Sprit-Erfahrung der Vortour bauen wir in Deutschland auf einen neu gekauften Anhänger einen ebenso neu erworbenen 1000-Liter-Tank mit den passenden Ventilen, um in Bolivien immer Diesel mitführen zu können. Die Einfuhr des Bausatzes ins Land ist unter anderem dank „Ley 830" nicht das Problem, aber die Straßenzustände und die Höhe umso mehr. Hänger und Zugfahrzeug kommen an ihre Grenzen, der Tank an sich aber leider auch. Denn was wir nicht bedacht haben: Bei großer Höhe dehnt sich der Kraftstoff extrem aus. Direkt vor einer Ortseinfahrt meldet sich das Überlaufventil: Diesel fließt den Plastiktank herab. Sofort lasse ich den Konvoi stoppen, in Windeseile muss jedes Fahrzeug rückwärts zum Anhänger rangieren und „tanken". Tatsächlich erreicht kaum Kraftstoff den Boden.

One consequence of the roadblock tactic was the obvious shortage of fuel. It is also something we had to consider as part of the planning process. It was important to know the following: diesel is certainly a common fuel in Bolivia. But anyone in a position to interrupt the supply of diesel can prevent trucks and other diesel-powered vehicles from moving – unless, of course, those vehicles are clever enough to be part of the Land Rover Experience Tour.

Still, with roadblocks everywhere, finding juice calls for a certain skill. Ciro explained to us that it had become something of a national pastime in Bolivia, with people storing diesel in old olive oil kegs, vinegar canisters or whatever else they could get their hands on. We just needed to find these people and offer them enough cash to part with their treasure – the rest was easy: an old hose, create a vacuum by sucking up the first drops, spit it out and Bob's your uncle – fuel in the tank.

A clever employee at a construction company came up with a particularly lucrative way of providing us with diesel. He broke the lock on the tank of his boss's Caterpillar front loader, which was half full, and filled up our Defenders. The deal was (apart from an immediate cash-in-hand payment) that we bring him over some spare parts for his own Defender when we returned on the main event. Which we duly did. Wherever I go, I pay my debts as soon as I can.

Speaking of bringing things over: after the constant search for fuel on the pre-scout, once we were back in Germany we decided to build a 1,000-litre tanker trailer equipped with the right valves to enable us to carry more fuel. Thanks to our special piece of legislation, "Ley 830", importing the trailer kit into Bolivia wasn't a problem, but the condition of the roads and the altitude would give us difficulties. The trailer and the towing unit were on the limit as far as weight was concerned, and the tank had another problem, for we had forgotten the effect altitude had on diesel fuel – namely expansion. As we were about to enter a village, the overflow valve on the tank began to drip. I stopped the convoy immediately and filled up as many of the tour vehicles as quickly as we could. Fortunately, we managed to avoid spilling almost any diesel.

Bunt geht's zu in den Dörfern und Städten Boliviens. Die fruchtbaren Gegenden sorgen für reichlich Obst und Gemüse. Übrigens: Der Sitz des Hutes namens „Bombín" zeigt an, ob die Dame verheiratet ist oder nicht – sagt man in La Paz. Sitzt er schräg, ist sie noch zu haben …

Life in the villages and towns of Bolivia is a feast of colour. Fertile regions provide rich harvests of fruit and vegetables. Oh, and by the way, in La Paz one says the way a "Bombín" hat is worn reflects whether or not the lady is married. If the hat is at an angle, then she is still "available".

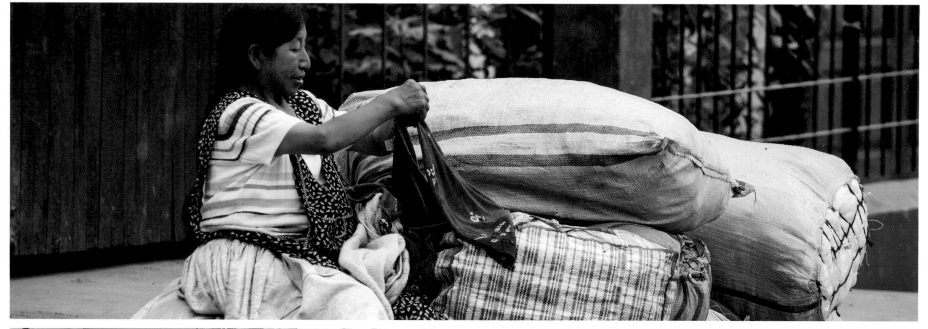

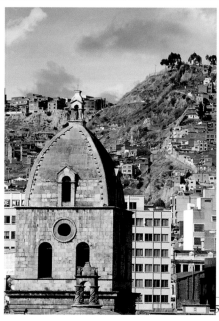

LIESA ROGGE

geb. 17.7.1993
Studentin der Tiermedizin

born 17 July 1993
student of veterinary medicine

Du bist die jüngste Experience-Fahrerin, die jemals auf einer (Vor-)Tour einen Land Rover gelenkt hat. Wie kam es?

Liesa: Wahrscheinlich, weil ich schon mit sieben Jahren bei Papa auf dem Schoß saß und so einen Offroader durch die Gegend gelenkt habe – das war im Jordanien-Urlaub. Aber auf den Pisten dort ist ja auch viel Platz, und kleine Fehler machen nicht so viel aus. Später bin ich auch in Kanada gefahren, aber da ist mir mehr der Grizzly mit den zwei Bärenjungen im Gedächtnis geblieben oder die Tat meiner Schwester Anni, die meinen geliebten Kuschelbär versteckt hat und ich ihn erst Monate später wiederbekam.

In Bolivien hast du dann schon völlig selbstständig einen Defender gefahren?

Liesa: Stimmt. In Deutschland musste ich noch das „Begleitete Fahren" absolvieren, in Südamerikas Wildnis konnte ich selber fahren. Aber auch nur, weil wir niemanden gefragt haben, ob es auch „Internationales Begleitetes Fahren" gibt. Immerhin besaß ich vorher schon den Traktorführerschein und habe ein Quad gelenkt, das wir als Trecker zugelassen haben.

Seit wann hilfst du deinem Vater Dag bei der Arbeit?

Liesa: Schon seit ich 16 bin. Natürlich zuerst im Büro: Papa hat angerufen, mir ein paar Berichte durchgegeben, und ich habe sie dann auf Facebook gepostet.

Und wie hast du die Tour in Bolivien erlebt?

Liesa: Ich bin auf der Vortour mitgefahren. Es war gleichzeitig faszinierend, anstrengend, nervenaufreibend, und oft hat etwas nicht so geklappt, wie es geplant war. Ich bin meistens nachts gefahren, das hat eine Menge Konzentration erfordert. Manchmal gab es nur zwei Stunden Schlaf – das ist eindeutig zu wenig. Irgendwann habe ich dann ständig meine Mama angerufen und ihr unter Tränen gebeichtet, dass ich nach Hause will. Aber ich würde es jederzeit wieder machen.

Wenn es nach dir ginge – welches Land sollte die Land Rover Experience Tour auf alle Fälle noch in den nächsten Jahren anfahren?

You are the youngest Experience driver to ever actually drive a Defender on a pre-scout recce. How did this come about?

Liesa: Probably because I'd already steered an off-roader sitting on my dad's lap when we were on holiday in Jordan. There was plenty of space on the tracks there if I made a mistake. Later on, I also drove in Canada but I have stronger memories from there of a grizzly bear with its two cubs, or my sister Anni hiding my favourite teddy bear, which I only got back months later.

In Bolivia you drove a Defender completely on your own.

Liesa: Correct. In Germany I had to complete the so-called "accompanied driving programme"; in the wilderness of South America I was able to drive on my own, but only because we didn't ask if "accompanied driving" existed abroad. That said, I have a licence to drive a tractor, and we have a quad at home, and it's registered as a tractor.

How long have you been helping your dad at work?

Liesa: Ever since I turned 16, at first mainly in the office.
Dad rang up and gave me some reports, and I posted them on Facebook.

What was your impression of the Bolivia Tour?

Liesa: I drove on the pre-scout recce. It was fascinating, tiring and nerve-wracking all at the same time. Things often didn't work out as planned. Most of the time, I drove at night, and that required a lot of concentration. Sometimes I only managed two hours' sleep at night – clearly not enough. At some point I just phoned mum, crying and telling her I wanted to go home. But I would do it again every time.

If you had to choose – where should the Land Rover Experience Tour go in future?

Liesa: Easy. Brazil.

DIE SCHWESTER

THE NUN

Independencia taucht ziemlich unvermittelt in Boliviens Hochland auf, gleich hinter einer Biegung eines Reifen mordenden Schotterweges. Ich sehe Hunderte grauer Dächer plötzlich im Nirgendwo zwischen Cochabamba und La Paz. Ein Blick genügt, um zu wissen: Hier auf 17 Grad, 8 Minuten und 4 Sekunden südlicher Länge und 66 Grad, 56 Minuten und 40 Sekunden westlicher Breite gibt es keinen Reichtum.

Deswegen ist Caritas-Schwester Verena Birnbacher für die Bolivianer fast eine Heilige. Und sie ist genau so, wie man sich jemanden vorstellt, der sein Leben der Nächstenliebe verschrieben hat. Wir lernen Schwester Verena – natürlich – völlig zufällig kennen. Unser Guide Ciro hat auf der Vortour seine alte Schule San Bonifacio in Independencia besucht, die von der Bundesverdienstkreuz-trägerin geleitet wird. Schwester Verena war früh aus Deutschland nach Bolivien ausgewandert und hat hier die Schule für Jungen und Mädchen gegründet. Es ist eine Art freiwilliges Internat. Die Kinder aus dem Umland müssen manch-mal bis zu drei Stunden zu Fuß gehen, um ihre Schule zu erreichen. Bolivien gilt als das ärmste und exportschwächste Land Südamerikas, zwei Drittel der Einwohner leben in Armut, 40 Prozent besitzen sogar so gut wie gar nichts. Darunter leiden besonders die Kinder – ohne Bildung haben sie keine Chance auf ein würdevolles Leben.

Mit Elan und Eigeninitiative hat Schwester Verena alles selber aufgebaut – was stets fehlt, ist Geld. Die Schwestern, Helfer und Sozialarbeiter führen uns herum, mitten in den Unterricht im Mädcheninternat. Es war einst ein reines Jungeninternat, das 1969 fertiggestellt wurde. Zwei Jahre später eröffnete hier das Heim Papa Juan XXIII für die Aus- und Fortbildung von Katechisten. 1974 weihten die Verantwortlichen dann das Mädcheninternat Santa Elisabet ein, weil Frauenbildung noch immer ein Fremdwort in Bolivien war. Ende der 70er Jahre hat man ein Studienkreditsystem eingeführt. So wurden bis heute mehr als 300 Lehrer, Ärzte, Ingenieure, Techniker, Schneiderinnen für ihren Beruf qualifiziert, die nun durch Rückzahlungen anderen Kindern die Ausbildung ermöglichen. 2007 fasste man alle Einrichtungen als Stiftung „Fundación Centro Social San Bonifacio" zusammen, in der heute mehr als 1200 junge Menschen lernen.

Die Schule lebt nur von Spenden der Kirche, von denen sie sogar noch einen Teil an die Kinder weitergibt und ihnen Klamotten kauft. Für mich ist es eine Selbstverständlichkeit, dass wir sie besuchen und einen Scheck dalassen. Doch Land Rover geht noch weiter und unterstützt mit fünf Euro pro Bewerber der Bolivien-Tour das bolivianische Rote Kreuz. Aber nicht nur das: In Deutschland hatte Schwester Verena eine Auszeichnung verliehen bekommen. Das Problem: Sie konnte sie nicht wirklich entgegennehmen, die Anerkennung bestand aus einer 200 Kilo schweren Gedenktafel. Und die ohne Begleitung von Deutschland nach Bolivien schicken? Sie wäre wahrscheinlich nie durch den Zoll gekommen. Natürlich haben wir das gute Stück in Deutschland gut verpackt, ins Land geschmuggelt und an Schwester Verena übergeben.

Behind a curve, while driving along the tyre-killing gravel roads in Bolivia's highlands, we stumbled across the town of Independencia. In this no-man's-land between La Paz and Cochabamba, we were suddenly confronted by a sea of grey roofs. My first thoughts were that behind the coordinates 17 degrees, 8 minutes and 4 seconds south and 66 degrees, 56 minutes and 40 seconds west was a lot of poverty.

As far as the Bolivians are concerned, Sister Verena Birnbacher, who works for the Caritas aid organisation, is almost a saint. She is the living embodiment of the concept of charitable spirit. We met her purely by chance. On the pre-scout recce, our guide Ciro had visited his old school, San Bonifacio, in Independencia, which is run by the wearer of the Order of Merit of the Federal Republic of Germany, Sister Verena. When she was younger, she had emigrated from Germany to Bolivia, founding the school for young boys and girls. It is a form of voluntary boarding school. The children from the surrounding region have to walk for up to three hours in order to get to school. Bolivia is the poorest country in South America, with the weakest export economy. Two-thirds of the population live in poverty, and 40 percent have nothing that they can call their own. Children are the ones who suffer most in this environment, as without any education they have no chance whatsoever of improving their situation.

Sister Verena had displayed considerable elan and resourcefulness in getting the project off the ground at all – however, she needed financial support. The nuns, assistants and social workers showed us around the school while lessons were being conducted in the girls' boarding school. Built in 1969, it was initially an all-boys' boarding school. Two years later, the Pope John XXIII home for the training and further education of catechists was founded. In 1974, they opened the girls' boarding school, Santa Elisabet, at a time when education for girls and women was still unheard-of in Bolivia. By the end of the '70s, a course credit system had been introduced. As of today, over 300 teachers, doctors, engineers and seamstresses have qualified in their respective careers and by putting money back into the school are enabling other children to benefit from an education. In 2007, the whole complex which today houses over 1,200 students, was reorganised as a charitable trust: the "Fundación Centro Social San Bonifacio".

The school lives from church donations, some of which are allocated directly to clothing for the children. It goes without saying that we wanted to pay them a visit and also make a donation. We went one step further – for every applicant on the tour, Land Rover donated five euros to the Bolivian Red Cross. There was something else, however. Sister Verena had received an award in Germany, a commemorative plaque weighing 440 lbs., but it had been impossible for her to come to Germany to take it back to Bolivia. Sending it via post to Bolivia was out of the question, as it would probably never make it through customs. We packed it well in Germany, smuggled it through ourselves and personally presented it to Sister Verena in Bolivia.

Es gibt keine Kurve im bolivianischen Hochland, nach der einem nicht der Atem stockt. Das liegt nur zum Teil an Höhen bis über 5 000 Meter; meistens ist es der Ausblick, der einen fesselt. Dass die Autos wegen der Höhenluft auch Leistung verlieren, ist da völlig zweitrangig – so kann man den Weitblick länger genießen.

All of the curves or switchbacks in the Bolivian highlands can be described as breathtaking. It is partly a consequence of being at well over 16,000 feet, but in the main it refers to the views, which are simply enthralling. What does it matter that the altitude affects the vehicles' performance? You have more time to enjoy the view as a result.

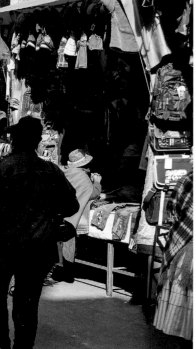

DER STEIN
THE STONE

Wir haben schon viele ungewöhnliche Städte gesehen, aber La Paz sticht ganz deutlich hervor. Zwei Gründe als Beispiel: Zunächst ist da die beachtliche Zahl von getrockneten Lama-Föten auf dem Hexenmarkt. Hier gibt es nicht nur Pülverchen aller Art, bei denen der aufgeklärte Europäer gar nicht wissen will, wogegen und woraus das Zeug ist, sondern auch diese staubtrockenen Tierkadaver, die einen aus hohlen Augen anblicken. Für die Bolivianer sind das Glücksbringer. Man vergräbt vor dem Hausbau in jeder Ecke des künftigen Gebäudes eines der Tiere, und alles wird gut. Beispiel zwei: Noch mehr Tiere hüpfen auf den Hauptstraßen herum. Tatsächlich, da sind Zebras. Drei, fünf, zehn. Und ein Esel dazwischen. Aber alle unterwegs auf zwei Beinen? Ja, im Regierungsauftrag. Denn der Straßenverkehr orientiert sich an der Maxime: „Erst ich, der Rest ist mir egal." Und das soll geändert werden. Also steckt Präsident Evo Morales Menschen für ein paar Peso in Zebrakostüme, und die sollen den Autofahrern beibringen, dass Fußgänger auf Zebrastreifen Vorfahrt haben, dass sie auch mal halten müssen und dass sie nicht jeden gleich umfahren dürfen, der versucht, die Straße zu überqueren. Wer es nicht kapiert, bekommt Besuch vom Esel. Und der schimpft dann kräftig.

Mit Schimpfe der harten Sorte bekommen wir es auf dem Weg nach La Paz, zum Ende der Tour, zu tun. Wir kommen gerade vom Titicacasee, diesem unglaublich blauen, riesigen Gewässer, das die bolivianische Marine (!) bewacht, und das wir auf abenteuerlichen Holzbooten mitsamt unseren Defendern gequert haben. Voller Vorfreude auf die übliche große Abschlussparty in diesem gastfreundlichen Land bekommen wir noch einmal zu spüren, was eine Blockade ist.

Wir wollen, nein, wir müssen nach La Paz, also versuchen wir, dort zu fahren, wo die Blockade noch nicht komplett steht. Das weitet sich zur Schnitzeljagd aus – Ciro und Hans huschen mit ihren Autos durch die Seitenstraßen der Vororte und melden über Funk, wo frei ist und wo nicht. 13 Wagen rasen dicht an dicht durch die kleinen Ortschaften, was den Bewohnern nicht wirklich gefällt. Einige – besonders Frauen – werfen mit kleinen Steinen, einige treffen unsere Wagen auch, sie hinterlassen aber nur kleine Lackschäden.

Aber an einer der großen Straßen ist Ende im Gelände. Steine und Menschen haben sich zu einer unüberwindbaren Barriere aufgebaut. Hans fährt vorne und entscheidet: durch geht nicht, also dran vorbei. Mit viel Speed pflügt der Konvoi über das Feld – was der anwesenden Besitzerin nun völlig missfällt. Ich fahre als Letzter und möchte mich gerne bei der Frau entschuldigen und ihr unser Tun erklären. Also bleibe ich neben ihr stehen und öffne das Fenster.

Keine gute Idee. Denn sie hat einen recht großen Stein in der Hand. Und droht, ihn zu werfen. Zuerst rede ich noch in Englisch, aber schnell verfalle ich etwas hektisch ins Deutsche. Denn ihre Faust mit bedrohlichem Stein und mein Kopf mit verletzlicher Hülle sind plötzlich keinen Meter voneinander entfernt. Und noch während ich rede und sie immer wieder Wurfbewegungen macht, gebe ich Vollgas.

Ich weiß nicht, ob sie den Stein letztlich geworfen hat oder nicht. Ich weiß nur, dass auch dieses Abenteuer für uns alle gut ausgegangen ist.

Wie immer bei der Land Rover Experience Tour.

We have seen many unusual cities, but La Paz is certainly at the top of the list, and for two reasons. The first is the remarkable number of llama foetuses at the Witches' Market. You can buy all manner of remedies and powders made from things best left undescribed, for ailments the enlightened European wouldn't want to know about, and, of course, dried animal corpses, staring at you through their empty eye sockets. To Bolivians, they are lucky charms; if one is buried at each corner of the site of a future house, everything will be all right.

The second: there was suddenly an unusual number of animals on the main roads, mainly zebras, and a mule in between, and all of them walking on two legs, clearly on government commission. The story behind the project was to be found in the way people drive – the rule of the road being "Me first – you loser". This had to change, so President Morales put people in zebra costumes for a few pesos. The idea was to teach car drivers that people at zebra crossings have right of way, and that drivers should always endeavour to stop and not wipe out anybody trying to cross the road. Should people have problems comprehending the message, the "zebras" would then send the donkey to scream its lungs out at them.

We experienced another form of screaming on the way back to La Paz as the tour was winding down to a close. We had just visited the wonderful blue Titicaca Lake, interestingly guarded by the Bolivian Navy (!), which we had crossed in our Defenders aboard rustic-looking wooden boats. We were looking forward to the big party celebrating the end of the tour in this wonderfully hospitable country when we hit another roadblock.

As I said, we were headed towards La Paz and began looking for a gap in the roadblocks. This rapidly deteriorated into a sort of paper chase as Ciro and Hans darted from one side road to the next telling us over the radio which roads were open and which weren't. 13 vehicles racing through tiny villages didn't go down well with the local population; some – mainly women – threw stones at the vehicles, which caused the odd scratch or two, but fortunately nothing more serious.

Things came to a halt, though, at the end of one of the larger roads where people and stones had converged to create an impenetrable barrier. Hans drove up to the front to decide what to do. The convoy then shot at speed across the fields, which, as far the woman who owned the land was concerned, was really the final straw. I was in the last vehicle and wanted to apologise to the lady. As I drove up to her, I wound the window down.

This wasn't a good idea, as she had a rather large rock in her hand that she seemed ready to throw. I started speaking to her in English, and then I panicked and started rabbiting at her in German as her rock and my fragile head were very near to one another. As I talked and she threatened to throw the stone at me, I put my foot down.

I don't know if she threw the stone or not. I do know that we all survived to tell the tale, which is just how it is on the Land Rover Experience Tour.

PETER MODELHART

geb. 16.12.1968
Geschäftsführer Jaguar Land Rover Deutschland

born 16 December 1968
Managing Director Jaguar Land Rover Germany

Wie wichtig sind die Experience Touren für die Marke Land Rover?

Peter: Sie sind essentiell und Teil des Kerns der Marke. Die Experience Touren und die dazugehörigen Reisen verkörpern alles, was Land Rover emotional ausmacht: Freiheit, Natur, Familie und das Entdecken – nicht das Erobern. Die Reisen öffnen die Augen über das Fahrzeug hinaus. Wir meistern schwierige Passagen, um Freiheit zu genießen. Sie sind sowohl etwas fürs Auge als auch fürs Herz. Das kann man nur mit einem Land Rover erleben.

Warum?

Peter: Die Fahrzeuge besitzen eine entspannte Größe, man sitzt auf langen Strecken völlig problemlos hinterm Lenkrad. Die Autos befreien vom Stress, egal ob man Fahrer, Beifahrer oder Fondpassagier ist. Dazu kommen die großen Glasflächen, sodass man von jedem Platz aus bestens sieht, was draußen los ist. Von dem Erfahren der herausragenden Land Rover 4x4-Technologie muss ich hier sowieso nicht extra schwärmen. Im kaufmännischen Sinn verkaufen wir damit die schönsten Probefahrten der Welt. Wer einmal so eine Reise gemacht hat, bleibt Kunde und Freund der Marke auf Lebzeiten.

Wo warst du selbst schon dabei?

Peter: Als Geschäftsführer von Jaguar Land Rover Österreich war ich bereits bei der G4 in der Mongolei auf der Pre-Scout-Tour, aber völlig mitgerissen hat mich die Reise durch Namibia. Da genoss ich eine nie gekannte Ruhe im Auto, und am Himmel gab es nicht mal Kondensstreifen, außerdem keinen Radioempfang entlang der Skelettküste. So eine Entschleunigung ist einfach einzigartig und gleichzeitig so unfassbar schön fürs Auge.

Welche Länder und Gegenden würden dich persönlich noch reizen?

Peter: Es ist naturgemäß schwer, die Jubiläumsstrecke zu toppen. Aber es gibt – ganz im Sinne der Experience Tour – noch viel zu bereisen, zum Beispiel vergessene Kulturstätten. Ich finde Kambodscha faszinierend, aber auch Chinas Hinterland, wo man noch nicht war, oder die russische Taiga. Selbst in Südamerika, wo wir schon oft fuhren, gibt es noch ganz viel zu erkunden: Wie weit kann man am Amazonas fahren, von welcher Seite geht man rein? Wir wollen auch weiterhin entdecken …

How important are the Experience Tours for the Land Rover brand?

Peter: They are essential and belong to the very core of the brand. The Experience Tours and the accompanying customer tours epitomise everything that is the emotion in Land Rover. Freedom, nature, family and the joy of discovering, not conquering. The tours open your eyes to a world beyond the vehicles. We take on difficult routes in order to really enjoy freedom. The tours are both a visual and an emotional feast. This is only possible in a Land Rover.

Why?

Peter: The vehicles are of a certain size, so you can relax. The driving position is wonderful, and that's an advantage on a long journey. The vehicles provide for a stress-free environment regardless of whether you are a driver or a passenger. Thanks to the large glass surfaces, the view is wonderful – from every seat. I probably don't need to tell about what it is like experiencing Land Rover's outstanding off-road abilities for yourself. In business terms, we are selling the best test-drives in the market. Anyone who has been on an Experience Tour tends to stay with the brand for life.

Which tours have you experienced yourself?

Peter: As MD of Jaguar Land Rover in Austria, I accompanied a G4 Challenge pre-scout in Mongolia. It was the journey in Namibia that really impressed me. I had never experienced this sense of calm in a vehicle before. The sky was free of condensation trails, and along the Skeleton Coast not a single radio station to disturb the peace and quiet. This kind of winding-down exercise is unique and a joy to witness.

Which countries or regions would you personally want to explore?

Peter: Naturally it is almost impossible to top the anniversary tour, but as far as the Land Rover Experience Tour is concerned, there is a lot still out there to explore. Lost cultural sites, for example. I think Cambodia is fascinating; or there's the Chinese interior, which we haven't been to as yet; or the Russian taiga. Despite more than one tour, there, South America still has a great deal to offer: how far into the Amazon can we travel, and what is the best way to approach it? The journey continues…

EPILOG
EPILOGUE

Wenn ich behaupten würde, zehn Land Rover Experience Touren hätten mich um 20 Jahre altern lassen, wäre das gelogen. Aber ebenso flunkern würde ich, wenn ich konstatierte, ich wäre dadurch jünger geworden. Würde jemand dagegen sagen, die Zeit hätte mich um 20 Jahre weiser werden lassen – nun ja, ich würde mich zumindest nicht nachhaltig dagegen sträuben. Richtig ist wahrscheinlich: Ich habe unglaublich viel dazugelernt. Ich habe so wahnsinnig viele tolle Menschen kennen und schätzen gelernt, denen ich sonst wahrscheinlich nie begegnet wäre. Ich kann Gefahren besser einschätzen als vorher, ich kann ihnen eher ausweichen, und ich weiß genau, auf wen ich mich hundertprozentig verlassen kann.
Na, wenn das keine gute Grundlage für die nächsten Jahre Land Rover Experience ist.
Ich verspreche es.

If I were to say that ten Land Rover Experience Tours had put 20 years on me, I'd be lying. It would be equally untrue to claim the opposite and say that they had made me feel younger. However, if someone were to point out that I had gained 20 years' worth of experience in the same time frame, I wouldn't argue with that. Truth be told, I have benefitted enormously from the experience. I have met and learned to respect a group of wonderful people whom under normal circumstances I would never have had the pleasure of meeting at all. My sixth sense for danger has improved dramatically; I am quicker to avoid trouble today than I was as a younger man, and I know on whom I can rely one hundred percent, which is probably a firm footing for all the Land Rover Experience Tours to come.
And that is a promise.

100 EXTREME

DIE INTENSIVSTEN MOMENTE AUS ZEHN LAND ROVER TOUREN

- **die gefährlichste Straße:** ein extrem schmaler Minenweg (Bolivien)
- **der gefährlichste Moment:** ein überlaufender Tankanhänger (Bolivien)
- **der schönste Sonnenaufgang:** in der Wüste (Namibia)
- **der schönste Sonnenuntergang:** in den Bergen (Kirgisistan)
- **der offenste Guide:** Tenzin (China)
- **die schwierigste Passage:** ein Flussbett (Argentinien)
- **der problematischste Einkauf:** auf dem Frischmarkt (Malaysia)
- **das furchtbarste Hotel:** lieber keine Beschreibung (Bolivien)
- **das beste Hotel:** ein Haus in Colomé (Argentinien)
- **das seltenste Tier:** ein wilder Puma (Kanada)
- **die tiefste Wasserdurchfahrt:** fast bis zur Mitte Seitenscheibe (Island)
- **die höchste Bergstraße:** Gyatso La mit 5 228 Metern (Tibet)
- **das schlimmste Essen:** Gammelfleisch zum Selberkochen (Bolivien)
- **das leckerste Essen:** diverse Restaurants (China)
- **der größte medizinische Eingriff:** ein schlimmer Verkehrsunfall (Mexiko)
- **die komischste Situation:** eine erfundene Technikgeschichte (Malaysia)
- **die längste Tagesetappe nach Zeit:** 19 Stunden (Island)
- **die längste Tagesetappe nach Kilometern:** 1 161 Kilometer (China)
- **der untalentierteste Fahrer:** ein deutscher Journalist (Guatemala)
- **die problematischste Benzinsuche:** täglich (Bolivien)
- **das größte Geldbündel:** Barzahlung beim Tanken (Usbekistan)
- **die höchste Bestechungssumme:** 2 000 … (aber wo war das noch?)
- **der längste Grenzaufenthalt:** 13 Stunden (Usbekistan)
- **die schwierigsten Visumanträge:** bitte nicht daran erinnern (China)
- **das teuerste Telefonat:** eine Satellitenverbindung wegen Luftschlauchproblem (Island)
- **die schwierigste Teilnehmeraufgabe:** eine Abseilaktion (Guatemala)
- **die teuerste Fahrzeugpanne:** das eigene Auto abschleppen (Namibia)
- **das größte Missverständnis:** zum Glück noch nicht passiert
- **der längste Umweg:** 500 Kilometer wegen einer Blockade (Bolivien)
- **die kürzeste Nacht:** zwei Stunden (Island)
- **die meisten Insekten:** mindestens Abermillionen (Schottland)
- **der fieseste Stich:** ein Blutegelangriff (Malaysia)
- **der ungewöhnlichste technische Defekt:** ein Kabelbaumfehler im Defender (Bolivien)
- **das höchste Bier:** auf 5 124 Metern (Bolivien)
- **die größten Grenzschikanen:** diverse (Ukraine, Usbekistan, China)
- **der dichteste Dschungel:** verschiedene (Malaysia, Guatemala)
- **die scheuesten Kinder:** bei der Dorfbevölkerung (Argentinien)
- **der albernste Unfall:** ein leichter Auffahrunfall Land Rover/Land Rover (Malaysia)
- **die steilste Straße:** der Kraterweg (Argentinien)
- **die engste Straße:** eine Bergtrasse (Bolivien)
- **das wildeste Überholmanöver:** an einer Grenz-Baustelle vorbei (Usbekistan)
- **die niedrigste Temperatur:** -23 Grad (Argentinien)
- **die längste verschneite Straße:** rund 1 000 Kilometer (Kasachstan)
- **die größte geleistete Hilfe:** an Schwester Verena (Bolivien)
- **das schlimmste Getränk:** Rotwein, der ein schlechter Rosé war (China)
- **der abartigste Brauch:** Trockenfisch essen (Island)
- **der naheste Moment des Verzweifelns:** schwimmende Autopapiere (Niemandsland Ukraine/Russland)
- **die fieseste Fingerfalle:** Kachelrand im Bad (Tibet)
- **die dreckigsten Klamotten:** völlig verschlammte Garnitur (Malaysia)
- **die treuesten Land-Rover-Fans:** die LET-Gemeinde (weltweit)
- **die beste Idee:** feuriges Spritfilteraufheizen unterm Defender (Chile)
- **die dümmste Idee:** Benzinabzapfen aus dem Spritfilter zum Grillen (Bolivien)
- **die aufwendigste Reparatur:** Motorüberholung beim Defender (Bolivien)
- **der schrägste Bewerber:** ein ungeeigneter Deutschrusse (Deutschland)

- **der/die älteste Teilnehmer/in:** eine 64-jährige Tierärztin (Deutschland)
- **die größte Fehleinschätzung:** eine vermeintlich tolle Abkürzung wählen (China)
- **der sympathischste mitreisende Promi:** Jessica Schwarz (Argentinien, Seidenstraße)
- **die merkwürdigste Anfrage an den Doc:** Arztgeheimnis (irgendwo)
- **das schwerste Auto:** die rund vier Tonnen wiegende Ambulanz (diverse Länder)
- **das leichteste Auto:** Land Rover Freelander (Malaysia, Jordanien)
- **der treueste Sponsor:** Continental und Haglöfs (Deutschland)
- **die größte Bewerberanzahl:** 30 000 für die Seidenstraße (Deutschland)
- **die schwierigste Bewerbercamp-Aufgabe:** nachts vergrabene Räder suchen (Deutschland)
- **die krasseste Bewerberlüge:** „Ich bin kein Eventhopper." (Seidenstraße)
- **die heißeste Temperatur unterwegs:** 43 Grad (Usbekistan)
- **die tougheste Teilnehmerfrau:** ein Journalist (!) aus München (Deutschland)
- **der härteste Teilnehmer:** ein LR-Fan aus Krefeld (Deutschland)
- **die längste Ansprache:** bleibt ein Geheimnis (geheim)
- **der langsamste Abschnitt:** 2 km/h im Durchschnitt (Guatemala)
- **der schnellste Abschnitt:** Autobahn Berlin-Polen ohne Tempobegrenzung (Deutschland)
- **der schlechteste Treibstoff:** Kamaz-Diesel-Fusel (Usbekistan)
- **der hilfreichste Tipp von außen:** bergab fahren im Rückwärtsgang (Malaysia)
- **der schrägste Mitfahrer:** ein Cocablätter kauender Bergbauer (Bolivien)
- **die gefährlichste Kurve:** Spitzkehre einer Minenstraße (Bolivien)
- **die längste Kolonne:** 18 Autos (Indien)
- **die längste Tour:** 16 000 Kilometer (Seidenstraße)
- **die wenigsten Tageskilometer:** 2 Kilometer (Guatemala)
- **die größte Hürde:** der Zoll (Jordanien)
- **der wichtigste telefonierte Satz:** „Wir haben's geschafft!" (Indien)
- **die größte Hilfeleistung:** Erste Hilfe bei einem schweren Verkehrsunfall (Tibet)
- **die längste Suche:** der verschwundene Hans (Guatemala)
- **der anstrengendste Meter:** letzter Schritt zum Pinkeln auf 5 200 Höhenmetern (China)
- **der beste Spruch:** „Sneidn wer rauuuus" (China)
- **der dümmste Spruch:** Teilnehmerin: „Wo sind meine Hupen?" (Nepal)
- **die größte Zeitverschiebung:** acht Stunden (Kanada)
- **der längste Tag:** Sonnenaufgang bis Sonnenaufgang (Island)
- **die geringste Autokraft:** 30 PS im Defender (Argentinien)
- **die größte Fehlkalkulation:** ein Touristenfallen-Abendessen (Russland)
- **die größte Fehlinvestition:** zu viele Ersatzreifen mitnehmen (Seidenstraße)
- **das bestangelegte Geld:** das Dankeschön an Zöllner (nahezu weltweit)
- **der überraschendste Laden:** eine Autowerkstatt (Bolivien)
- **der meistkonsumierte Drink abends:** Bier (weltweit)
- **der coolste Moment:** Eine Neun-Mann-Geburtstagsfeier im Discovery (Schottland)
- **das schärfste Essen:** in einem Restaurant in Golmud (China)
- **der verrückteste Guide:** Adil aus Kashgar (China)
- **die skrupelloseste Tat:** ein heftiges Insektengemetzel (Malaysia)
- **das sicherste Gefühl:** erzeugt von offiziellen Inoffiziellen in Toyota Land Cruisern (China)
- **die heftigste Kommandoübernahme:** eine Flugzeugkanzel-Okkupation (Argentinien)
- **die ungewöhnlichsten Tankwarte:** auffällig unauffällig verkleidete Zivilpolizisten (China)
- **der größte Erfolg:** die Seidenstraßen-Tour (Deutschland, Polen, Ukraine, Russland, Kasachstan, Usbekistan, Kirgisistan, China, Tibet, Nepal, Indien)

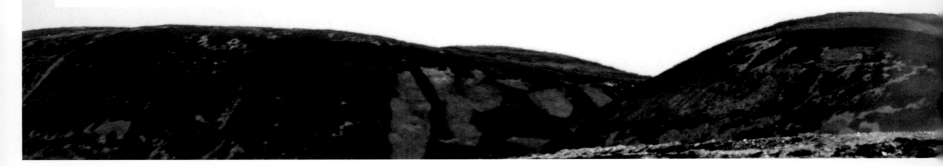

100 EXTREMES

THE MOST INTENSE MOMENTS IN TEN LAND ROVER TOURS

- **the most dangerous road:** an extremely narrow mining road (Bolivia)
- **the most dangerous moment:** a leaking tanker trailer (Bolivia)
- **the most beautiful sunrise:** in the desert (Namibia)
- **the most beautiful sunset:** in the mountains (Kyrgyzstan)
- **the most candid guide:** Tenzin (China)
- **the most difficult route:** a dry riverbed (Argentina)
- **the most difficult shopping trip:** a fresh produce market (Malaysia)
- **the worst hotel:** better left unsaid (Bolivia)
- **the best hotel:** a house in Colomé (Argentina)
- **the rarest animal:** a wild puma (Canada)
- **the deepest river crossing:** water almost halfway up the side windows (Iceland)
- **the highest mountain road:** Gyatso La 17,152 feet (Tibet)
- **the worst food:** rotten meat that we had to cook ourselves (Bolivia)
- **the best food:** numerous restaurants (China)
- **the most serious medical task:** a serious road traffic accident (Mexico)
- **the funniest situation:** a phoney technology story (Malaysia)
- **the longest driving stage (in hours):** 19 hours (Iceland)
- **the longest driving stage in miles:** 721 miles (China)
- **the least talented driver:** a German journalist (Guatemala)
- **the most difficult search for fuel:** every day (Bolivia)
- **the largest wad of cash:** paying for fuel (Uzbekistan)
- **the largest bribe:** 2,000... (but which country was that again?)
- **the longest wait at a border:** 13 hours (Uzbekistan)
- **the most difficult visa application process:** don't remind me (China)
- **the most expensive telephone call:** a satellite link to discuss a problem with an air hose (Iceland)
- **the most difficult participants' special task:** abseiling (Guatemala)
- **the most expensive breakdown:** towing our own vehicle (Namibia)
- **the biggest misunderstanding:** it hasn't happened yet (fortunately)
- **the longest detour:** 310 miles because of a blocked road (Bolivia)
- **the shortest night:** two hours (Iceland)
- **the most insects:** millions (Scotland)
- **the most painful bite:** leeches (Malaysia)
- **the most unusual breakdown:** a short circuit in the wiring loom of a Defender (Bolivia)
- **the highest beer:** 16,811 feet (Bolivia)
- **the worst border shenanigans:** numerous (Ukraine, Uzbekistan, China)
- **the thickest jungle:** various (Malaysia, Guatemala)
- **the most shy children:** villagers (Argentina)
- **the most ridiculous accident:** a rear-ender involving two Land Rovers (Malaysia)
- **the steepest road:** the crater route (Argentina)
- **the narrowest road:** a mountain road (Bolivia)
- **the craziest overtaking manoeuvre:** past a building site at the border (Uzbekistan)
- **the lowest temperature:** -23 degrees Celsius (-9 degrees Fahrenheit) (Argentina)
- **the longest road covered in snow:** 621 miles (Kazakhstan)
- **the greatest delivery service:** Sister Verena (Bolivia)
- **the worst drink:** a red wine that was a very poor rosé (China)
- **the most disgusting tradition:** eating dried fish (Iceland)
- **the moment of greatest despair:** watching our vehicle documentation float in the water (no-man's-land between Ukraine and Russia)
- **the worst finger trap:** the bath rim (Tibet)
- **the dirtiest clothes:** tour kit completely covered in mud (Malaysia)
- **the most loyal Land Rover fans:** the global LET community
- **the best idea:** "flame grilling" the fuel filter underneath the Defender (Chile)
- **the worst idea:** drawing off diesel from the fuel filter to get the barbecue going (Bolivia)

- **the most complex repair job:** engine overhaul on Defender (Bolivia)
- **the most off-the-wall candidate:** a particularly unsuitable German of Russian descent (Germany)
- **the oldest participant:** a 64-year-old vet (Germany)
- **the greatest miscalculation:** a "fantastic" short cut (China)
- **the nicest VIP we ever took with us:** actress Jessica Schwarz (Argentina, Silk Road)
- **the strangest request made of the doctor:** medical secret (that goes for the country, too)
- **the heaviest vehicle on the tour:** the ambulance, weighing around four tonnes (numerous countries)
- **the lightest vehicle:** Land Rover Freelander (Malaysia, Jordan)
- **the most loyal sponsors:** Continental and Haglöfs (Germany)
- **the largest number of applications:** 30,000 for the Silk Road (Germany)
- **the most difficult selection camp task:** hunting buried wheels at night (Germany)
- **the most blatant applicant lie:** "I am not an event hopper" (Silk Road)
- **the hottest temperatures on tour:** 43 degrees Celsius (109 degrees Fahrenheit) (Uzbekistan)
- **the toughest female participant:** a male (!) journalist from Munich (Germany)
- **the toughest male participant:** a Land Rover fan from Krefeld (Germany)
- **the longest speech:** remains a secret (classified)
- **the slowest section:** 1.2 mph (average) (Guatemala)
- **the quickest section:** the motorway between Berlin and the Polish border (no speed limits) (Germany)
- **the worst fuel:** Kamaz-diesel (Uzbekistan)
- **the best driving tip ever:** driving downhill in reverse gear (Malaysia)
- **the most bizarre passenger:** a coca-leaf-chewing miner (Bolivia)
- **the most dangerous corner:** a switchback on a mining road (Bolivia)
- **the longest convoy:** 18 vehicles (India)
- **the longest tour:** 10,000 miles (Silk Road)
- **the shortest distance travelled in one day:** 1.2 miles (Guatemala)
- **the biggest obstacle:** customs (Jordan)
- **the most important sentence on the phone:** "We made it" (India)
- **the most significant rescue operation:** first aid at a serious road traffic accident (Tibet)
- **the longest search:** Hans after he went AWOL (Guatemala)
- **the most exhausting walk:** taking a leak at 17,000 feet above sea level (China)
- **the best adage ever:** "Cut it out" (China)
- **the daftest quote:** participant "Where's my horn?" (Nepal)
- **the greatest time difference:** eight hours (Canada)
- **the longest day:** sunrise to sunrise (Iceland)
- **the least horsepower:** 30 hp in the Defender (Argentina)
- **the greatest miscalculation:** dinner in a tourist trap (Russia)
- **the biggest investment error:** too many spare tyres (Silk Road)
- **the best investment:** thank-you money to customs officials (everywhere)
- **the most surprising shop:** a vehicle workshop (Bolivia)
- **the evening drink consumed most:** beer (everywhere)
- **the coolest moment:** a nine-person birthday party in one Discovery (Scotland)
- **the spiciest food:** a restaurant in Golmud (China)
- **the craziest guide:** Adil from Kashgar (China)
- **the most ruthless thing we ever did:** massacring insects (Malaysia)
- **the greatest feeling of security:** the unofficial officials accompanying us in their Toyota Land Cruisers (China)
- **the most dramatic takeover:** the cockpit of a light aeroplane (Argentina)
- **the most unusual filling-station attendant:** the oh-so-obvious undercover policeman (China)
- **the greatest success:** the Silk Road Tour (Germany, Poland, Ukraine, Russia, Kazakhstan, Uzbekistan, Kyrgyzstan, China, Tibet, Nepal, India)

IMPRESSUM & BILDNACHWEIS

IMPRINT & PHOTO CREDITS

© 2013 Jaguar Land Rover Deutschland GmbH
© 2013 teNeues Verlag GmbH + Co. KG, Kempen
Editor: Land Rover Deutschland

Forewords by Christian Uhrig, Head of Marketing Land Rover Germany
and Dag Rogge, Head of Land Rover Experience Germany
Text by Roland Löwisch
Translation by Graham Paul Entwistle
Copy editing by Dr. Simone Bischoff; Schmellenkamp Communications
Design, Layout & Prepress by Christin Steirat
Editorial coordination by Nadine Weinhold, Juliane Schröder
Production by Dieter Haberzettl
Imaging by Tridix, Berlin
Photo editing by Julia Preuss, Betti Fiegle

Wir danken allen, die dazu beigetragen haben,
dass zehn Land Rover Experience Touren so sicher
und erfolgreich stattfinden konnten.

Special thanks to all those who made the ten
Land Rover Experience Tours possible.

Jaguar Land Rover Deutschland GmbH
Am Kronberger Hang 2a
65824 Schwalbach/Ts.
Germany
Phone: +49 (0)2131 151 23 70
lrhilfe@jaguarlandrover.com

PHOTO CREDITS

Cover photos by Craig Pusey
Jordanien/Jordan: Dag Rogge, Hans Hermann Ruthe
Island/Iceland: Nick Dimbleby, Dag Rogge, Hans Hermann Ruthe
Winter Experience: Nick Dimbleby
Namibia: Thomas Grimm, Dag Rogge, Hans Hermann Ruthe
Mundo Maya: Thomas Grimm, Dag Rogge, Hans Hermann Ruthe
Kanada/Canada: Thomas Grimm, Dag Rogge, Hans Hermann Ruthe
Schottland/Scotland: Craig Pusey, Dag Rogge, Hans Hermann Ruthe
Argentinien/Argentina: Craig Pusey, Hans Hermann Ruthe
Malaysia: Craig Pusey, Hans Hermann Ruthe
Bolivien/Bolivia: Roland Löwisch, Craig Pusey, Hans Hermann Ruthe
Seidenstraße/Silk Road: Pierre Johne, Craig Pusey, Hans Hermann Ruthe

Satellite maps: Google™ earth
Jordanien/Jordan pp. 52/53 © 2013 Shutterstock, Inc./nicolpetr
p. 56 © 2013 iStockphoto LP./stevenallan
p. 60 © 2013 Shutterstock, Inc./Marco Tomasini
p. 61 © 2013 Shutterstock, Inc./Max Topchii
p. 62 © 2013 Shutterstock, Inc./Rossillicon Photos
p. 65 © 2013 Shutterstock, Inc./sbarabu
p. 67 © 2013 Shutterstock, Inc./Waj
Island/Iceland pp. 70/71 © Tepper; Natalie/Arcaid/Corbis
Mundo Maya pp. 114/115 © 2013 Shutterstock, Inc./Zai Aragon

Published by teNeues Publishing Group
teNeues Verlag GmbH + Co. KG
Am Selder 37, 47906 Kempen, Germany
Phone: +49 (0)2152 916 0, Fax: +49 (0)2152 916 111
e-mail: books@teneues.de

Press Department: Andrea Rehn
Phone: +49 (0)2152 916 202
e-mail: arehn@teneues.de

teNeues Digital Media GmbH
Kohlfurter Straße 41–43, 10999 Berlin, Germany
Phone: +49 (0)30 700 77 65 0

teNeues Publishing Company
7 West 18th Street, New York, NY 10011, USA
Phone: +1 212 627 9090, Fax: +1 212 627 9511

teNeues Publishing UK Ltd.
12 Ferndene Road, London SE24 0AQ, UK
Phone: +44 (0)20 3542 8997

teNeues France S.A.R.L.
39, rue des Billets, 18250 Henrichemont, France
Phone: +33 (0)2 4826 9348, Fax: +33 (0)1 7072 3482

www.teneues.com

© 2013 teNeues Verlag GmbH + Co. KG, Kempen
ISBN: 978-3-8327-9801-7
Library of Congress Control Number: 2013954795
Printed in the Czech Republic

MIX
Papier aus verantwortungsvollen Quellen
Paper from responsible sources
FSC® C005833